C000282896

Behind Closed Doors

Behind Closed Doors

Stories from the Coaching Room

Edited by Erik de Haan,
Ann Baldwin, Nicola Carew,
Stephanie Conway, Jude Elliman,
Jacqui Hazell, Andrew Martin,
Saskia Mureau, Paul O'Connell,
Nick Pounder, Paul Rutherford
and Christina Wanke

First published in 2013 by Libri Publishing

Copyright © Libri Publishing

Authors retain copyright of individual chapters.

The right of Erik de Haan, Ann Baldwin, Nicola Carew, Stephanie Conway, Jude Elliman, Jacqui Hazell, Andrew Martin, Saskia Mureau, Paul O'Connell, Nick Pounder, Paul Rutherford and Christina Wanke to be identified as the authors of this work has been asserted in accordance with the Copyright, Designs and Patents Act, 1988.

ISBN 978 1 907471 77 3

All rights reserved. No part of this publication may be reproduced, stored in any retrieval system or transmitted in any form or by any means, electronic, mechanical, photocopying, recording or otherwise, without the prior written permission of the copyright holder for which application should be addressed in the first instance to the publishers. No liability shall be attached to the author, the copyright holder or the publishers for loss or damage of any nature suffered as a result of reliance on the reproduction of any of the contents of this publication or any errors or omissions in its contents.

A CIP catalogue record for this book is available from The British Library

Cover design by Helen Taylor

Design and typesetting by Carnegie Publishing

Printed in the UK by Ashford Colour Press

Libri Publishing
Brunel House
Volunteer Way
Faringdon
Oxfordshire
SN7 7YR

Tel: +44 (0)845 873 3837

www.libripublishing.co.uk

CONTENTS

Praise for *Behind Closed Doors*

Behind Closed Doors is as enlightening as it is provocative. The authors have skilfully and eloquently brought the rigour of academic study to what they quite rightly describe as the "messy business" of coaching. It is a truly human and authentic account of the subtleties and sensitivities of the coaching journey. This is a journey that deserves reflection and each chapter provides a new layer of insight and learning. This book certainly warrants a second reading – you will want to go back into the very personal accounts of coaching practice described therein and in doing so stimulate and enhance your own reflective learning as a coach.

Johanna Fullerton
Business Psychologist & Director
SEVEN, Psychology at Work

Behind Closed Doors is a fascinating book that at once makes you feel both privileged and humbled. The *business* of working with the hopes, fears and real-life challenges of an executive coaching client is always an honour, but to get inside the head and heart of the coach, as this book enables us to do, is to examine the true meaning of vocation. The coaches in this book care deeply about their clients and their profession and this collection of 11 chapters will provide any coach with an incredible resource of insights to enhance their practice and transform the quality of their client relationships. Well done to all involved, the fluency of the writing and editing makes this an accessible text that I will use often.

Simon Phillips
Managing Director, Champions Club Community

Behind Closed Doors is in my opinion a very inspiring and honest book. It is the first book that I know about that describes how coaches struggle to do their work; about what really happens in a coaching relationship. It is a "must-read" for reflective practitioners interested in doing a humble inquiry together with their clients.

Professor Yvonne Burger
Vrije Universiteit, Amsterdam

Behind Closed Doors is an unusual and intimate coaching book that gives a unique insight into what happens within executive coaching relationships, through the reflections of Executive Coaches. I found it fascinating and absorbing and note with some admiration the Coaches who have literally bared and shared their souls and practice in the pursuit of learning and learn I did! The Prologue quotes Socrates who said that the "unreflected life is not worth living" and then suggests that the "unreflected coach is not worth hiring" and that resonated strongly with me. The value of this book and there is much to value is in essence: how this group of coaches reflected on their own life story, noticed how this showed up in their coaching and the impact it had on the coaching relationship and coachee outcomes. There is great learning in this book for Executive Coaches who are curious about the treasures they can harvest from inquiry and reflective practice.

Niamh Shiells
Chair, Association for Coaching Ireland

INTRODUCTION

W H A T really happens inside executive coaching? What would we see if we opened the walls and doors of confidentiality that surround the coaching room? A conversation, a chat, a tussle, pep talk or lecture? And how would what we see relate to what goes on within the people involved? How does what goes on inside the coaching room relate to what is felt and thought at the same time? How does what happens in coaching relate to what happens out there in the organisations that have yielded such rich strains for conversation? And how does simply asking these questions about coaching actually alter what goes on in the coaching room? Would such questions strengthen relevant reflection, or would they distract from the goals and the objectives of coaching?

It is our impression that these questions are rarely asked *about* coaching, and that they are rarely asked *in* coaching, and that their appearance in the coaching literature is even rarer. Reading coaching books and articles, one sometimes gets the impression of an utterly sanitised domain of recipes, theory, models and bullet points, which is largely concerned with coaches and how they ought to do the work – yet rarely about coachees and how they struggle to do their work. Much of the venerated literature in coaching seems to leave out all the mess, the grit, the doubt and the tentative, ambiguous, material that for us is so central, if not the essence of executive coaching. We have set out in this book to do something about this, and to offer the first messy, incoherent, incomplete, gritty and doubtful account of executive coaching interventions.

We believe it is about time that 'real coaching' gets documented. There has been an enormous growth in the field of executive coaching; a growth that is more than hype as it has now lasted over 20 years. Obviously, coaching is seen by many as a particularly effective and tailored form of leadership development.

1

Organisations are also increasing their internal investment in coaching even where external coaching may be afforded only for the most senior executives. Growth areas include managers as coaches, internal coaching resources, supervision and leadership team coaching. This trend is encouraging many to look for ways to enhance the effectiveness of their coaching interventions. There are plenty of 'how to' coaching texts (of mixed quality) and an equal supply of academic texts (of mixed accessibility). Yet, in the sea of material, there are very few publications that show the reality of coaching in action. In other words, there is a dearth of usable case studies in the executive coaching literature. When the curtain *is* pulled back a little, practicing coaches – and the people who retain their services – can learn much about the impact of different interventions and different styles. Through case studies professionals can learn where change happens and where potential 'stuckness' may occur.

This book comprises 11 inquiries into executive coaching practice, each based around a commonly encountered theme, ranging from listening and motivation to emotions and transitions. It contains a wealth of real-life case studies from experienced practitioners which are analysed to reveal the value they hold for the development of coach and client alike.

INSIDE THE COACHING RELATIONSHIP

This book aims to connect theory with practice by showing what happens 'inside' coaching relationships and how what happens 'inside' influences both the people in the room and, through them, the outcome of coaching. It is a deep immersion into current coaching engagements through the lens of rigorous inquiry and action-research methodology.

The 11 chapters come from the highest-ranking dissertations over the first five years of the Ashridge MSc in Executive Coaching (a total of 80 submissions). There were 12 dissertations that achieved a mark of over 75% and only one of these withdrew from the book project because of the personal nature of the work.

Within the chapters, scores of case studies are presented, each of which is unique and a world within itself, offering a view into a coach's personal practice through a specific theme, e.g. humour, listening, emotions, power, and motivation.

The cases are eminently readable, relevant and mostly represent successful coaching engagements that changed for the better both the authors and their clients.

The intent of publishing these accounts is primarily to show practising executive coaches ways to be more effective in building a relationship with a client, in reviewing this relationship, and in using the relationship to achieve more meaningful and significant coaching outcomes.

The chapters of this book offer emerging understanding in three interrelated aspects of coaching:

1. The coach's experiences, including reflections, feelings, doubts and insights

2. The relationship's trials and transitions, including atunement, ruptures and critical moments

3. The effects for the client, including benefits, change and insight.

In our view the book also highlights the importance of development, training and supervision for coaches who – even in a business context – are privy to personal issues, private concerns and considerable emotion.

For the protection of confidentiality, the cases are presented without author attribution, and all client and organisational names have been changed. But the truth of each story has been retained.

LEARNING IN THE RAW

This is *not* a book of easy answers. The aim is to challenge, disturb and excite by showing learning as it happens, from 'I haven't a clue' to moments of profound insight. In this way we hope to encourage thinking about the way we are when we are in relationship with another.

What distinguishes the coach/authors in this book from many other coaches is the extent to which they try to be conscious of what is going on in the room as the conversation develops. They use this rich relational experience to make sense of the interplay between them and their coachees. They pursue a level of purposeful mindfulness which allows the learning for both parties to be relevant, dynamic and centred around the 'here and now' and not a retrofit into preconceived models and frameworks.

Coaching is a messy business; two people bring fears, doubts, uncertainties and anxieties into a room and try to make sense of it all. In short, it is about being human. That humanness is often missing in management and even in coaching, hiding behind the apparent certainties of models and frameworks.

In the many vignettes that follow, the humans behind the coaches *are* present – warts and all.

BEHIND CLOSED DOORS: STRUCTURING WHAT WAS FOUND

The structure of the book builds up from presence with a client, to affecting the client and ourselves, to encountering and overcoming challenges with the client – just like an ordinary coaching relationship might do.

In the first part of the book we find three chapters that are curious about being with the client. Chapter 1 studies how a coach's effort to listen, to clients and to self, sheds light on what belongs to whom. Chapter 2 looks into the question of how much we want to disclose with our clients and what the consequences of self-disclosure or of not disclosing may be. Chapter 3 similarly explores the consequences of being present more fully, in this case with humour, playfulness and even sarcasm.

The second part of the book follows naturally: what happens when coach and client start affecting each other over time? Four chapters look at the life of emotions within coaching relationships: Chapter 4 is all about making emotions explicit, Chapter 5 about doing so in a culture that is not used to thinking explicitly about emotion, Chapter 6 about the impact of vulnerability and power differentials and Chapter 7 about finding a 'secure base' to help processing the growing emotion of a coaching relationship.

The third and final part of the book is about putting in place four more aspects that every coaching relationship needs. They are the kinds of things one might look at once the 'secure base' is 'good enough' (Chapter 7) for client and coach to begin working together. Building and developing awareness (Chapter 8), goals and objectives (Chapter 9), motivation (Chapter 10) and change and transitions (Chapter 11) are the topics of these chapters in Part 3.

The three parts of the book are preceded by a prologue about the nature of the inquiry process on which all the authors have embarked – and are followed by an epilogue celebrating the freshness of these inquiries. The epilogue poses the question how we as coaches can maintain with our clients the freshness of our inquiry.

Here is a short introduction to every chapter in the book with 'she' and 'her' referring to both male and female coaches:

PROLOGUE: ON INQUIRY, THE GROUNDWORK OF COACHING

The prologue highlights the links between the fields of executive coaching and phenomenological inquiry, which are both reflective practices aimed at enhancing understanding, meaning making and (self-) insight. It shows how working on one's own 'inquiry question' or 'learning objective' in conversation with others may prepare oneself for working on the 'learning objectives' of others in a coaching relationship.

PART ONE: INQUIRING INTO BEING WITH THE CLIENT AND THE RELATIONSHIP

1. *Listening: What is needed for me to listen well and what happens with me and my clients when I do?* We listen and make sense of the world through

our unique lens and life experiences which manifest as our prevailing assumptions, behaviours and interpersonal relations. This interplay is hugely significant for those of us who work as coaches as we often share our insights and interpretations of our clients' stories with them as an explicit intervention in the coaching session. This case study explores how an awareness of what the coach brings into the room helps us to distinguish 'what comes from whom' and to tune into the 'vital' aspects of our clients communication, transforming the coaching relationship and outcomes.

2. *Disclosure: What happens when I bring 'me' in the room, overtly, covertly and unintentionally?* This study explores how self-disclosure can be a helpful, conscious part of the coaching relationship. It emerges that the author's attempt to avoid countertransference in the sessions with coachees had the potential for interfering with creating an effective working alliance. Without feeling a sense of who we are as coaches, coachees may lack the sense of intimacy that gives them courage to explore deeply. Reciprocal self-disclosure, or something personal about the coach that is shared as part of the relationship, could be one way of helping coachees to make sense of what they are revealing. Along this very personal journey there were many challenges and pitfalls but out of it came the potential for richer and more productive working relationships.

3. *Humour: What happens in moments of humour with my clients?* What does it mean to have a well-developed 'sense' of humour as a coach? Humour can build strong rapport and open up new discoveries for both the coach and client. It can move beneath the surface reality, unearth hidden emotions and birth new ideas. This case study explores how humour can be used both positively and negatively within coaching rela-tionships – as a source of fun and creativity, and its potential to become a habit, closing down openness and being used to avoid what really needs to be discussed.

PART TWO: INQUIRING INTO THE EVOLVING COACHING RELATIONSHIP

4. *How does my exploration of emotions affect my clients' experience of coaching?* In this case study, which includes discussion of the limitations of a company manager also acting as an internal relational coach, the internal coach explores self-awareness and emotional inclusion. Becoming aware of a tendency to control, to ask leading questions and to become directive in coaching, the coach seeks to 'drop the mask' and be

more open, curious, and aware of his affective response to the client. These emotions and feelings are expressed verbally and non-verbally and are shared with the purpose of creating authentic contact and deepening the relationship in the service of the client.

5. *How do I work with emotions in a setting where expressing emotions is not so common?* Many coaches encounter people in organisations for whom emotions have an ambiguous connotation. Rationality is highly favoured in many business environments, and the expression of emotion is frowned upon. How can a coach be effective in this setting, when working with emotions can be especially useful? This case study shows how gender differences play a role, addresses the balance between structure (highly valued in technical companies) and 'going with the flow', and explores what is required of a coach in managing her or his own emotions.

6. *How do power and vulnerability manifest themselves in my coaching relationships?* This coach believed her coaching approach was professional and avoided any control of her clients' agendas. Yet her inquiries showed her that she did take control in many different ways, and that her practice of keeping 'the real me' behind barriers was a hindrance to the client relationship. Through reflection, research and experimentation in real coaching sessions, she began to appreciate that more open, vulnerable and power-brokered relationships created much improved coaching experiences for her clients and much deeper connections and understanding between coach and client. Through their feedback her clients taught her how to be a better coach.

7. *How do I create a secure base in my coaching relationships?* In attachment theory, John Bowlby identifies a secure base as vital for a child's social, emotional and intellectual growth. Building on that principle, this case study identifies conditions and enablers needed to create a secure base in coaching, and explores the importance of safety and security for both coach and client in the coaching relationship. In a very personal journey, it explores the impact of life script on the coach's capabilities and the conditions she needs in place to experience safety and a secure base.

PART THREE: INQUIRING INTO SPECIFIC CHALLENGES FOR THE COACHING RELATIONSHIP

8. *Developing awareness: the role of somatic experience in building client awareness.* Much has been written about the role of attention and

awareness in coaching, but attention to and awareness of *what* is often unclear or narrowly defined. The emphasis on cognitive skills in problem solving – the dominant mode of thought in most organisations – leads to a focus on conscious thought and language as the main signifiers of being. This case study highlights the oft-forgotten aspects of somatic experience, and how increasing awareness of what the body communicates to both coach and coachee can have a profound impact on both the participants in a coaching relationship.

9. *Developing self-congruent goals: 'doing less, being more'.* Agreeing goals is a core dimension of an effective working alliance: 'how can I achieve defined business objectives while still remaining myself and striving for self-identified, personal goals'? This case study inquires into the process of setting and working towards self-congruent goals as a core element of intentional personal change. By accepting the challenge of the organisational goals while consciously staying in touch with the inner centre, a creative tension can be generated. Organisational goals can then form a dynamic framework and invitation to step out of the comfort zone into a space of stretching and learning. The question of 'What do I want to accomplish?' might then turn into 'Who do I want to become?'

10. *Developing motivation: a journey of awareness, insight and new thinking.* This research started by looking at the impact of the clients' motivation on the coaching relationship, driven by a concern that perhaps some clients weren't motivated enough to gain a benefit from coaching. In addition to exploring their motivation, the inquiry reveals the impact of the coach's and sponsor's motivation and the impact of sometimes conflicted motivations of one or more parties. The awareness of these dynamics on the coaching relationship and the coaching outcomes for all members of the coaching triangle potentially is profound.

11. *Developing transitions: gaining perspective on personal change.* Our worlds rarely stand still for long as we seek to make sense of and adapt to change. The continual search for ever higher efficiency and effectiveness often means that before the last changes are embedded, benefits realised and closures achieved, we are off again in the pursuit of nirvana. This study examines how identifying the distinct stages of a transition can help a client understand her responses to change and aid the coach in supporting her through her journey. It also charts how a coach's recent experience of change has influenced what she brings to the client relationship.

EPILOGUE: DEVELOPING OUR CAPACITY TO BE AFFECTED IN RELATIONSHIP

The epilogue draws together the many strands of learning, inquiry and coaching in the book in the light of the longer-term development of an executive coach or consultant. What makes a good coach? How can a good coach preserve her freshness and stance of inquiry? The epilogue speaks about the contradictory aspects of developing at the same time both a thinner and a thicker skin, to conclude with some questions about 'the skin we live in' as executive coaches.

We would like profusely to thank Emma Wishart for her invaluable help in bringing together both us as a team and the manuscript as a book, with careful editing.

Dear reader, may you now enjoy the fruits of our reflection on the emerging sense of being present in a coaching relationship and weave these stories into your own coaching relationships!

Yours

Erik de Haan, Ann Baldwin, Nicola Carew, Stephanie Conway, Jude Elliman, Jacqui Hazell, Andrew Martin, Saskia Mureau, Paul O'Connell, Nick Pounder, Paul Rutherford and Christina Wanke

Erik de Haan
London, 2012

PROLOGUE

ON INQUIRY, THE GROUNDWORK OF COACHING

*Of none of our future statements do we positively affirm that the fact is
exactly as we state it, but we simply record each fact, like a chronicler, as it
appears to us at the moment.* (S.E. I.4) *

T H I S book is homage to the simple practice of 'just' sitting at the feet
of your own experience. The eleven authors of this book have done
nothing more, and nothing less, than staying attentively with their practice
as it unfolds, staying in touch with their experiences as they are. They have
experienced how easy it is to rush in and label, categorise or judge, how
tempting to prejudge or evaluate these experiences, even to act on them in a
variety of ways. They have experienced how easy it is to get carried away by
experience, rather than taking the time to just observe and be present, or in
other words, without taking the time 'to just experience'. In short they have set
themselves a challenging task, namely to 'just' experience their experiences.

ABOUT THE SCHOOLS, THEIR IRRECONCILABLE DIFFERENCES AND THE LIMITS OF KNOWING

The domain of practice of this book is *executive coaching*, the branch of
organisation-development consulting that specialises in providing one-to-
one helping conversations for leaders and professionals. There is a strong

---

* Sextus Empiricus writes this at the beginning of his text on scepticism: *Outline of
Pyrrhonism,* a text to which I will return several times in this Prologue in direct
quotes from the Loeb Classics translation (in italics). I will refer to it briefly by
S.E. – e.g. this citation is at S.E. I.4, *Outline of Pyrrhonism* Book One Section 4. Of
Sextus Empiricus very little is known and he is usually described as a Greek
physician and philosopher living in Alexandria, Athens and Rome around the
year 200 AD. He wrote in Greek and drew on five hundred years of sceptical
philosophy, a tradition that started with Pyrrho from Elis who travelled with
Alexander the Great on his campaigns in the East.

parallel between the practices that led to this book ('just sitting attentively...' etc.) and what coaches may do with their clients, namely 'just' to sit with them and be present with their experiences and their sense-making of their experiences, and their own sense-making of being present with all of that. 'Just' sitting at the feet of experience matches the simplest offer that executive coaches may make to their clients. In this book executive coaches make this simplest of offers to themselves and to the development of their practice.

It is a rather minimalistic thing to do in coaching, 'just' sitting with experience. Schools abound with competing ideas about what else coaches and clients should be doing together:

- *Solution focused coaching* tells us to avoid 'problem traps', look on the bright side, at what works, when problems are not there, and imagine even brighter futures with e.g. the 'miracle question': 'how might you know that you have found what you are seeking?' (Greene and Grant, 2003).

- *Performance coaching* tells us to ask for goals first and foremost, then to establish the tension between those future goals and present reality, then to move on to ways in which we can reduce that gap, and finally to remind ourselves of what exactly we are going to do to reach the goals (Whitmore, 1992).

- *Rational-emotive coaching* tells us to dig in to our 'false' cognitions, self-beliefs, and limiting assumptions, challenge them and adopt a stoic stance in the face of adversity, keeping our emotions as much as we can under our control (Sherin and Caiger, 2004).

- *Person-centred coaching* tells us to offer an exuberance of warmth, respect and understanding from within, to any issues and situations that our clients may offer. In fact, in this conception of coaching we need to be as unconditional and pure in our love and understanding as a loving parent (Joseph, 2006).

- *Relational coaching* tells us to investigate and reinforce the productivity of the relationship from the client's perspective, and explicitly to explore with the client the present coaching relationship (De Haan, 2008a).

This is only a very short selection of models and methodologies, with the first three taken from various cognitive-behavioural schools, the next one from a humanistic orientation and the final one being broadly integrative with origins in psycho-analysis.

There is not a lot of evidence about what would be helpful to do in coaching to back up these various claims. Moreover, what evidence there is can be contested as there have been very few quantitative-research studies in the field. Even if one trusts the evidence from, say, trials with control groups then there are still good reasons to be sceptical about how much of that can be translated back to practice. That evidence is based on simple digits collected after or at unique points in a long and rich coaching journey.

To make matters even worse, what evidence we do have points at *equivalence* of all these various models and schools. 'Everybody has won, and all must have prizes" – or put slightly ironically: clients and coaches are going to get extremely busy in their coaching room trying to do all these many things that are now shown to be effective, many things that are arguably incompatible.

There is a long history in executive coaching, and more generally, in helping conversations, of presenting specific ideas, schools, techniques and interventions as somehow 'effective' or 'evidence based'. At the same time we – the authors of this book – remain convinced that it is far too early for any single approach or technique to claim a unique evidence base.

> *The schools frequently admit only such facts as can be explained by their own theories, and dismiss facts which conflict therewith though possessing equal probability.* (S.E. I.183)

Due to this situation which is in my view very likely to continue, it is ultimately very hard to say about any piece of coaching that it is 'good' coaching (or 'helpful', 'effective', 'adroit', etc.), even for experts. In order to attest that any coaching is good, one needs a criterion or criteria. For any criteria one wishes to apply one needs a demonstration that the criterion is actually related to what is good in coaching, i.e., to outcome, or effectiveness. For such a demonstration one needs to know in general terms what makes up a good intervention or a good assignment, and why. As professionals I believe we should be honest and remind ourselves regularly that we remain clueless as to all of the above.

> *If, then, one cannot hope to pass judgement on the afore-mentioned impressions either with or without proof, the conclusion we are driven to is suspension; for while we can, no doubt, state the nature which each object appears to possess as viewed in a certain position or at a certain distance or in a certain place, what its real nature is, we are unable to declare.* (S.E. I.123)

---

* The present state of affairs in helping conversations was already intuited by Rosenzweig (1936) and to sum it up he coined this phrase from the 'Dodo verdict' in *Alice in Wonderland* (Chapter 3).

Despite the lack of certainty about what works, we keep finding that coaching is generally considered helpful and shown to be effective and also that panels of experts and lay people (such as in our own Ashridge Coach Accreditation Process) tend to agree remarkably well on those matters. Nevertheless, the reasons for agreement are not known and have not been demonstrated. Moreover panels of accreditors do come across occasional nasty surprises of profound disagreement in co-assessing live sessions of coaching.

In my view this is a state of affairs that calls for a 'minimalist' conception of coaching, where we 'just' sit in doubt about what 'helpful' means, and try to remain present with our experience, the experience both within the 'material' of coaching and also as emerging in the here-and-now interaction in the room.

ABOUT THE REAL FREEDOM AND UNDERSTANDING ONE CAN ACQUIRE BY NOT KNOWING

After reading so many textbooks with good ideas about what to do in the coaching room, to forget about all that and suspend our judgements can really free us up. As in every profession, it appears to me very wholesome to try in this way to relieve ourselves of all dogmatism. Freed up from preconceived notions and dogmatic tenets we become more aware of how little we can really know about our contributions and we become as sensitive as we can be to what our experiences might be telling us in this very moment as we do our work.

This book is a testimony to what one may gain in this way, by just making contact again with our experience as it occurs to us. The authors of this book have all strived to be acutely aware, even critically aware, of their experience as it unfolds right there for them. They have reflected on their coaching experiences before, during and after sessions, with as little pre-judgement as they could muster.

In this way their coaching experiences were examined, re-examined and allowed to become part of their coaching journeys in a lively and reflective way. The authors of this book hope that these experiences may now inform yours, as you strive to make sense of them and reflect upon them in your own way, whilst reading this book.

It was Socrates who said, in defence of his philosophical way of life,[*] that the 'unreflected life is not worth living'. We believe similarly that the 'unreflected coach' is not worth hiring. And to make it even more Socratic: the reflected coach is not worth hiring either. That would still make the person

---

[*] As romanticised by Plato in the *Apology*, 38a.

who hires into a passive 'customer' of a reflective coach. What is on the other hand worth doing in our opinion is engaging reflectively and humbly... together with your reflective and humble coach.

I would like to describe this practice of 'sitting at the feet of one's experience' in a few more words. The practice has many forerunners and many followers, in a great variety of traditions of thought. I will here follow the Sceptical tradition, which is one of the oldest and seems closest to our present-day ideas about reflective inquiry.

In fact, in ancient Greek the translation of 'inquiry' would be the word 'scepsis' which is usually translated into English more fully as 'suspension of judgement in investigation' (S.E. I.30). Scepsis can also be translated with 'examination' and with 'doubt'.

Inquiry means, first and foremost, taking leave of what opinions and views we may have and holding lightly all 'knowledge' we may think we possess. For a genuine inquiry we need actively to open up space. This opening up of space the sceptics call 'deferring judgement':

> *Accordingly, the sceptic, seeing so great a diversity of practices, suspends judgement as to the natural existence of anything good or bad or (in general) fit or unfit to be done, therein abstaining from the rashness of dogmatism; and he follows undogmatically the ordinary rules of life, and because of this he remains impassive in respect of matters of opinion...*
> (S.E. III.235)

To open up space for inquiry, we may even need to depart from certain convictions that are important to us, about how one 'ought' to live, how one 'should' coach, or what reflections are 'better' than others. Much more room for inquiry will be opened up if we can park our opinions on the good and the bad, the effective and ineffective, and the ethical and unethical, even if only temporarily.

> *For the man that opines that anything is by nature good or bad is forever being disquieted: when he is without the things which he deems good he believes himself to be tormented by things naturally bad and he pursues after the things which are, as he thinks, good; which when he has obtained he keeps falling into still more perturbations because of his irrational and immoderate elation, and in his dread of a change of fortune he uses every endeavour to avoid losing the things which he deems good. On the other hand, the man who determines nothing as to what is naturally good or bad neither shuns nor pursues anything eagerly; and, in consequence, he is unperturbed.* (S.E. I.27)

We also need to suspend or defer our judgements regarding inquiry itself and what it is yielding. This is why the findings of inquiry are quite often liberating and innovative. They are also impossible to generalise or turn into 'knowledge' (generalisable, replicable facts or essential truths), precisely because inquiry is such a highly personal, unique and liberating expedition.

> No practice can be perceived in its purity or essence. There is the
> relationship with the perceiver and the present state of the perceiver that
> impacts on the perception, and there is also the context and the other
> practices in view which impact on the perception. (S.E. I.135)

Finally, complex definitions and jargon are best avoided, as they have a tendency to close down the space for reflection with elaborate and esoteric language.

> Thus for instance, to take a silly example, suppose that one wished to ask
> someone whether he had met a man riding a horse and leading a dog and
> put the question in this form – 'O rational mortal animal, receptive of
> intelligence and science, have you met with an animal capable of laughter,
> with broad nails and receptive of political science, with his posterior
> hemispheres seated on a mortal animal capable of neighing, and leading
> a four-footed animal capable of barking?' – how would one be otherwise
> than ridiculous, in thus reducing the man to speechlessness concerning so
> familiar an object, because of one's definitions? (S.E. I.211)

The sceptics had a number of 'invocations' to help them to stay rigorously with the practice of undogmatically attending to experience, such as (see S.E. I.107 onwards):

1. 'Not more': do not attend to one aspect more than to another. Or: for what reason would this view or this perspective be more important than that one?

2. 'Non-assertion': assertively non-assert that one thing is like this or like that, to remind oneself that ultimately one is not able to affirm or deny any assertion or evidence, as a counter-example may yet emerge.

3. 'Perhaps, possibly, maybe': an emphasis on qualifying terms that make sure we are reminded that we don't have ultimate knowledge or final truths.

4. 'I suspend judgement': reinforcing the basic premise which creates space to observe and to reflect, in a fresh way.

5. 'I determine nothing': I am in a state of mind where I come to no conclusions and where I do not, nor would I want to, determine anything.

These are the practices for which the executive coaches writing this book have aimed in their inquiry work. A state of mind of suspending judgement about experience means you do not deny it whilst you also do not affirm it, you don't embrace it nor do you flee it, you don't value it nor do you devalue it – in short you aim to be perfectly still and tranquil with regard to your present experience, neither moving it along nor being moved by it.

On a more practical level, the contributors of this book have made a number of distinctions whilst opening themselves up for experience:

- Their clients' and sponsors' experiences; the experiences of their clients' organisational counterparts such as colleagues, line managers and customers; and their own experiences with their clients.

- Individual reflection, co-created reflection (in dialogue) and gathering fruits from outside reflection by third parties; in other words first-person, second-person and third-person inquiry (Reason and Torbert, 2001).

- Individual or first-person reflection entirely within themselves or reflection with others (such as their clients) into how they are experienced by those; in other words, the 'inner arc' and 'outer arc' of personal inquiry (Marshall, 2001).

Of all the many traditions of philosophical scepticism that have practiced these and similar paths to inquiry-based understanding (Buddhism, Cārvāka, Jainism, Al-Ghazali, Montaigne, etc.), I would like to draw particular attention to *mindfulness*: inquiry into the present moment, as practiced in Buddhism. Both traditions I am referring to in this Prologue – Buddhist meditation and Pyrrhonic scepticism – are over two millennia old: one a great tradition from the West and one from the East, and they come together in their ability to create space and tranquillity for the inquirer (*ataraxia* or peace-of-mind/serenity in scepticism; *bodhi* or awakening/enlightenment in Buddhism).

Amongst the earliest suttas of Buddhist scripture there are instructions to mindfulness practice and they describe the liberation felt by just attending, or just noticing, in a very similar way to Sextus Empiricus. Here is an example:

Thus he lives contemplating feeling in feelings internally, or he lives contemplating feeling in feelings externally, or he lives contemplating feeling in feelings internally and externally. He lives contemplating origination-

things in feelings, or he lives contemplating dissolution-things in feelings,
or he lives contemplating origination-and-dissolution-things in feelings. Or
his mindfulness is established with the thought: 'Feeling exists,' to the extent
necessary just for noticing and remembrance and he lives independent and
clings to naught in the world. Thus, indeed, O bhikkhus, a bhikkhu* lives
contemplating feeling in feelings. (Sathipattana Sutta, 29 BC).

Whilst the sceptical tradition helps us to move away from dogmatic views
and to defer our judgements, so that we can begin to attend to experience
itself, the Buddhist tradition goes deeper and writes in more detail about
how it is to attend fully and inquire into experience in the present moment,
as it unfolds. Chapters 8 and 9 of this book make explicit reference to this
Buddhist tradition, and more links between Buddhist traditions and the
inquiry process can be found in Bentz and Shapiro (1998).

SPECIFIC HELP WITH UNDERTAKING AN INQUIRY: BEYOND RIGHT AND WRONG

The first problem for practitioners, who want to 'just' sit with experience, or
undertake a 'pure' or 'sceptical' inquiry, is that they will want to do it well. As
with anything they would undertake they will want to make a good job of it.
Right there, at the very start, they begin interfering with their own inquiry,
as they start asking themselves questions about what a good inquiry might
be, which methods to use, and how to make the best use of time, models,
guidance and other resources. The idea of doing an inquiry well is a fallacy,
and sets up the polarities of good and evil, and the dogmas of established
doctrine, from which one wants to move away. It is possible to sit at the feet
of your experience rigorously, or intensely, but it is hard to do it 'rightly', or
'correctly'†.

The second problem is the choice of an inquiry question. A question
limits space rather than opening up space. To choose a focus constrains the
essential freedom of inquiry, and thus goes against the spirit of inquiry, even
if ever so slightly. Strictly, it is not necessary to have an inquiry question in
order to sustain an on-going inquiry. Yet it is very hard to sustain an inquiry

---

*   A 'bhikkhu' is a practitioner or a monk; literally a 'beggar'.

†   Thus we can assess the fruits of inquiry afterwards as we do at Ashridge with e.g.
    the dissertations of the Ashridge MSc in Executive Coaching, such as the ones
    you find summarised in this book. We can judge an inquiry afterwards, or at least
    the written-up inquiry, in terms of what we infer about the quality of inquiry
    (retrospectively), and in terms of other aspects as well... but if we judge an inquiry
    as it happens we seriously obstruct it because by judging we take it away from its
    central purpose.

stance without a question, even if that is doable. An 'area of focus' might do instead of a question, as for example the concentration on our breathing when we engage in certain forms of meditation. An example of a focus might be 'the start of meetings', so in an inquiry process I might be interested just in what happens at the start of meetings. A clear bounded area or well-defined question limiting the topic of inquiry helps to contain the experiences, structure the work and measure its progress, yet needs to be held lightly whilst one is engaged in the inquiry. Insight from other domains might just enter into the inquiry process and serve the process rather than distract from it.

Every author in this book has chosen a clear and well-defined inquiry question, which has helped them to progress the inquiry and complete it in a matter of months.

The third problem of inquiry is its impermanence. A pure inquiry is like the flow of our attention or like our heartbeat: always in motion, never fixed, self-directed as well as responsive. If an inquiry stops flowing, then it dries up, ossifies and turns into 'dogma': it stops being an inquiry and its life saps away before our eyes. On the other hand, once you embark on or ignite any inquiry process you will notice that you enter a natural cycle. A healthy inquiry therefore, is necessarily circular yet also has elements of freshness, more like a spiral.

It is possible to have an unhealthy inquiry as well which is circular, when we are fretting about something or when we are navel gazing. In these cases you have an inquiry that turns in on itself, an inquiry curious of itself only, which stops being fresh, stops yielding new data.

If you have ever tried engaging in a meditation practice, you will have noticed that your attention drifts off and then returns. Something unsettles you, brings you out of your meditation, and then you recalibrate or re-find your meditative stance. Inquiry is exactly the same and this is why we often talk about 'inquiry cycles'. Inquiry cycles exist on many levels and time-scales all at once. The smallest cycle is straightforward: take an object in your field of view and try to focus your full attention on that object. You will find that within seconds your attention goes somewhere else, or if not away entirely it may go to a detail or some abstract property of the object; then you will remind yourself, and your attention will flow back to the object. This is the simplest and briefest example of an inquiry cycle. On a larger scale an inquiry cycle can be seen as one particular meeting that you are going to study from a certain aspect, or even a longer experience like a journey or an assignment. You will try to stay with the meeting and with the focus of your inquiry for the time it takes, and you will find yourself drifting in and out of focus. At the end of the meeting or journey that particular inquiry is over as the engagement is over. Similarly you could set an hour apart to do an inquiry, e.g. set an alarm to remind you of your timing. Again, this would be a structured inquiry cycle. You would experience many cycles during the hour, yet the hour itself would also be a clearly defined cycle. At the end of the hour you will find yourself in the same place, yet somehow enriched or changed by new perspectives, sentiments, experiences, all that happened, all that was fresh and all that changed your initial outlook.

The richness of cycles of inquiry is impossible to describe, and ever changing. There are cycles of bodily sensation, cycles of emotions, cycles of thought and deliberation, just to name a few. More so, all these cycles are ever-present and ever-changing, whether we attend to them or not. This is part of why we will not be in the exact same place after we complete what we think of as an inquiry cycle: if we sense we complete one circle we are still mid-way on other cycles which are of different duration or intensity. Take the example of focusing on an object on the table: at the end of that exercise, having completed the cycle of attending to that object, your heart has beaten many cycles, your breathing has probably completed some cycles as well, and yet you only progressed little in the day let alone longer cycles on the calendar or a life-span.

Within all these manifold nested cycles there is one movement which is of particular relevance to sitting at the feet of your experience. This is the cycle of your attention, in other words your presence with the inquiry itself. Noticing yourself as you are inquiring you may notice how your concentration grows and wanes. You immerse yourself in your inquiry one moment, you don't even think about it a moment later. These cycles of 'concentration' and 'distraction', which we could also call cycles of experiencing and reflecting, are ever present. They are like the tides of your mind, a continuing ebb and flow of offering attention, drawing it back, becoming lively, letting go, switching on, switching off, immersion, reflection, in endless cycles. In my experience something interesting happens each time the waves of attention flood your inquiry and then flow back again. If you notice carefully you will see that there is a small 'correction' every time this happens: a conscious shift of attention, a small critique within your inquiry, or a tiny assessment of what you are just experiencing. In my experience we shift from inquiry to meta-inquiry and back during each one of these moments. We focus and then we think about our focus, and then we focus again. We cannot do both at the same time: we cannot attend *and* reflect on our attending, we cannot inquire *and* reap the fruits of our inquiry. These things happen sequentially, not in parallel. To find, learn, change or progress in the inquiry one needs both, one needs immersion and one needs realisation. In other words it is on the cusp of this oscillation that something new happens, or some opportunity for inquiry gets lost, time and time again.

During these cycles not only the fruits of inquiry change, also the questions of inquiry change. The impermanence stretches out to the inquiry itself and its focus. Engaging in inquiry may change the question or focus of inquiry, and that is fine. Indeed, often it is a good sign if the initial question for an inquiry is changed by the inquiry itself. It is a good indication that something meaningful, something refreshing and new, may have taken place during the inquiry.

Here is a summary of these three challenges of inquiry, which can also be seen as three pillars one has to have in place for any inquiry:

1. We need to suspend judgement regarding the inquiry itself, and hold lightly whether we are doing 'it' right or not

2. We need to find some anchor in a particular object or area of inquiry, often expressed by our 'inquiry question'; also, we need to suspend judgement with regard to this anchor itself and appreciate its impermanence

3. We need to navigate our way through nested cycles of inquiry, reaping insights or findings of more permanence from the ever-present fluctuations, oscillations and transitions of attention.

NOT KNOWING AND INQUIRY CAN FREE YOU UP FOR EXECUTIVE COACHING TOO

Sextus Empiricus distinguished ten broad areas about which to be sceptical – or to inquire, which he says may be broken down into three categories:

1. We may be sceptical of *ourselves* as 'subjective' perceivers

2. We may be sceptical of the 'objective' *world* around us

3. We may be sceptical about the *relationship* between perceiver and the world (S.E. i.38; italics mine).

In executive coaching, similarly, we may be sceptical about ourselves as the observer-participants, the other person and the 'material' of coaching, and the relationship between the two collaborators, or the coaching relationship. So if we follow through the same 'minimalist' inquiry as described above within our executive coaching work, we now sit at the feet of our experience with our coaching clients and gently inquire into:

1. Our own state of mind, feelings, impressions, and in particular our 'felt' bodily sense as we are engaged in the coaching relationship

19

2. Our client and partner, and the material he or she is bringing to this coaching session at this very moment

3. The relationship of coaching as it unfolds and what is going on within that relationship that may shed light on one of the other fields of inquiry.

The inquiry process that Sextus Empiricus recommends and that the authors in this book have followed with regard to their coaching practice, prepares one for a purer, more grounded stance during coaching. We may not change anything in our coaching approach, yet we develop a more reflective stance towards what we are doing. We notice the material, our responses to the material, our attraction to certain aspects and moving away from other aspects, our values and judgements building up, and our secondary responses to these responses to the situation and the material, etcetera. We try to stay as much as possible with the experience itself and our direct impressions, and hold any of our judgements, hypotheses, memories, and thoughts, as they are bound to emerge incessantly, as lightly as possible.

As an example let us look at my process notes from the first few minutes of the eighth and last encounter with a client:

> *Case Example* Just before the session I realise first that I am slightly rushed as I arrive shortly before, and then I find out that something has gone wrong with room reservations so that we are in a different room than usual. I notice my own feelings about this and some tension building up. I also notice how I am making a conscious effort to calm down. Then I am aware of my client walking in. I notice facial expressions, indications of mood, anxiety. I notice the different environment of the 'new' room, and I find myself wondering how my client is responding to this room change. My client tells me he has asked and was granted a reduction of responsibilities in his job. I notice his delight and his confidence, and also his slight embarrassment. A memory comes up, from an earlier session; regarding the expert-witness work my client enjoys doing outside of his job. He will have more time for that. I notice myself wanting to make a note, apparently not wanting to lose that thought. I venture an observation on the new arrangement. I notice my client finds my observation challenging. I notice tension in my chest. I keep noticing how my client seems cautious and slightly taken aback. I am not sure whether I have lost him here. Something seems to be brewing inside him. I decide to say something about the effect of my observation. I name an emotion he recognises. We are now both more relaxed. There is a similar feel of confidence and embarrassment now between us as I noticed within the client just a minute ago. I notice myself wondering how the client wants to use this final session.

In a study of 86 descriptions of critical moments from coaching practice written up by inexperienced coaches (De Haan, 2008b) I have found that critical moments of beginning coaches are strongly characterised by *doubts*. More experienced coaches tend to feel more secure about their critical moments, and even if they are tense and anxious in their most critical work, they have been shown to be a lot less doubtful than beginning coaches (Day, De Haan, Sills, Bertie and Blass, 2008). What the coaches in this book are trying to do is to keep those doubts fresh and vivid with regard to their lived experience, by inquiring into their experience in an open and curious way, deferring judgement as much as possible. They try to retain this position of curiosity, ambiguity and doubt, which lies at the basis of every coaching contract, over a longer period of time.

Reflective, sceptical inquiry can be used on many levels. It has been used in this book to develop coaching practice and in the interest of the authors' own longer-term professional development as executive coaches. It can also be used on a session-by-session level as we offer our clients this most basic offer of a coach: grounded, open and reflective presence. Thirdly, inquiry will be used by our coaching clients as well, to deepen their reflections on their circumstances. We may at several times during coaching assignments help our clients actively to develop a more reflective stance, by noticing together with the client and inviting the client to notice. Executive coaching then consists of building up a stream of reflectiveness and doubt alongside the convictions and action orientation of the client.

> *Case example.* I remember one senior board-level client in the telecoms industry with whom I worked with for several years, who radiated his executive presence and control, and quite often approached me in a manner similar to how he would approach, say, an IT contractor, letting me know about his progress and where he might have a query for me. I responded with little more than just my observations, letting him know what I had understood of his progress and of his queries, and also how I noticed his stance towards his progress and also towards me. On his final feedback form he described the impact of my reflective presence: 'I think the moments where difficult questions were asked about my behaviour or honest feedback about what I have said, stand out for me. I enjoy the direct feedback during our conversations, about the job and the whole environment around it'.

There is another way in which a sceptical stance in the vein of Sextus Empiricus is groundwork for coaching. Executive coaching material often starts off in a rather dogmatic and formulaic way, in the shape of repetitive thinking about experiences which appears to be dished up to 'entertain' or

21

'cover' the coaching session. Coaches enter from a position of advantage here, as they come fresh to the material. By remaining fresh and inquisitive they can tear down stilted thinking and rash conclusions, to open up space for new reflection on the client's original experiences. Sextus Empiricus has shown us the way as to how to do this, in books with titles such as *Against the dogmatists*, *Against the professors*, and *Against the logicians*.

If inquiry is the groundwork for coaching, then based on the previous section we can intuit the groundwork for this groundwork. In that section it was suggested that the underpinning foundations of inquiry are:

1. Letting go of the pressure to do it right

2. Having a clear anchor or inquiry question, which in a coaching session might be to understand what the client brings

3. Navigating and extracting insight from impermanence and nested cycles.

In other words, sitting at the feet of your experience means opening up space by suspending judgement, anchoring your perspective and letting go, reaping from experience and again letting go, and opening up space again, and so on in continuing cycles of experience and inquiry.

I end with the same quote and with the same emphasis that the material of this book is 'just' tentative, 'just' lived personal experience: mostly observations and hypotheses – with very few conclusions. We have left it like this on purpose: to facilitate its entry into *your* reflections, *your* experiences, and to leave you something on which you would enjoy building and improving:

> *Of none of our future statements do we positively affirm that the fact is exactly as we state it, but we simply record each fact, like a chronicler, as it appears to us at the moment.* (SE I.4)

Erik de Haan

PART ONE

INQUIRING INTO BEING WITH THE CLIENT AND THE RELATIONSHIP

CHAPTER 1

PERSONAL REFLECTIONS AND LEARNING FROM THE PROCESS OF LEARNING BY DOING

INTRODUCTION

M Y exploration and learning throughout the period of my inquiry was chaotic, confusing and at times extremely distressing. However this chaos and confusion yielded fantastic moments for both me and my clients. It led me to reflect on previous coaching relationships as a source of learning and increasingly...as I learnt more, I viewed them through a different lens. One example in particular springs to mind. One of my previous clients had experienced intense instability and tension within our sessions. He was trying to get his boss to respect his ideas and give him more autonomy generally within his dealings with customers. My coaching record showed that the road map and pre-set goals around which we had contracted were featuring less and less in our sessions. I had noted that this period of our alliance had been a very stressful time for me also. My journal detailed that I believed it to have been created by the tension which is created between the need (quite often from my clients) to be working within a structure and the potential that relative spontaneity and expanding boundaries can bring. Little did I know at that time that in order to achieve that potential for my clients that most of the work was sitting with me. ...because I brought this tension into the room! At that time, I lacked awareness of this as my own behaviour. I was unable therefore to make use of this, unable consciously to deploy a strategy to 'raise awareness, to name or confront the transference, respond reparatively or to allow the transference' (Sills and Joyce, 2001).

This set the self-insight and reflective theme of my coaching inquiry. My approach to continuously question and improve has stayed with me and is now habitual. I now consider the practice of habitual reflective inquiry to be one of the key differentiating characteristics of great coaches.

Throughout this inquiry, I developed a level of awareness which allowed me to acknowledge my own need for structure and process and to make use of this insight for my own benefit. It helped me to understand the origins of so much of my energy prior to and during coaching sessions. Moreover it gave me a valuable insight into this as a fundamental way of being for me which had the potential to inhibit my ability to listen well and be present with my clients. I saw that it unfolded in *my* need for structure and goals, for my coachee.

Beginning to learn from and to live with ambiguity and free-flow has in itself been an enlightening and significant learning experience for me. To start this inquiry and not to coerce my findings entirely toward a pre-determined outcome has proved to be enormously challenging and provided me with a significant insight into this, my prevailing behaviour. Specifically it enabled me to experience the strength of my propensity to start with the end in sight and the limited extent to which I was actually able to concentrate on the 'here and now'- and this went straight to the heart of my interest into this inquiry question:

> *How do I behave when I am listening well and what conditions need to exist for me to listen so as to be in the service of my clients?*

SOME INTERESTING THOUGHTS ON MY PROCESS OF INQUIRY

Over four cycles of action research I was able systematically to research, act, and experience and reflect. I took learning and insights from one coaching experience into my next coaching session. Overall, these learning cycles were rich, although extremely challenging, as a methodology. Increasingly I sought to 'be in the moment' more and yet by virtue of this methodology consciously was taking prepared material (predetermined thoughts and new insights) into the coaching room with the explicit intention of practicing and (following the sessions) reviewing my effectiveness. Interestingly...

> *Overtime, I became more effective as I prepared less!*

Previous to this inquiry I would spend a lot of time considering which approach to deploy in my coaching session, basing my assessment on my thoughts from the previous sessions and my judgement on what was 'best' for my client. Over time, with a desire to be less directive and less preoccupied, I would invariably attempt to shift away from my focus to solve my client's issues toward a focus on my client's resourcefulness – a more client centred but still solution focused approach, totally in the service of my client. This was my espoused intent.

THE FATEFULNESS OF MY INQUIRY QUESTION AND WHAT I HAVE LEARNT ABOUT WHAT IT SAYS ABOUT ME AS A COACH – SOME BACKGROUND

I have come to realise that my overwhelming and somewhat unconscious desire to 'fix' was characterising my coaching. When I look back I now see that the extent to which I enabled my clients to find their own solutions was minimal. I paid little attention to the coaching relationship itself and was somewhat blind to the benefits which such a focus could bring for me and my clients.

My underlying intention had always been to create an environment for my clients to explore their topics and for them to reach a deep level of personal insight into their own effectiveness and behaviour. However I began to examine whether my espoused approach to coaching was a reality in the coaching room. During the past 18 months, I had found myself cognitively more at home with a more humanistic and person-centred approach to coaching, 'with a vision of psychology that would have a place for human capacity for creativity, growth and choice' (McLeod, 1998). I discovered that I continuously created barriers to enabling this. This inquiry has enabled me to dismantle them. I came to accept that for many coaching engagements I arrived in a state of 'already knowing'. This inquiry has shown me just how difficult I find it to be in the moment, to experience 'what is' and take on board new learning and experiences as they arise. If I could embrace the process of Action Research as a methodology then it, in turn, would serve me well in my pursuit of a more person centred approach as it required me to experience a sense of 'immediacy' (O'Neill, 2007) into my coaching.

THE BEGINNING OF MY INQUIRY – PREPARATORY READING AND EXPLORING

DEVELOPING BEST PRACTICE LISTENING 'THE CHECKLIST'

At the onset I sought to put together 'the checklist/best practice' for good listening. This behaviour I came to realise was immensely significant for me. I was thinking (as I always do) that the answer will be out there somewhere – and not within, that is not within my own knowledge/experience. During my initial reading, I was being gloriously informed by concepts and ideas which I was using to structure a checklist of areas to enhance my listening. In particular, I found Van de Loo (2007) a useful reference. In this article he cites empathy, intuition (mentalising), free floating attention, transference and countertransference as the 'fundamental dynamics' which result in the coach and coachee engaging in an interactive synchrony and the establishment of a direct and personal relationship which is the 'royal road' to understanding and helping the client. I came to consider that my 'capacity to think and make inferences about people and their lives' (Van de Loo, 2007) was inadequate because there was too much of me (my own relationship with what was being said) in the meaning making.

SIGNIFICANT INSIGHTS FROM A SUPERVISORY SESSION

During a supervision session a colleague helped me see that I was engaging in an on-going search to seek *credibility and worth* in my work and in my ability. At the onset of this inquiry, I had begun to understand the origins of these feelings and came to view them as in accordance with the Joyce and Sills view of 'the field of relational dynamics' which maps 'the link between relational dynamics established in the past, and those maintained in the present – both inside and outside the consulting room' (Sills and Joyce, 2001). I came to accept my playing out in my current coaching relationships of the lack of regard I perceived others had for me. My origin, I judged, came from my perceived abandonment as a child, and lack of love and support generally as a child and developing adult – which, for me, still evoked many insecurities and has many unresolved aspects. Specifically, I came to acknowledge that this complex burden of self-doubt which I carry weighed heavy on my ability to have belief in what I do and who I am. Significantly, in my capacity as a coach, it was holding me back from developing my own integrated approach to coaching. I discovered that I sought continuously to characterise what I do in accordance with a stated and existing model – I desperately wanted to latch onto something as a means of validating how I coach. The constant exploration of 'why?' and 'what goes on for me when?' type questions during the inquiry process was rich mining for me, but it was also a raw exposé of what lay beneath the surface.

THE ANSWER ...OUT THERE SOMEWHERE?

What emerged was a fear of not being good enough or being able to find a solution or way forward for my client. This had undesirable effect on my ability to listen well with and to my clients. Through supervision, I discovered that habitually I gave little value to my own unique talents and gave little thought to what I bring. I looked around constantly for the right way to be and for approaches which I could assign to specific situations. I would plan as if with a menu and select from it as I went – in a very preoccupied state much of the time. I discovered that I developed a compelling and almost irresistible behaviour throughout my initial research period whereby I found myself looking for the *'golden bullet'*. I had sought desperately to be seen as credible and legitimate in my consulting and coaching work and so would often need to feel as if I had input some tangible solutions or direct the way forward. Not very humanistic or person centred! I was confused!

THE ANSWERS – WITHIN!

These revelations were painful. I came to see the extent to which these feelings are very much a part of who I *was* and how I regarded myself from day to day. I am of the opinion that the fatefulness of my choosing my inquiry topic is as much to do with a deep desire to confront this minefield or forever be deeply sad. During this distressing time I tried to capture (understand) and confront my anxieties. I had been captivated intellectually by the framework which Malan's triangle (Malan, 1979) gave me in understanding my anxieties and how they manifested in and characterised my coaching behaviour – low self-esteem and desire to fix things and rescue people. It prompted me to appreciate more of how my 'script' (Lapworth, Sills and Fish, 2001) was playing out in my life.

Around about this time the following words flowed:

> *Malan and Me*
>
> I'm not good enough for this precious privilege ....
> It bemuses me a lot why I feel the need to assist,
> For at the conscious level of me I have little regard for me.
> So I've hidden me from them...pretending that a greater guide is here
> For fear that if all they get is me, it will leave them in despair
> I've spent my life unloved so there's no respect for me –
> So why should they unfold their secret fears to me?
>
> *Excerpt from Learning Journal: 30th July 2009 (informed by the work of Malan, 1979)*

I was beginning to understand the very personal challenges which I faced in my desire to becoming a better listener and a great coach.

I can only try to live by my interpretation of the current meaning of my experience and to try to give others the permission and freedom to develop their own inward freedom and thus their own meaningful interpretation of their own experience. (Rogers, 1961)

CHAPTER 1

DEFINING MY SCRIPT IN AN ATTEMPT TO MANAGE (IGNORE) IT

My predominant behaviour at this phase of my action research was to connect with my new coaching behaviours so that I might define these 'awakenings' (as I had labelled them), with the intention of managing them in the coaching sessions. I had a sense that they should be managed out somehow and so this was my intended use for the 'script checklist' in my coaching sessions which followed. My hypothesis was that in order to be present I somehow needed to be 'absent'! At a deeper level I was feeling that there was little value in 'my' stuff and it was in the way.

WHAT IT IS TO BE ME – MY NOISE

I began to summarise my script not in accordance with the plethora of definitions afforded to us from the world of transactional analysis (Berne, 1964), (Berne, 1961), (Berne, 1972) and other offerings related to the structure of personality (Stewart and Joines, 2002), but on the basis of how I experience me. I had a strong desire to break old habits, to validate and account for myself – from how I feel and experience the world. This was an incredibly difficult but ultimately liberating summary piece to write.

MY VERY PERSONAL 'AND SO' SCRIPT

- You are not interested in me for my sake, only in what you can get from me – **and so** I will have to give you things.
- I do not matter – **and so** I will not attempt to have any of my needs met
- I am not very good – **and so** I will need to prove to you that I am /I can fix everything –you'll see
- I am nervous that I will let you down – **and so** I will focus on the things I can fix/we will follow my agenda.
- You do not like me – **and so** I will hide away from you and try to be what I think you want me to be
- You will reject me soon – **and so** I will not get close
- I will hide me from you – **and so** I will not let you know what I am thinking
- Anything nice you say will be a lie – **and so** I won't hear it
- I will focus on the negatives – **and so** I will fantasise about how incompetent you think I am.

...**and so**...I will 'be strong' and 'be perfect' (Kahler and Capers, 1974).

At the onset of this 'experiment', I had already concluded (once again starting with the end in sight!) that being absent, not present, is the key to effective listening /coaching. To leave all my insecurities and perceptions behind will enable me to go unburdened and *clean* into the coaching session. Somehow it seemed that, armed with the knowledge of the origins of my self-doubt and how this manifested in my coaching work, I could now set about the job of leaving all that behind (and outside the coaching room) and getting on with some real coaching. As if it was as easy as that!

IN SESSION: MANAGING MY 'SCRIPTY BEHAVIOUR' AND TRANSFERENCE

The session was a difficult one for my client as she wanted to contemplate a decision to exit a family member from the business. There were very obvious (to me) organisational root causes for the incidences which had led to this situation. And I worked hard to keep them from the conversation. My client spent a lot of time communicating to me how she would do anything for her daughter. The other four directors wanted to exit this person – and so my client had to make a choice between staying in the business herself and starting up again. She only saw the either/or option and this is how she set the agenda for our discussion.

I was acutely aware of feeling very cross and envious towards this family member and my 'noise' was loud during the session. I judged her behaviour to be inexcusable. The unconditional commitment and support that my client had shown toward her daughter evoked a sense of longing in me. There were many opportunities for my script to be ignited in conversation with my client and I commented in my journal, in a congratulatory manner, on how I felt a sense of being in control and in a state of containment. I was left wondering the extent to which transference and countertransference was playing out during this session. Specifically, 'was this a realistic response to the here and now' or my own 'unfinished business about this sort of person' (Sills and Joyce, 2001). My preoccupation with keeping my 'noise' silent had potentially deprived me of the opportunity to explore this with my client. I recognise that this had been a feature of most of my sessions during this phase of attempting to manage (hide) my script and suppress my insecurities.

My supervisor had previously helped me to see that this was inhibiting the wider 'relational' aspects of my coaching and so I committed to enhancing the coaching relationship and its dynamics by attempting to go with the flow more. The post session feedback from my client felt like progress!

- 'You seem to be the only one who sees how difficult this is for me'

- 'You got me thinking out of the box..... helped me see a different solution'

31

The latter was said in relation to my reframing her view of the either/or option. Finding a solution whilst not abandoning her daughter had been her primary session objective – well that's how I heard it! ...and so I allowed myself to consider the way forward she decided upon as an effective outcome for her. It pleased me that I had been able to get 'in sync' with my client's objectives and help her resolve his dilemma. She had really needed me to do this *with* her as she was unable to think of a way out of this predicament because of the strong emotions she felt. It reminded me that I do have a very strong tendency to be empathetic with my clients and have seen this as a major contributor to establishing a good environment for them to explore and for honest dialogue.

This experience prompted me to balance my search for a checklist with an appreciation of what I am already doing naturally and intuitively when I am listening well. I started to integrate those behaviours into my checklist. This was a change in focus for me and I started to see how much I apply this negative approach to my work and life generally – with a bias towards my deficiencies. I was 'the product of a lifetime of working on deficiencies' (Block, 2000). Significantly, and in addition, I realised that this propensity to focus on deficiencies was also a feature of my approach with my clients. I sought to pay attention to this and to achieve more of a balance with what is good already. I was still very aware of how my prevailing feeling of low self-worth was a part of me, but somehow there was more in the background and it did not make me feel uncomfortable and anxious as before. I reviewed previous client feedback and noted for the first time how positive most of it was. I had been blind to this before.

A NEW WAY OF BEING...COACHING AND LEARNING IN PRACTICE

It felt strange to consider that my coaching relationships could serve me and assist my learning, development and growth. I came to realise (and welcome) that:

> We in fact are often more changed by our consultation than our client, and that is how it should be. (Block, 2000)

I began to take 'stuff' for me to work on into the coaching room and not just carry a focus on inputs and outcomes for my clients. I became very aware of what I was working on – my own development agenda – and would often share this with my clients.

After a prolonged and difficult period, this shift enabled me to experience how knowing myself more, and paying attention to my needs, made for a better 'service' for my clients – ultimately. During my next sessions, I sought to carry a renewed sense of my capabilities (not deficiencies) together with my desire for immediacy and authenticity. I began testing out a new behaviour, a new way of being, namely to acknowledge and discuss my feelings with my clients...in session and with others more generally.

THE BEGINNINGS OF A NEW WAY OF BEING WITH MY CLIENTS

The onset of the next session with my client was very ambiguous and, uncharacteristically, I let it be! Internal organisational events had overtaken our contract and I had no idea what would happen...including whether our relationship would continue. In order to be authentic I shared how I felt with him. I wanted to be collaborative in *our* learning journey. For me, initially this threatened my need to be seen as credible and expert (old habits die hard!) but in airing my concerns I turned my noise down and was able to listen and something shifted in my client ...It seemed to give my client permission to talk more freely. The level of disclosure and honesty which he displayed was a new way of being for him too! This was a major behavioural shift for my client as well as a major source of learning for him. It had been created out of a level of self-disclosure and personal authenticity which I had never experienced or allowed before. My client had benefitted enormously from me just being me.

SOLUTIONS AND CERTAINTY FADING – 'VITAL' CLARITY EMERGING

I realised that my previous pursuit of solutions was also a result of my *wanting certainty* and predetermined outcomes in the sessions. I realised that, previous to this inquiry, I had been unable to manage my tension and any ambiguity within the sessions. My reluctance to express my own discomfort prevented me from listening. During this session, I was more than ever tuned in to my client (more occupied with the dynamics in the room than my own biography or 'script') and a new phenomenon emerged. I noticed 'non–conversations' and the throw-away lines used by my clients. I discovered that in many instances this previously discounted dialogue was in fact very significant. My ability to catch it in the moment and assist my clients in doing the same enabled the real conversation to take place. It was not an insight into my own learning or behaviour but instead an enhanced noticing of my client.

> *...It struck me that as I have progressively come to understand more my own behaviour I was now more able to focus on and tune into my clients – to the peripheral of what they say, to their thinking out loud in an off-guard way.*

Here is a snapshot of one my clients' off-guard moments:

- *I'm not scared of getting it wrong...anyway* – and then she reverted back to the flow of the 'proper' conversation

- *Don't care if they don't like me. Just need to do what is right for the business* – added as I was leaving our session

I have since learnt to catch these throw away lines and to share them with my clients. They have invariably led to very meaningful discussions and self-insights for my clients and they have occurred in almost all sessions since.

COMMON TENSIONS AND AWKWARD MOMENTS

During this phase of my inquiry I embarked on an on-going process to identify the uncomfortable times I experienced in my coaching. My plan was that, if I could identify my 'common tensions', I could differentiate between those in the room which were mine in origin and those transferred from my client. I began to embrace and discover the phenomenon of transference from a Gestalt perspective that is 'the past that is still active in the present and its interaction with the here and now' (Sills and Joyce, 2001). It felt that this was a heightened form of listening and understanding for both me and my client, as if by listening to myself more I would be able to hear my clients better. My journal notes denote that some conversational subjects and interactions in particular seemed to 'get in the way' of my listening and ability therefore to be present, and I learnt to recognise this as 'my own transference profile and vulnerability' (Sills and Joyce, 2001).

Over the next two months, I compiled an account of when I felt awkward during coaching conversations and committed to enhance my coaching effectiveness by managing what I came to call 'my reactivity' and 'my ambiguity'.

Collectively these accounts depicted times when I was not at my best and I have come to embrace them as 'commonly experienced tensions'. Below are a few which I noted:

Common tensions which stop me from listening: and my response

- Discussions about families: I feel jealous and cross

- Encountering aspects for which I have no immediate solution or intervention/one in the drawer: I panic and stop listening

- Hiding my true feeling: I spend a lot of energy controlling this and denying the dynamics of the relationship and not using this rich data and transference/countertransference as input to the conversation

- Offering my own opinion: knowing when to, and this was my familiar and ongoing 'coach or consultant' dilemma.

WHAT COMES FROM WHOM...ABANDONING THE CHECKLIST

My aim going forward was to be able to differentiate between the tensions which my clients were experiencing and those which were mine in origin. In essence *'what comes from whom'*? This was the beginning of a process to develop a way of utilising my feelings, not hiding them or leaving them behind, and as a result I felt much more authentic. Significantly, I came to realise that a 'neutral or empty mind is an illusion' (Van de Loo, 2007). It was also the start of my abandoning the creation and use of a 'checklist'. It seemed benign now!

PUTTING ME BACK IN THE ROOM!

I set out to discover ways of managing the tensions I experienced in an authentic and genuine way. I discovered an approach, which I continue to develop as a prevailing way of being. It has changed fundamentally my self-belief and effectiveness as a coach. During the sessions which followed, I attempted to bring my own *'signature presence'* (O'Neill, 2007) into my coaching. By developing this 'signature presence' my aim going forward was, and still is, to be me – however I am turning up! I continue to this day to develop a tolerance for the host of emotions and scenarios which I had identified and which I knew had the potential to throw me off balance.

PUTTING SOME NEW BEHAVIOURS INTO PRACTICE

Listed below is a summary of some of my behaviours during some coaching sessions. They arose within session in a way which I would describe as immediate, fluid and natural. I am able to reflect that together they constitute conditions which enable me to listen well and stay on track. Significantly, they most certainly were not part of how I coached prior to this inquiry.

- During a period of intense ambiguity for both me and my client, my client drew a picture to describe his view of the business and its way forward. Also it was very important for him to own this view. So I shared with him my nervousness in recommending this approach and how I perceived he may react to it, to my lack of solution and my fear of him thinking I was inadequate....we discovered that there was a prevailing view in the business that he wasn't very good at strategy/

planning, which then we discussed and worked on. His picture was great and so was mine.

- The team session went ahead without an agenda. There was a request to 'just see where we get to' and 'we just need to see where we all stand'. So it began with no agenda, no models and no predetermined solutions. I did not even have an orientation for the meeting, except to create an environment for courageous and honest dialogue. In an attempt to strengthen my presence, I did however set myself a goal for the session which was simply to share my concerns with them openly and immediately and the others all followed in this vein.

I was able to listen effectively because I maintained both an awareness of what was happening (my own anxiety) and an on-going tolerance to it and sharing of it. I was constantly regrouping in a state of 'Interactional equilibrium' (O'Neill, 2007).

CLIENT FEEDBACK

I shared my inquiry subject with my clients and asked them to contribute to it with some feedback. Allowing them to see me learning made me feel vulnerable and not the expert and so I shared this with them also. Their response to what felt like a gesture of vulnerability was amazing! My effectiveness with them is borne out by the feedback excerpts shown below:

> As far as your involvement is concerned I think your honesty and your understanding of each member's position made it much easier to address a very difficult situation and enable everybody to speak their mind without too much stress.......This would have been difficult to achieve without your input and openness

Specifically on my listening skills they commented:

> I think good listening from a coach could be defined as knowing when to put up and when to shut up. This is always difficult to assess especially when a meeting is fired emotionally as well as practically

FROM 'SOLUTIONS' TO 'RELATIONSHIPS'

Over time, I managed to get to a point where I was more aware than ever of what was happening for me and my clients. Our discussions increasingly focused on this as an aspect of the coaching conversations. The relationship and its immediacy were in effect allowing both of us to make sense of the unique dynamic of what was being created and explored. Interestingly, there are some clients with whom I cannot be this way. Exploring this has helped me realise that honesty in the coaching relationship is a prerequisite to my clients' feeling safe and respected. I often consider in this regard that you reap what you sow.

Paying attention to and being in relationship with my clients I believe has enhanced significantly my effectiveness as a 'relational' coach (De Haan, 2008). Increasingly I can 'trust the coachee to fully make use of and exploit contributions by the coach' (De Haan, 2007). I have been able to experience how 'common factors' (Lambert, 1992) such as empathy, respect and relationship are a major contributor to successful coaching outcomes.

> *The relational coach observes from minute to minute what is going on in the relationship with the coachee* (De Haan, 2007).

CONCLUDING THOUGHTS ON MY JOURNEY

Major changes have occurred in my personal and professional relationships as a consequence of this inquiry. I am discovering all the time what it is 'to be me'. Throughout this inquiry I was able to assess my effectiveness and my behaviour and, as I took learning from one 'experiment' into the next (coaching session), I entered into a process of continually reorganising myself. Progressively, I had more courage to express what I was feeling and to use my intuition in a free flowing manner.

> *I came to see that possibly my own self-doubt had been the biggest barrier to my listening effectively. I noticed that as I gave myself permission to ' be' and stopped assuming how others may view me, I felt less preoccupied and more in the moment.... and began to enjoy life a lot more as a consequence.*

I cannot say that I have reached a point where in my coaching I can 'come totally without memory or desire' (Bion, 1961) but ......I have reached a point where I am more present and aware.

At the onset of this inquiry, I felt I could 'serve' my clients better by concealing feelings. This behaviour has come full circle. I am back in the room more completely than ever. I feel that in this state I am able to provide a relationship for my clients where a high degree of trust flows from my own authenticity and honesty. I am increasingly able to enhance my clients' sensemaking by making use (through discussions with my clients) of my own emotions and intuitions and insights. I am coaching in a very different way now.

Previous to this inquiry, I continually built and reinforced a barrier wall crafted with material from my personal and coaching relationships. I spent a lot of energy trying to peer round and over it but the more I tried, the thicker and thicker the wall seemed to become. I now feel as if I sit on top this wall when I coach. I have dismantled parts of it and removed the odd brick here and there but I am on top of it peering over more often than not.

*If I can create a relationship characterised **on my** part:*
by genuineness and transparency, in which I am my real feelings;
by a warm acceptance of and prizing of the other person as a separate
*   individual;*
by a sensitivity to see his world and himself as he sees them;
then the other individual in the relationship:
will experience and understand aspects of himself which previously he has
*   repressed,*
will find himself becoming better integrated, more able to function
*   effectively,*
will become more similar to the person he would like to be,
will be more self-directing and self-confident,
will become more of a person, more unique and more self expressive,
will be more understanding, more accepting of others,
will be able to cope with the problems of live more adequately and more
*   comfortably.*

(Rogers, 1961)

CHAPTER 2

DOES SELF-DISCLOSURE BY ME HELP MY CLIENTS? THE 'ME' IN THE ROOM – OVERT, COVERT AND THE UNINTENDED...

Mask illustration designed and created by LEKIDDO
Copyright © LEKIDDO, 2013. All rights reserved.

A s a little girl my father said to me:

When people ask 'How are you?' they don't really want to know.

He was not to know how his throw-away remark would impact on his daughter. Over the coming years I was trusted with more family secrets than I should have been, and witnessed the violent collapsing of my mother's mental health and my parent's marriage. My problems seemed unimportant. Already I had the defence mechanism that started childhood private fears of being poisoned which developed into panic attacks and I believe is a significant contributor to the Chronic Ulcerative Colitis I have had since my 20s. All of those pathologies I kept to myself.

So keeping my own counsel is a strong part of me. Now I am examining how this affects my coaching.

So – does self-disclosure by me help my clients?

MY HISTORY WITH THE INQUIRY QUESTION

Many years ago I chose a coach who I hoped would help me in developing my business and support me the way I believed I was supporting my clients. I never felt totally comfortable with her but told myself that this would be part of the grit that would open up new thoughts. Typically then, I did not discuss this with her but 'told myself'.

At meeting four or five, I was talking about my relationships with my coachees.

Me: *My clients won't know much about me but I feel very intimate with them. I know a lot about their lives and emotions.*

Coach: *Why 'won't' they?*

Me: *Because I believe in concentrating totally on them and their issues and don't believe that anything about me should impact on their process.*

Coach: *So you don't think that a coach should tell you anything about themselves?*

(I felt tension in this question)

Me: *No*

Coach: *Well that makes me feel very uncomfortable as you know a lot about me – my house, my dogs and my situation...*

This could have been a moment of self-disclosure from her but actually it felt aggressive and uncomfortable.

From then on I felt the need to make her feel more at ease and realised that the coaching relationship had ended.

This experience confirmed all my prejudices about self-disclosure. It had a bad effect on me so, I determined, my clients would not be *overtly* treated to this experience. Re-living this I now understand we both conspired to create this bad experience: I did not declare my discomfort in the relationship and then felt the need to smooth over the tension; the coach took this event as a personal comment, not as a piece of information, and didn't use it to help me develop. This countertransference was more revealing than any of her other self-disclosures about which she now felt uncomfortable.

My comment '...but I feel very intimate with them' on reflection concerned me. Do they feel intimate with me?

This defined a pattern in my life – I took the role of rescuer – rescuing her from her discomfort – and in doing so we both conspired and I became the victim, the looser in the deal (Karpman, 1968).

40

Recently I found a Drivers questionnaire that I completed, many years ago now, when I was 21 – the results showed 'Be Strong' was clearly my highest driver followed by 'Please Others' (Stewart and Joines, 1987). This combination could explain why it was so easy for me to fall into the trap of self-concealment (Be Strong) reinforced with the belief that it was for the benefit of the client (Please Others). So, I developed my early theory that I best served my coachees when my present-self focused totally on the coachee and my past-self felt to not be present.

But me, past and present, will be in the room: *overtly* in my physical presence; *covertly* in the influence that I inevitably have; and *unintended* when I am not conscious of my presence and am not respecting how I might be impacting on the coachee.

And I am aware that I have felt that clients would not be interested in my experiences, something which I needed to explore and then return to.

So, I undertook my action research project to understand what effect self-disclosing, or the lack of it, has in my coaching relationships.

CORE INQUIRY

CYCLE ONE – REFLECTIVE INQUIRY OF RECENT PAST COACHING EXPERIENCES

I wanted to find out how much self-disclosure would be normal for me in my coaching, expecting to find little *overt* self-disclosure in line with my espoused theory. But I needed to understand how much of what I have called the *unintended* and *covert* self-disclosure is present in my work.

My experience with Mary was typical. She came to me as she had had a difficult couple of years transitioning from a high earning, high status woman in the media world to a different way of life led by her spiritual beliefs.

The point that stands out dramatically to me was when she told me a symptom of her bad year was she developed Irritable Bowel Syndrome (IBS) – and she particularly pointed out 'the embarrassment of it.' I was sympathetic but did not mention that I have that experience too.

I recall in that moment considering mentioning it but chose not to as I feared that Mary may see it as 'one-up-man-ship,' something like 'you may have had IBS but I have chronic Inflammatory Bowel Disease!' (IBD) I felt I may have taken her expression of a bad year away from her.

What difference would it have made if I had?

'It is the process of expending energy to keep information from other people that defines secrecy,' (Kelly, 2002). This word 'secrecy' I find upsetting – it is a side of self-concealment that feels much more unpalatable – much more dysfunctional. My concealment of the shared experience of IBD from Mary took energy – it felt like a secret.

41

Listening back to this session, what I heard was that I relied almost entirely on tone of voice, positive reflections about the coachee and some laughter to establish empathy.

Is this enough? Am I making an assumption of self-disclosure relating to empathy and therefore an additional assumption of it being an important part in a positive working alliance?

CYCLE TWO – SECOND PERSON INQUIRY WITH COACHEES

I was worried how this heightened sensitivity to self-disclosure in a therapeutic context would impact on how I could coach – would it take away my awareness of what was happening in that moment for the coachee and result in a session that was unsatisfactory for both of us? Would this consciousness of my agenda make it difficult to establish a working alliance? In my reflection notes before my next session I wrote:

> ...danger that I am walking into a narcissistic place where boundaries may be blurred by my own self therapy...

This highlighted a strong paradox – in the past I have not *overtly* brought myself into the coaching sessions and so the relationship with my clients may have been professional though, possibly, not fulfilling its potential. Now, in my research, I am struggling consciously to self-disclose in order to see how it would enrich the working alliance and risk the very thing that I have been avoiding – that the coaching does not focus on the coachee.

One of the clients I chose to involve in my inquiry, Rory, was someone I already knew from coaching in the past. I felt that we already had a good relationship and this new coaching period would mean we could recontract to include my inquiry. I had offered him coaching at a reduced rate as it assuaged my fear that it might not be as 'good' coaching because I had my own agenda. I soon regretted this later realising that already I had given Rory a message that perhaps this was 'second rate' coaching, that I had less confidence than before. My self-disclosures had started with 'the *unintended*' – a disclosure unknown to me but known by the coachee.

To create a base-line before the coaching started, I gave him a sheet of paper headed: 'What I know about, assume about or believe about my coach' and asked him to take two minutes to write what he wanted. I felt immediately that he wasn't comfortable doing this, he went very quiet, his body language was awkward. Soon he looked like he was struggling, which made me nervous. This inquiry into me had made us both uncomfortable. This nervous feeling is not how I feel when my coachees are struggling on their own problems. This discomfort was about me being in the focus. When he handed it back to me I can hear that I tried to dampen the stress with an over-jovial tone, 'That's brilliant!' I didn't look at it; I felt it would taint the session, and I put it aside.

Rory's agenda for his coaching was to explore a sense of impotency in his new role and he had not yet got over his last experience of redundancy. I reflected back to him about his feelings of redundancy, but never did I offer an empathetic reflection on my own experience; that I was brought up hearing powerful positive experiences following redundancy (from my father's outplacement business) but, when it happened to me, it rocked me too. A self-disclosure could have helped him co-create meaning from the redundancy experience as 'disclosure is facilitated by reciprocity' (Farber, 2006). It did not occur to me – I was not in touch with my feelings of it. Was my own potency tied up with having a sense of being expert? I was very disappointed and frustrated with my impotence towards my goal.

On the journey home I was excited to see what he had written in the pre-meeting list of what he knew about me, and pulled out the piece of paper for the first time. He wrote the six points below:

1. Has inside knowledge about my industry and can therefore respond to specifics.

2. Gets me to answer the questions rather than answering them herself.

3. I believe she cares about what she does.

4. I assume she is interested in continuing to develop her own skills not just others.

5. I know her to come highly recommended.

6. I know she follows up on what she promises.

I felt deflated and disappointed. Rory did not see or remember anything that he knew about me. I thought there were several explanations I should consider.

Perhaps Rory thought I only meant in the coaching session (we had not started discussing coaching at that time). Alternatively the 'small talk' may not have registered with him. What I felt on reading it, even after what seemed to be a successful coaching relationship nine months ago, was that nothing much about me had stayed with him. Why did I feel so deflated when I knew that my espoused theory was to not reveal myself? His comments were around professionalism, I felt pleased about that, but they were sterile. I have to now consider that this reflects what they see of me – professional and, because there is not much self-disclosure from me, the relationship is one dimensional.

Reflections on second research cycle

I am troubled about the non-disclosure of my experience of redundancy. Unlike the experience with Mary above when I censored it in my mind, this time it did not occur to me in the session at all. I saw the opportunity only after hearing the session back particularly listening for self-disclosure. I have a great deal of experience of the pain of redundancy both as an outplacement coach and personally in my career. I have felt my confidence shatter because of it even when it was not a surprise and I was one of several people affected. With Rory it was not in my conscious, I had shut off that side of me.

Even after the first use of it I can tell the questionnaire is the wrong path for me in my inquiry. It didn't elicit the kind of feedback I had hoped; it seemed too forced and highlighted a distance. This distance seems to parallel my own relationship with self-disclosure. I know I need to be bolder and ask directly what I need to know.

My disappointment with the answers he gave stopped me from asking Rory to explain them. Now I see the real information from this was in this feeling of disappointment. I had approached this with my agenda, my hypothesis. A truly collaborative research would have helped me understand what information Rory was actually giving me.

I read that in Rogerian terms the lack of self-disclosure is possibly seen as a lack of showing myself as a person rather than a role (Brockbank and McGill, 2006). That made me feel uneasy, it suggests to me that I am more involved in being a *professional* Coach rather than a *good, fully effective* coach. The difference between the two seems to be a Relational quality.

CYCLE THREE – FURTHER SECOND PERSON INQUIRY WITH MY COACHEES

In the next three sessions with my coachees I hoped to 'exercise' my self-disclosure technique by trying at every opportunity. These sessions were with Rory and Will, a new client. They were both people to whom I warmed, and I felt that I could have an honest and thoughtful dialogue with them on their experience of our coaching. This, too, would have the potential for learning and growth for me. I had to weigh up the benefits from the potentially ethical dilemma of providing the best possible space for their own development and my needs.

On the way to my next session with Rory, I was apprehensive. As usual when I am uneasy, I arrived 20 minutes early because being late makes me anxious (what will they think of me if I am late!) and walked around for a bit. This was calming. Spot on time I arrived at his offices and received a warm welcome.

I felt elated after this session; self-disclosures came naturally, didn't seem indulgent and were pertinent to the coaching. Reviewing the recording later there were six moments of self-disclosure. Two were statements of immediacy and one of these I have identified as a critical moment (De Haan, 2008) when I revealed the way I was feeling about what he was telling me. This is referenced later. The other four were more existential including a common connection with another country (explained more fully below). Of these self-disclosures two were outside the coaching session and two as part of it. So – in terms of my changed behaviour I can point at the two within the coaching session as a breakthrough; the two outside the session were probably richer as I felt myself less guarded and freer to chat – I could hear at the time it was more a conversation of equals. It was just one meeting, and I felt a little stupid, was that all it took?

At our next meeting I was feeling much easier, less tense; still reminding myself to offer a self-disclosure when possible. There were three self-disclosures within the coaching session. Two of these were responses to his frustration about difficulty in getting motivated. In my discussion with Rory he felt one was useful (putting on the walking shoes is the hardest part of my long walks) but the other one he didn't like. It was about someone I knew who was very agenda-focused and how I admired him but couldn't follow his methodology. This story did not touch Rory and at the time he told me so and again in our post session discussion. My post-session personal reflection was mixed – noting my greater sense of boldness to put myself into the coaching session, but as coaching interventions I thought they were problematic.

I am now mindful that this raises the issue of clarity of what is a positive self-disclosure and the danger of metaphor or stories originated by me. So, in this case Rory identified with the walking analogy so that was useful, but the agenda story missed the mark and he felt I was not on his wavelength. My initial reaction to his feedback was that this was 'bad' self-disclosure. In supervision I have seen that I can lean on my metaphors too much. Steve Connor, of Birkbeck College, University of London, put this succinctly at the time of writing 'A metaphor is a way of not quite saying what you mean.' (Connor, 2010) As a coach it is incumbent on me to be clear and to help the coachee understand their own metaphor. On reflection and listening to the session, we seemed to pass that mistake without tension and carried on exploring how he gets things done. So it was a momentary mistake and even that had information about what motivates my coachee.

The third was a more *overt* self-disclosure. Rory was explaining how he can get very busy doing 'things' but denying the really important longer term projects. I, too, am very prone to this and without a deadline I can fill any space. What I said was 'I share your pathology; we know what we have to do...' I cringe hearing this back. It was an intervention from my head and not my heart.

What I would have liked to have said was 'I relate to what you are saying, I

CHAPTER 2

too find it easy to find things to do and more difficult to take the time to look at the big picture. But sometimes people like us know what we should be doing but something else gets in the way – would it be helpful to look at that?' That would have been a more empathetic self-disclosure and then to work with the coachee to help them work through their own issues.

Rory's feedback
Our session was during the World Cup and we joked about which countries were getting our support – and thus we discovered that both our partners come from the same country …and so for the next seven minutes we talked about this beautiful place. I have included this moment because it was an important self-disclosure that Rory singled out (below) as a relationship building moment. It was a moment where I joined his world.

In a discussion with Rory about my Inquiry into self-disclosure he said (my choice of words in bold):

> *For me the interpersonal stuff is important as I suspect that is how I build up a rapport and it is more than just a transactional thing.* **I discovered** *by accident that we have a connection. The conversation that we started was very easy because you know what I am talking about and it is light-hearted. And I think the sessions are more powerful the more I know about you and I think we sort of* **stumbled upon** *that… For me, I like to know about what people are up to and that makes you a more interesting person. I almost wonder if I'd had known up front I would have gotten even more about you as a person and I* **would have got more from coaching.**

He could have got more from the coaching… this was the message I needed to hear. I chuckle to myself too, because he felt that he had discovered by accident and stumbled upon the disclosures. So, my disclosures were unobtrusive, even reserved. Some were by accident but some were the outcome of preparing myself to make disclosures.

WILL
Soon after this event I had my first coaching session with Will. With a new confidence in my ability to work with self-disclosure I was more relaxed and approached this session with curiosity.

Will was late for the meeting. Every ten minutes someone came to apologise. While sitting waiting I wrote in my reflection diary 'getting very irritated – 40 minutes late! Writing this to remember how I feel because probably won't tell him this meeting but may be useful to remember for a later session.' As I saw it then, it would have been an intrusive self-disclosure before we would have developed a relationship and he may have felt the need

46

to repair our relationship. But I am glad that I noted my feelings rather than put up with it – it was a self-disclosure to me.

Will arrived, flustered and charmingly apologetic. I immediately forgot my irritations. It turned out to be an extremely productive meeting part of which I explain later.

Later in my reflection diary I wrote in bold and boxed this:

> *...fear of what will happen if people see me angry... overriding influence is not wanting conflict – be strong, please others... ...if I am not in touch with my feelings then at what level do I touch my clients? How relational can it be? And do I not self-disclose because I'm not in touch with my feeling... and the client isn't sparking my feeling?*

I was very emotional as I wrote that and immediately listed 'things I feel angry about'. It contained 15 moments which I had never addressed with the people who were the focus of this anger. This sparked in me a fear of exploding with uncontrolled feelings, the kind I recognise occurs rarely but dramatically with a sibling when unresolved family issues come to be represented by each other in a maelstrom of countertransference.

This acceptance of my anger with Will rather than suppressing it created a strong reaction. I am glad I did not broach it in this meeting with so much potential for unconscious countertransference.

> *I come to the somewhat uncomfortable conclusion that the more psychologically mature and integrated the therapist is, the more helpful is the relationship that he or she provides.* (Rogers, 1980)

Addressing my emotional wellbeing is as important to my practise as it is to me.

Will's feedback

Later in our coaching relationship Will told me that he was extremely grateful for my flexibility in working around his needs, especially for his timekeeping. His formal feedback was that he had 'A positive feeling coming out of the sessions – surprisingly cathartic.' and 'A strong sense of stepping out of the day to day. We spent a good amount of time around the issues raised, and I left each session feeling this was valuable introspection and 'time out'.'

Will's sense of stress at the time was part of his problem and I gave him the opportunity to explore these issues. If I had have focused on what was a symptom of this, i.e. his time keeping or lateness, even if I was able to prevent any countertransference, I may have created a feeling of guilt or even shame in him. This would have interfered with our work and it may not have been so cathartic.

47

I recognise that my decision not to discuss it may have its roots in my old paradigm – but even in this, the fact that I wrote down my feelings at the time was a major step forward for me and allowed me to make a conscious decision rather than an unconscious reaction – thus reducing the likelihood for harmful countertransference.

CYCLE FOUR – FIRST PERSON INQUIRY INTO MY LEARNING FROM THIS RESEARCH

Reflecting on all the work on this Inquiry to date I conceptualised a theory to serve me and my practise.

My self-disclosures can help my coachees to make sense of what they are revealing to me. This feels most powerful when the coachee starts with their disclosure or something that the coachee is trying to express. My reciprocal self-disclosure then has more relevance and is likely to resonate with the coachee's reflections. When initiating an *overt* self-disclosure I risk burdening the coachee with the feeling they have to respond to my needs.

> *An empathetic therapist points sensitively to the felt meaning which the client is experiencing in this particular moment, in order to help him or her focus on that meaning and carry it further to its full and uninhibited experiencing.* (Rogers, 1980)

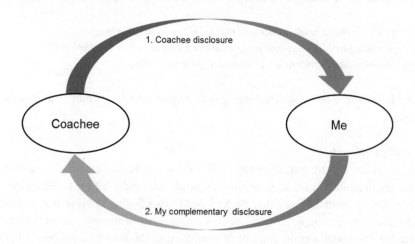

Fig 1: The role of self-disclosure in empathy

I now have a better understanding of how earlier I came to link self-disclosure and empathy. Empathy is a kind of sharing another's experience at some level and self-disclosure can be a way of voicing this. But self-disclosure

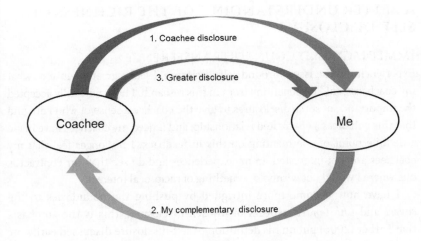

Fig 2: Overt self-disclosure as a catalyst for greater coachee disclosure

and empathy are different. They are linked only in that good self-disclosure will feel empathic. If I had disclosed to Mary I have experienced IBD and understand how distressing it can be, then it may have helped her have stronger confidence to talk about her issues with me – not necessarily about IBD but in general.

This is what Stern (2004) calls 'intersubjective sharing... as they encounter each other in this shared present moment a re-entry loop is created between the two minds.' So the process is recursive. Earlier I described how elated I felt after the session with Rory. Looking back I think this is only partly due to meeting my expectations for the inquiry. I believe that not only are my coachees benefiting from this widening of the intersubjective field I, too, gain and grow from this shared experience.

But my experience with my own coach reminds me that even responding to a disclosure, rather than initiating it, is not a protection for inappropriate self-disclosure.

So within the coaching sessions generally the most valuable *overt* self-disclosure is a response to a disclosure by the coachee, when you have indication from the coachee that this is something with which they will identify. I am aware that this means an a-symmetry in the relationship; asking the coachee to self-disclose freely whereas I am being purposeful in my self-disclosure and their disclosures often move me profoundly.

In order for this Inquiry to be for the betterment of my practise my journey was taking me to the *covert* and especially *unintended* self-disclosure to which I needed to pay more attention.

49

A BETTER UNDERSTANDING OF THE RICHNESS OF SELF-DISCLOSURE

IMMEDIACY AND COUNTERTRANSFERENCE

Experiencing these issues around self-disclosure, I feel a greater sense of what my coachees could be benefiting from in this research. I have now fully accepted the importance of some disclosures to give the coachee a sense of who I am and that this enhances a co-created relationship, and indeed my coachees have made a definite point of commenting on this in feedback. I no longer feel that my coachees are 'not interested' in my experiences and do see that our contract is one where I would not withhold something of reciprocal interest.

I have now become more intrigued by pushing the boundaries to the *covert* and *unintended* aspects of my self-disclosure. This is the emphasis that Farber (2006) put on his definition of self-disclosure discussed earlier or that Wosket (1999) cites as *'the intentional use of self.'*

Returning to the examining of self-disclosure in my recent coaching sessions, the disclosures which had most impact were much more of the immediacy type (Hill and Knox, 2001). This use of self involves putting my personal characteristics into the frame so that they become potentially significant in the coaching process (Wosket, 1999).

That is a kind of *covert* self-disclosure, a feeling or sense. This, when expressed, is a self-disclosure as I am disclosing something of me – expressing it as something that has come from me but may have significance in this coaching context.

In the second session with Rory we had a critical moment (De Haan, 2008) arising out of immediacy.

Rory had been talking about decisions he had made recently. These felt to me to be laboured, over-analysed and nearly all became disastrous, and responded to this feeling by saying, 'I sense you overriding your intuition.' Rory replied, 'Yeah... Yeah... That's quite an interesting thing you've mentioned...'

For 15 minutes he ran through amazing pieces of serendipity in his life. It was a wonderful one man conversation. Then he asked about intuition 'what is that... a feel in the gut or little voice... how does it manifest itself?' I heard a slight panic in his voice. I felt excited that something important was beginning to open up. I thought this was akin to the Stern 'now' moment. 'This is a present moment that pops up and is highly charged with immediately impending consequences. It is a moment of Kairos, heavy with presentness and the need to act' (Stern, 2004).

Again, in the first session with Will, we had a similar experience. I was feeling confused and overwhelmed in our session. He was talking in a rapid-fire, staccato way. I didn't know if it was the way he always talked or a symptom of his stress. My immediate reaction was to struggle with understanding – it was my job to listen *to* the client and help construct a meaning to his words, at least that was what my old paradigm told me. I remember taking a deep breath to listen to how I felt. I told him I felt like I was on a fast 'train' that I couldn't get off. This started a productive discussion. Will realised that other people may experience this too, he had already received feedback that not everyone could follow his 'train' of thought. I followed this with more immediacy relating to how I felt when he was speaking more slowly and clearly. He told me:

> ... *I am now talking in a different way, I probably would never have realised ... which means the next time I'd have done the same thing ... That you are able to spot the unsaids underneath I think is really helpful.*

At the end of our coaching programme he told me that this was one of the most helpful and memorable points of our coaching. A self-disclosure of an immediacy type sparked this critical moment.

Stern (2004) sums it up for me 'the longer the therapist can stay with the present moment and explore it, the more different paths to pursue will open up... the result is a greater appreciation of experience, and a less hurried rush to interpretation.' I wasn't feeling that I had to force an interpretation; the coachee did all that work. This felt much more powerful and more relational.

At supervision coaching too, when experimenting with self-disclosure the same impact has been commented on by my peers and supervisors. They observed greater confidence in my coaching and that I develop a strong relationship with my coachees.

I am happy to feel more aware of me and my coaching persona and am bringing more of myself in to the coaching sessions. It seems to work. And I need to be vigilant that the needs of the coachee are paramount – this faith in immediacy as a coaching catalyst is one tool. It has to have authenticity to be effective and therefore I must continue to listen to me at the same time as listening to my coachee. It must be co-created.

I started my Inquiry particularly focusing on *overt* self-disclosure – and made the connection that perhaps my relationship with my coachee was diminished by my reticence to self-disclose. Now I feel that self-disclosure is valued by my clients.

My interest in self-disclosure is now not so much about revealing something about me and my experience to a coachee, as I have shown it will occur naturally where I can remain in touch with my feelings and present with the coach. It is then not a piece of information that I chose to disclose – but rather something that arises out of the relationship. Wosket (1999) claims that the 'intentional use of self', that is bringing her persona into coaching relationship, was a revelation to her practice. But, she qualifies; seldom does this mean *overt* disclosures about herself. Zachrisson (2009) endorses this and hypothesises that 'private' information about a therapist is best kept at a minimum to allow the patient to fantasise. I am not convinced that this principle should extend to a coaching relationship although I am not immune to wondering about my coachees' other lives to complete the picture they have allowed me to share.

Wosket (1999) movingly describes the family events that resulted in her withdrawn character and her ability to not be overwhelmed by her own or her client's feelings. I identify with this experience and see my introverted self-sufficiency as part of my persona that people identify as someone they can trust and share their 'secrets' or own self-disclosures with – a characteristic that I am sure is helpful to me as a coach. I am learning to embrace it. My experience with anger makes me aware to be clear of the difference between suppressing my feelings (old paradigm) and disconnecting but not rejecting my feeling (as with Will's lateness).

MEANING MAKING FOR AND WITH PROFESSIONAL COACHES

There are a large number of papers written on self-disclosure mostly from a psychotherapy environment. An excellent summary is in *Self-disclosure* (Hill and Knox, 2001) and in the slightly more recent Myers and Hayes (2006). They both applaud the trend for therapists to be 'crossing the threshold of anonymity' (Hill and Knox, 2001) but with judgment and not to be over used, agreeing that more research is needed on the subject.

Farber (2006) quotes some opinions that claim infrequent self-disclosures seem more special to the coachee and they may feel less vulnerable whereas frequent self-disclosures seem to decrease their potency.

Stern (2004) believes that intersubjectivity, or the emotions shared between two people in a relationship, is 'one of the major motivations that drives a psychotherapy forward'. He uses many examples of intersubjectivity feedback loops both for the healthy emotional growth of babies and children and for continuing personal growth of us all. Intersubjectivity involves not only 'I know what you know' but 'I know that you know that I know' – that is a direct awareness of each other's experience that will become an implicit knowing. Self-disclosure is part of this communication. Stern goes even further, stating that it is so hard-wired into our being to want to have an intersubjective encounter that 'the question becomes not how we **do** it, but how do we **stop**?' (his emphasis).

Lapworth, Fish and Sills (2005) emphasises the special relationship that therapists and thus, I am projecting, coaches, have with their clients.

In therapy, clients have the experience of being listened to and of listening to themselves in the presence of another for whom they have no responsibility whatsoever. This absence of distraction caused by a need to attend to the desires of the other is what distinguishes the experience from that of talking with a friend or colleague when attention is inevitably drawn to their experience or to the need for fairness in attention and sharing.

So, as I understand it, sharing with my coachee information that would burden them could change this quality of the special relationship.

In summary the overall conclusions on self-disclosure based on therapist experience seems to be:

- Self-disclosure is generally favourable when used:
  - Within a strong relationship or
  - To advance the reflexivity of the client and
  - Sparingly.

- Self-disclosure is often damaging when used:
  - When the relationship is weak or
  - In a challenging phase of the relationship or
  - Too early in the relationship or
  - To increase the intimacy of the relationship or
  - Too frequently.

(Hill and Knox, 2001; Farber, 2006; Myers and Hayes, 2006; Blickle et al, 2008)

This then highlights the importance of self-disclosure being a helpful, conscious part of the relationship. It also flags up the necessary control of professionalism and ethics.

If I use self-disclosure then it must be with caution and for the benefit of the client/coachee. In the process of this inquiry I have to prioritise the opportunity for growth of my coachees and seeking betterment of my practise is secondary but undoubtedly related.

PERSONAL CHANGE AND LEARNING FOR MY PRACTICE

From the outset of this Inquiry I realised that I couldn't prevent self-disclosure, in fact in trying hard to reduce the potential of countertransference to a minimum, I have come to the uncomfortable conclusion that I may have been '**present** as an attentive listener ... but **absent** as a personality.' (Wosket, 1999, quoting Rennie, 1998; original emphasis).

Therapists report countertransference in 80% of their sessions (Hayes et al., 1998). Getting in touch with my past was what I was fearful of inflicting on others who played no part in its origin.

Clinical neutrality, for example, may be a defense against a strong counter-aggression aroused in the coach or consultant by the clients. Neutrality becomes invested with a counter-transference element: the helping professional is determined to keep his stance of neutrality. He has lost his 'free-floating responsiveness (Van de Loo, 2007).

So if countertransference is difficult to avoid, even for the most experienced therapist, perhaps the belief that I could was making me less vigilant, opening up the possibility for the *unintended* self-disclosures.

Either my self-disclosures can strengthen our working alliance or they may see me in a less positive light. Learning to accept I won't always connect with potential clients will be important as equally with others I will develop richer and more productive working relationships.

I am also appreciating that *covert* revelations can be more personal than *overt*. They relate to the heart of me rather than the commentary of everyday things and events. And as such they move the coachee more too.

My earlier belief that professionalism was the best way to create a good working relationship with my clients missed the point. The opposite is true, coachees who feel a working alliance with their coach, report a better outcome (De Haan, 2008). My experience with Rory and Will now encourages me to accept that the exposure of my personality and the chemistry between us was at least as important as any technique.

I have learnt some profound things specifically because of this research. At the beginning I said I was aware that I felt coachees are not interested in my experience. I was both right and wrong. What we are both primarily interested in is their own learning. What I have learnt is that how and when self-disclosure by me can help their learning and disclosure. Moreover, I have learnt that this is not a one-way street 'We become aware of our own internal states as we discover others have them.' (Stern, 2004) This journey has been a powerful one for me.

> **"One thing I noticed was that writing honestly about running and writing honestly about myself are nearly the same thing."**
>
> **Haruki Murakami**
> **in 'What I talk About When I Talk About Running'**

CHAPTER 3

WHAT HAPPENS IN MOMENTS OF HUMOUR WITH MY CLIENTS?

INTRODUCING MY INQUIRY

THIS inquiry first started with an underlying niggle that just would not go away. I began to question whether my humour, so welded into my coaching practice, served my clients well. It has taken courage to step back and look at an aspect of myself so ingrained that it seems like breathing to me. I was afraid that I would lose or negatively affect part of myself through focusing upon it in this way.

Now, I am grateful that I took that risk. I have developed greater confidence in reflecting honestly upon my own practice and I am experimenting with new ways of working with my clients.

It is my hope that as you read this chapter, it may lead you to reflect further on your own practice. Perhaps, it will be about how you use humour as a coach? Possibly, it will lead you to examine a 'niggle' you may have that lies at the heart of who you are and how habitually you like to coach. Either way, I hope that you will sit back and enjoy reading my inquiry and that it will trigger some new thinking for you.

MY INQUIRY

I use humour actively in my life, not simply in my coaching. I believe I have a well-developed sense of humour. It is part of my 'identity' and is present in all my relationships. Humour for me appears to be a curious bag of seemingly mixed intentions and reactions.

I view myself as someone who is creative and can usually see the funny side of things. With less ease, I see myself as someone who can be hurtful and malicious, sometimes using humour defensively, as a witty or spiteful put-down remark that establishes a sense of superiority.

My clients often tell me that humour creates rapport, helps them feel at ease, and affects their mood positively, often breaking negative states and reframing what is going on. It also enhances creativity in the sessions. This feedback mirrors the themes that Knight describes about humour in her chapter on 'Healing through humour' (Knight, 2009). Hardingham describes good humour as a 'habit' that connects coach and coachee, builds mutual understanding and raises 'energy levels' (Hardingham, 2004).

This is the positive side, but what about the darker, more negative aspects to humour? I am *not* so aware of this or when it 'plays out' in my coaching sessions.

On occasions, my clients give me feedback directly and through their body language that the humour has been inappropriate. Inadvertently I touch somebody's weakness or expose a secret through a 'throwaway' humorous comment.

On other occasions a different reaction occurs. These unintentional 'light-hearted' humorous interventions reveal unconscious elements in my clients that create an unexpected breakthrough in thinking or a cathartic emotional release (Heron, 1975).

So, what emerges seems hit-or-miss to me. Therefore, I want to become more aware of how and when humour emerges with my clients, and to be more sensitive and respectful in my use and timing of my interactions.

This led me to my inquiry question:

What happens in moments of humour with my clients?

It is clear that humour means many different things to everyone. The range of experiences that people consider humorous is legion: irony, satire, sarcasm, farce, jokes, comics, cartoons, slapstick, buffoonery, jesting, pranks, lampooning, gallows humour, parody, idiom, riddles, malapropisms, spoonerisms and wisecracks.

For this inquiry I did not intend to tell jokes, or create a context in which I am the comic and my client is the audience. The humour with my clients is usually completely unplanned and context-specific, often about the client's world or an aspect of our co-created relationship. It is an *emergent, spontaneous* and an *informal* humour.

Being recently diagnosed with diabetes, I discovered that one of the best strategies for managing this long-term, chronic condition is to cultivate a sense of humour. Humour contributes to people's feelings of wellbeing, an observation that dovetails with the literature on the 'therapeutic' benefits of humour in medicine (Seaward, 1992) and which resonated with me as I adjusted to being a diabetic.

From this literature, I discovered a *practical* definition of humour that serves me well for this study:

Humour is an experience that results in laughter, smiling, or a feeling of amusement along with one or more of the following: a decline in tension, mood elevation, pleasant diversion, or a sense of well-being (Napora, 2010).

I also learnt from the work developing out of the 'emotional intelligence' debate and the 'positive psychology' movement that humour plays a vital role in many aspects of what Daniel Goleman *now* calls 'Social Intelligence'. Humour lubricates social encounters, relaxing people and creating a mood of optimism (Goleman, 2006). Martin Seligman identifies 'humour' as one of the core strengths that characterise people with a 'healthy' optimism (Seligman, 2006).

From my reading about humour, I understood that there are *three* broad theories of humour. I wondered how these might emerge in my coaching sessions with my clients:

1. Humour often involves establishing some sort of social advantage over others, that is to say humour reinforces social status by demonstrating superiority or some form of saving face.

2. Humour can contain what Freud called 'the return of the repressed', that is to say that humour involves a 'leakage' of repressed (unacceptable) sexual or aggressive feelings (Freud, 1905).

3. Humour generally involves some form of 'dissonance'. It is frequently reflective of a set of (perceived) potentially incongruous conceptualisations.

It became clear to me that, whatever the emphasis, looking beneath the surface of humour was going to be my challenge. I took on this challenge by looking at coaching sessions with three clients and by interviewing ten coaches about how they used humour with their clients.

GETTING STARTED – MY OWN 'HISTORY' OF HUMOUR

Before starting work with my clients, I examined the role humour played in my own history during a personal coaching session. We focussed upon my reactions as a teenager to frequent moves, new schools and to living with my grandmother and her schizophrenic sister. We also explored how I had developed an amusing banter with my powerful father during the times when he was *not* suffering from bouts of deep depression.

I realised for the *first* time how I had used humour in my family and with my peers to help me to:

*   Handle issues of inclusion and exclusion, often being the new girl at school (Vucetic, 2004).

- Deflect painful or difficult emotions, especially shame. Jennifer MacKewn says 'shame-binds' (MacKewn, 1997) and I discovered a way to use humour to anesthetise unpleasant feelings of shame and distract attention from myself (Sills et al., 1995).

- See and negotiate my way through issues of 'unreality' in a system; what appeared outside my home was different to the reality inside. I learnt about the importance of recognising 'incongruities' that were present but hidden and unspoken about. I used humour to bring these out. Peter Berger sees this as one of the *critical* functions of humour (Berger, 1997).

- Gain a sense of power in a system where I felt I had little choice and was a victim of other people's decisions. I recognise *now* that I used humour as a means to get out of 'victim-mode', moving into a relatively 'benign' and 'socially acceptable' 'persecutor' role in the TA Drama Triangle (Stewart and Joines, 1987).

- Cope with and deal with the politics and power, learning how to handle an Alpha-male (my father) without being intimidated (Ludeman and Erlandson 2004 and 2006).

Through this coaching, I also saw sadly an *underlying* theme of needing acceptance from others; my humour masked this vulnerability. At the same time, I marvelled at the strength of my resourcefulness in using humour to keep me going and in building friendships against these odds.

THE COACHING SESSIONS WITH MY CLIENTS
Phenomenological inquiry starts with an act of suspending judgment, 'bracketing off' prior experience and not jumping to conclusions (Beyer, 2011). So, once I had assimilated the reading and collected the above insights, I knew that I had to put them to one side, in order to work with my clients in a *phenomenological* way.

I invited three clients to have three coaching sessions with me (nine sessions in total, each of two hours):

- In the *first* meeting with each of my clients I reflected upon the spontaneous, emergent, 'unplanned' and shared moment-by-moment humour interactions.

- In the *second* session I introduced an 'experimental' factor (a 'gift' for each client) into the field conditions.

- In the *third* session, I added another *new* aspect: a set of photographs, as a creative and different way to mark the ending of our time together (MacKewn, 1997).

At the end of each meeting, I drew a graph with the session duration across the horizontal axis and significant coaching moments on the vertical axis. I asked my clients to identify when the significant or critical moments (De Haan, 2008a and 2008b) had occurred and to 'plot' them on the graph.

I also discussed with my clients when they thought humour had been present and plotted these on the graph. In this visual way, I was able to see aspects of the relationship between humour and the critical moments.

Linking back to the Kolb Learning Cycle (Kolb, 1984) I worked this learning pattern iteratively. From the 'concrete experience' my clients shared with me I created 'in-the-moment' reflective exploration; using the graph I created 'abstract conceptualisation', and in the actual coaching sessions I encouraged 'active experimentation'.

These nine graphs showed the themes for each client in their sessions and the patterns of similarity and differences between the three clients.

CLIENT SESSIONS

CLIENT ONE – SARAH

Introduction
Sarah was a director of a charity, where there were major job-cuts and another organisational restructuring so that all people at her level had to reapply for their roles. Her coaching objectives were to come to terms with her strong reactions of anger to her current situation and to be clear about the role for which she wanted to apply.

The sessions with Sarah
At the beginning and end of each session it was clear that we used a light touch of humour, expressing warmth and establishing an easy rapport. Figures 3 – 5 show how this lightness seemed to pave the way, *paradoxically*, for a follow-on phase of seriousness and deeper exploration. This was a thoughtful and more intense mid-section of the session, where there was an opening of negative feelings beneath Sarah's anger, and feelings of vulnerability and uncertainty. There was a palpable shift in the room at this juncture (De Haan 2008a and 2008b).

At the close of the session, the humorous asides served to break that state of intensity. They marked an end point of the intimacy and 'reality' co-constructed in my room, as well as the return to the 'real world'.

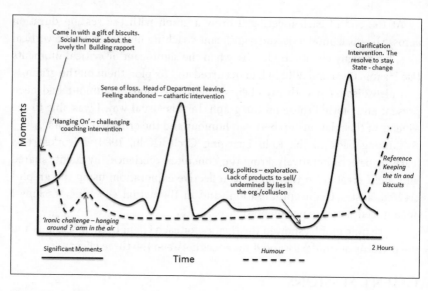

Fig 3: Sarah Session 1 – Significant coaching moments and humorous moments

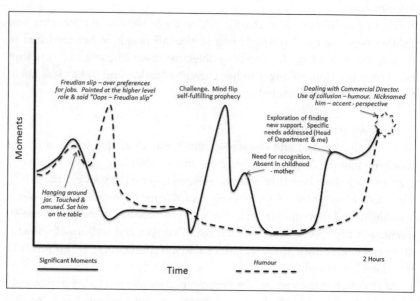

Fig 4: Sarah Session 2 – Significant coaching moments and humorous moments

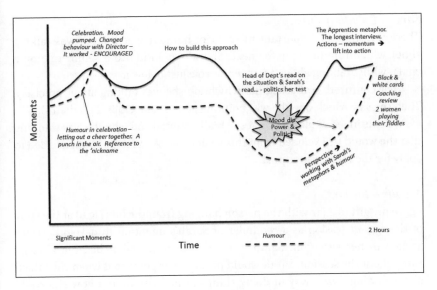

Fig 5: Sarah Session 3 – Significant coaching moments and humorous moments

A throwaway comment

A throwaway comment by Sarah in her *first* session – 'I am just hanging around to see what happens next' – created another incident of humour. It reflected Sarah's lack of apparent agency and feeling of being a victim in the system (Stewart and Joines, 1987). I challenged Sarah as to whether this was really what she was doing. She was surprised and said 'Did I really say that?', at the same time as holding her arm up about her head and bending it into the shape of a clothes hanger. I did the same to mirror the action. We both laughed and wiggled our arms about as clothes hangers for a few moments.

This led to a useful exploration of what was *hooking* her into this sense of powerlessness. It uncovered a complex mix of relationship challenges present for Sarah within her department and the wider organisation. We explored the organisational politics, the games being played and the interplay of characters that were entering the scene during this restructure. For me, this was a creative way of using humour to bring to the surface some of the hidden and darker sides of Sarah's world. She was operating in an emotionally 'toxic' organisation and we explored strategies to navigate the 'cross-currents' (Appelbaum and Roy-Girard, 2007) and what Gerard Egan calls 'the shadow side' (Egan, 1994).

61

Sarah's Freudian slip

There was another important moment of humour when Sarah was talking about which role to apply for next. She was pointing to a senior role on a chart, whilst talking about a *less* senior role just below it.

I felt confused, so I asked her which job she was talking about precisely. Then she saw which one she was pointing at and said 'Oops, Freudian slip!'

We continued exploring what she really wanted and why she was thinking that she would be excluded from this senior role. As a result Sarah decided to apply for the more senior post.

My gift – the jar

I gave my gift of a jar with the person hanging from the lid (Fig 6) at the start of the *second* session as a reminder of Sarah's intention to develop greater agency in her situation. Sarah was amused by it and it became a 'prop' throughout the session. Sarah would pick it up or point to it when she talked about finding a *new* way of doing things in her system and how she could develop more of an impactful presence. 'No more hanging around!' became her theme-tune. The jar served as a symbol of hope and reminded of her own newly found agency and efficacy (Duncan et al., 2004).

Fig 6: My gift to Sarah – The jar

Black humour and was I enjoying it too much?

In session two, Sarah described a colleague's intimidating behaviour. In his presence she felt hyper-vigilant and defensive.

As she spoke about this, she began to talk very fast and mimicked his voice. I mimicked her back, amplifying it and encouraging her to show me more of how he talked and behaved. This intervention is in line with Mindell's work concerning *primary* and *secondary* processes in clients (Mindell, 1985). Mindell advocates that, beneath the *first* level of what a person presents, there is often an unacknowledged *secondary* and far less conscious process wishing to be expressed. This is often seen in body movements, presenting body symptoms, voice tones and dreams. *Amplification* of any of these can draw out the underlying messages and release *new* energy and more conscious awareness (Mindell, 1985). Freud, by contrast, describes the same phenomenon using the reverse terminology; the surface behaviour is the 'secondary', whilst the deeper behaviour is the 'primary' (as first discussed in *The Interpretation of Dreams* (Freud, 1900)). *Both* underline the importance of looking beneath the surface of a client's behaviour to discern the 'hidden' or the 'repressed' motives and drives.

Then, I made a paradoxical shift from the high energy, playful, collusive humour and challenged Sarah to own the 'hidden' negative feelings that she was expressing towards her colleague. Sarah stopped and looked surprised at this shift. After seconds of silence she announced, 'He really insults me and cannot respect him when he behaves like this to me. I will *not* let him treat me like this.' I saw a new resolve in the muscles of her face and the tone of her voice. This paved the way for a new wave of self-confidence.

Through acknowledging and naming her own intense, repressed negative feelings, Sarah was able to release the bottled-up energy. The playful, darker-edged humour had created the ground for the challenge (Heron, 1975) that had enabled her to move from a victim (fearful, 'adapted-child-state') into an adult state. I had used humour to break states – her mood and her Ego-state (Stewart and Joines, 1987). Then we explored how to change her own behaviour and habitual responses to this colleague in order to break the existing pattern between them.

g this to supervision

I could *intellectually* justify the reasons as to why I had encouraged amplify the mockery of her colleague but I was concerned about h I had enjoyed this *black* humour and the *delicious* sense of superi-ad been expressing towards him. On reflection, I realise that this n reaction but I was also picking up her feelings and the release experiencing. It seems to be easier for me to acknowledge picking up sadness, anxiety, fear, doubt or joy from my client rather than feelings of revenge, malice or superiority. I thought that these *darker* emotions were often harder to acknowledge in myself.

I explored this idea with my supervisor, who challenged me to acknowledge how effective I had been in using humour in this way.

I realised that I had played with paradoxes of lightness and seriousness, and of inferiority and superiority. I discovered this was, surprisingly, one of the most *powerful* aspects of emotion-releasing interventions that I use in my coaching. The *timing* of that shift, however, was crucial in moving from active confluence to challenging differentiation (MacKewn, 1997) and there clearly needed to be a deep level of trust present for this to work well.

Coaching review

In her review Sarah chose from the selection of photographs one of two women playing violins, while one was balancing on the shoulders of the other one. Sarah explained that working with me had given her an enormous 'leg-up', just at the right time! She saw things differently and she was more assertive with colleagues. The coaching had helped her reconnect with what she was good at and to feel confident enough to apply for the new role. We both considered the coaching to have been effective in building up Sarah's confidence and emotional resilience.

CLIENT TWO – NICOLA

Introduction

Nicola was an experienced CEO of a Youth Charity. Her coaching objectives were to develop a new volunteer communication strategy that would stick and that she could take back to her leadership team.

The sessions with Nicola

As with Sarah, a light humour was used at the start of each meeting to build rapport and to ease the way into the coaching (Figs 7 – 9). Although the humorous interchanges between us at the start of the sessions were still light, Nicola may have been exerting her control with me. On reflection ⌐ was probably more intimidated by her forcefulness than I realised sessions.

I will use the *three* interchanges from the start of each of the me⌐ examples of how Nicola liked taking control:

- In her *first* session, she moved into a seat *opposite* me rather chair I offered her to my right, making a joke about her ma⌐ melting in the sun.

- In her *second* session, she took over by drawing on the white board.

- In her *third* coaching session, she greeted me waving and exclaiming 'Get with the programme!' I took the *hint* that lay underneath the light, humorous comment and wasted *no* time in getting with *her* programme on the white board again.

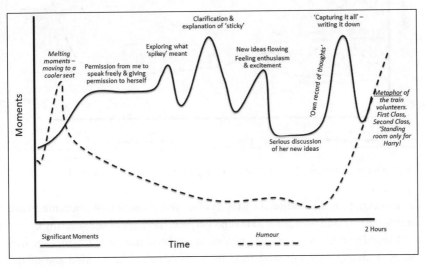

Fig 7: Nicola Session 1 – Significant coaching moments and humorous moments

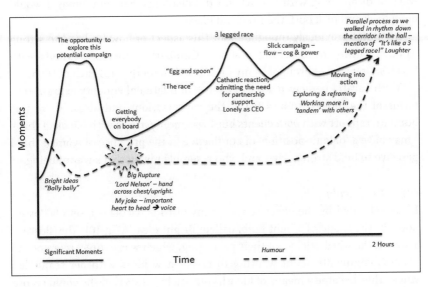

Fig 8: Nicola Session 2 – Significant coaching moments and humorous moments

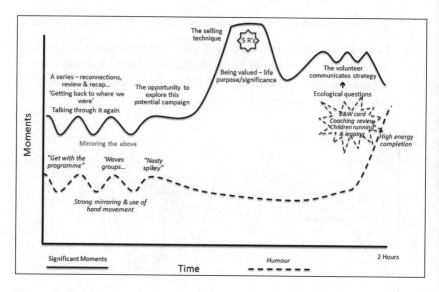

Fig 9: Nicola Session 3 – Significant coaching moments and humorous moments

It was not until I studied the graphs of all the sessions that I became aware of this pattern and how she had taken charge at the start of our meetings.

I wondered if there was an echo of my upbringing here: my mother had Nicola's strong opinions and tone in Nicola's voice did remind me of my mother. Throughout my life, up until my mother died three years ago, I was wary of disagreeing with her; when I did challenge her sometimes, I would hang back and pick both the time and place.

I had not previously thought about this aspect of how I related to strong women within my coaching practice. Comparing Nicola's sessions with Sarah's, I saw how I brought in my presence differently with each of them.

With Sarah I perceived a greater sense of relational equality expressed in terms of the mutual to and fro of the conversations and ideas. There was humour, rapport with *both* clients but I was more *passive* with Nicola. I think I may have a 'default-position' of confluence in the presence of women that I perceive to hold strong views and who resemble my mother's way of being.

My gift to Nicola

I was delighted by the effectiveness of my gift for Nicola – a set of 'Post-it' notes in the shape of a light bulb, called 'Bright ideas' (Fig 10). The 'Post-its' also had the word 'sticky' on their packaging, which was a *direct* reference to Nicola's comments about wanting to create new ideas with her team that stuck. They became a means of identifying 'sticky' ideas that she could record and take back to the organisation.

Fig 10: My gift to Nicola – Bright ideas

The rupture in this coaching session

It was in this coaching session that I made what I thought was an amusing comment that caused a perceived rupture in the flow of the coaching (Carroll and Gilbert, 2005 – 2011). Nicola was describing how good it felt to get out her ideas about the potential communication campaign. Suddenly she turned from the white board towards me and, with one hand across her chest; she began to talk intensely to me. I watched and drew her attention to what she was doing with her hand, to the 'Lord Nelson' hand movement that she was expressing across her chest. This was a clumsy intervention and she seemed offended by me.

I felt embarrassed and apologised quickly. She slowed down and explained that she was putting her hand to her heart because she was speaking honestly. I asked Nicola to carry on and ignore my remark. She continued.

I wonder *now* if I was trying to avoid her disapproval or displeasure. Perhaps if I had stayed with our *mutual* reactions, there might have been value in exploring what was happening between us. My vision of Nelson is of a lonely, isolated figure on a precarious column. Sometimes the images I imagine convey a 'hidden reality' and this one could have been depicting some of Nicola's leadership isolation. Indeed, later during that meeting, Nicola became tearful, admitted she needed more support in her role as CEO and we went on to explore how she could set this up.

Coaching review

At the end of the third session during our coaching review, Nicola was drawn to a photograph of children in Paris running in the street.

She picked it for the freedom, energy and forward movement that she said she had experienced in our sessions. She appreciated being able to express herself with me and step outside her pressured life. She had liked the 'multi-dimensional' way we had worked together. Nicola was pleased to have developed her volunteer strategy and felt confident going forwards.

Certainly, these sessions had catalysed new, creative thinking and Nicola came out with a robust, potentially effective plan of action. The organisational benefit and the effectiveness of these coaching sessions were difficult to evaluate then; if her strategy is successful and 'sticks', then the results will definitely be seen over the next year financially and in terms of recruiting new volunteers into the organisation.

CLIENT THREE – JOE

Introduction

Joe was friendly, small man with a big, extroverted personality. He was an experienced CEO of a UK Charity and wanted to explore what was happening at work and where his next steps might lie.

The sessions with Joe

Joe and I always started our meetings with light humour but he moved quickly and deeply into the serious midsections of the session (Figures 11 – 13), where political aspects of his organisation and their implications were discussed in depth. The intensity and seriousness of the organisation were paralleled in his sessions. He explained that there was little humour present for him at work. He found the idealisation of him as a leader by others, coupled with the behind-the-scenes loneliness, hard to handle. He felt isolated in his role and had been reading the work of Simon Walker about 'undefended leadership', which he had found helpful (Walker, 2011). We explored these issues in depth.

There were *two* interesting aspects to working with Joe that were *different* from my other two clients: firstly in the gift that I gave him, and secondly in a private fantasy that I risked sharing with him in the last session.

The present I gave him was a book about 'listening to your life' (Fig 14). Joe had been talking about wanting to do this in the first session. I knew that this *serious* present was different from the other more playful presents.

He was touched that I had got the book for him. This gift was not as productive as both the other gifts in terms of the coaching as it could not be

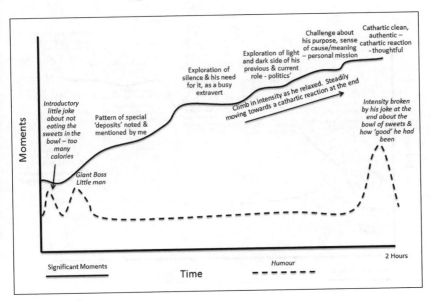

Fig 11: Joe Session 1 – Significant coaching moments and humorous moments

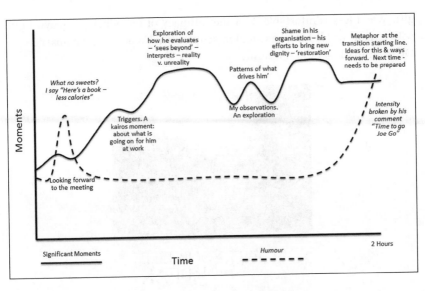

Fig 12: Joe Session 2 – Significant coaching moments and humorous moments

used immediately in the session – both the pot and the 'Post-it' notes were playful and acted as 'props', building the creativity in the moment.

I asked myself if it was a gender issue as to why I had given Joe a *serious*

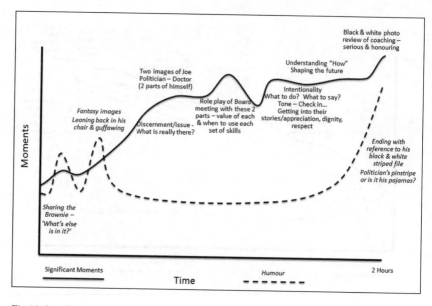

Fig 13: Joe Session 3 – Significant coaching moments and humorous moments

gift. Was I less comfortable with the intimacy of introducing a playful gift with a man? Did I think he would misconstrue it? Would I feel embarrassed? On examination, I did not think so.

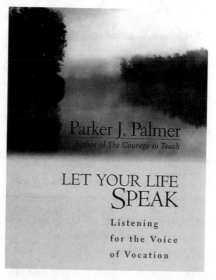

Fig 14: My gift to Joe – 'Let Your Life Speak'

                                        ⌐ have given him instead and quickly decided
on   ⌐d-mugs and a bag of Italian coffee. This was to do
w   ⌐nagined Joe. At this stage of the research however, I
h   che courage to share the quirky fantasy I had with Joe
h   ⌐s *not* until I had taken it to supervision that I risked sharing it
i   ⌐rd coaching meeting.

The fantasy images

My fantasy was a split-image in my mind of Joe as two, small, slightly rotund men! There was a cartoon-type feel to *each* image. On one side, Joe was wearing a black, Italian designer suit with a big white tie, looking like a smooth politician. On the other side, he was grinning and friendly, dressed in a white doctor's coat with a stethoscope and a small black tie.

My supervisor asked me whether there was some counter-transference going on? The irony, struck me that I had given Joe a book about 'Letting your life speak' and had *not* thought about what this image was saying to me about myself, rather than about my client! I knew these *two* aspects of myself: the friendly, caring 'doctor' that I was ready to embrace and the sharp 'politician' that I was far less ready to accept. I recalled how I used humour with my father successfully to navigate political crosscurrents at home. I realised that these *two* parts of myself were figural in my intuition and they had resonated with these two aspects of my client. Joe and I were mirroring aspects of each other and there was some 'transference and counter-transference' in the midst of our relationship (DeYoung, 2003).

I think that this phenomenon, particularly the fantasies, has a dream-like psychical energy to it. As Freud says, we unconsciously censor during the daytime yet beneath this, the unconscious may have much to say to us in the symbolism of our dreams:

> *The task of dream-formation is above all to overcome the inhibition from the censorship* (Freud, 1905)

This idea was a breakthrough for me. I was beginning to integrate *two* powerful ways of working in myself – the caring-side of me with the less acknowledged sharper political-side.

My supervisor suggested that I might consider sharing this image with Joe. I plucked up the courage to tell Joe my fantasy. He was amused – he leaned back in his chair guffawing with laughter and explained that when he was younger, he had wanted to be a medic (it was an unfulfilled dream) and that he also loved Italy and Italian suits! He knew that he could read the politics and the agendas around him but he longed to be able to express more of his the caring side, more of the doctor in him. He wanted to bring *both* sides of himself out.

As a result of bringing my fantasy into the open, we had an effective session exploring both sides of Joe's character. We set up a role-play around the two parts, an adaption of the two-chair work – two actors moving in for their strategic contribution in his forthcoming board meeting that he was anxious about attending (Yontef and Jacobs, 2005). We explored how he could integrate and use both aspects of himself more in this context.

In terms of the difference it made, the sharing of the fantasy was more of a gift to Joe than the book. The effectiveness of that session encouraged me to explore my fantasies, with both my supervisor and, potentially, with my clients. However, I am still cautious, as I am mindful of what Elaine Robinson says about the risks of imposing your own inappropriate metaphors and images on clients (Robinson, 2010). She suggests using the client's *own* metaphors (as a general rule).

On reflection, a key guide for as to whether the fantasy or metaphor is worth sharing is if it persists over a number of meetings. The use of supervision to discuss it before sharing it with the client and of talking through the implications will be vital too (Hawkins and Smith, 2006).

Coaching review

I gave Joe the set of photographs. He chose an image of a lone musician playing his cello on a mountain. His said he had gained new perspectives. He had been lonely and I had stood by him whilst he found his own music again. We co-created a thinking environment (Kline, 1999).

In this respect, the coaching was impactful and meaningful, although we did not effectively explore future career options. We will continue the coaching at a later date.

I now turn to the other facet of my inquiry: the interviews with the other coaches.

THE INTERVIEWS WITH TEN COACHES

All of the ten coaches I interviewed admitted that they had *not* thought much about humour in their work before this point. They said that there was humour in their sessions and that it happened spontaneously. They cited humour as a rapport-builder and as a way of reframing issues. Only two discussed wry humour, taking a deliberately paradoxical stance in order to tease or goad their client (De Haan and Burger, 2005). None mentioned the value of black humour, power issues or how humour might be used as an avoidance strategy on their part.

OVERALL CONCLUSIONS OF MY INQUIRY

WHY HUMOUR CAN HELP

Towards the end of this inquiry, I made an interesting discovery about the potential power of humour in coaching.

I attended a seminar on the neuropsychology of change given by Professor Paul Brown (Brown, 2011) that seemed to have a direct link to the value of humour for coaches in working with people to help them change. Brown is interested in 'brain plasticity', in the ways humans can learn, building on earlier work on the *three* 'types' of brain we all possess: the reptilian brain (or brainstem), the mammalian brain (the limbic system) and cognitive brain (the neo-Cortex). Our emotions are mediated through our limbic system and our amygdala. Social interaction is governed at a basic level by what he calls 'limbic resonance'; we encounter people and our reactions to them are governed physiologically by the non-verbal clues we display.

Brown argues that there are *eight* basic emotions (fear, anger disgust, shame, sadness, surprise, trust, excitement). Of these, *five* (fear, anger, disgust, shame and sadness) are the emotions of survival, governing threat avoidance and defensiveness, *two* (trust and excitement) are the emotions of engagement, and one (surprise) is the emotion that can be a bridge to the two other clusters of emotion. The link with humour is powerful; humour often has an element of 'discontinuity' that evokes surprise along with other potential types of encounters, such as challenge, newly felt bodily sensations and lateral, creative thinking.

I see that when humour emerges between my clients and myself causing a reaction of incongruence or surprise, it may create the possibility for change by evoking what Brown calls the *'potentiating emotion of surprise'*. He suggests that this is one of the key ways in which learning can take place – when humour emerges well in the coaching relationship; we are co-creating the 'limbic resonance' and physiological conditions for finding new ways of seeing the world.

In the light of this, I wonder whether minimising humour or infrequently considering it serves a purpose in professionalising the *seriousness* of coaching within a relatively new emerging discipline. The current coaching literature seems to illustrate an apparent lack of attention to humour. If the current neurological research findings and Brown's ideas are valid, then perhaps a fuller consideration of the use of both *black* and *white* humour may be needed in the development of coaches in the future.

CHAPTER 3

THE INTERVIEWS WITH TEN COACHES

This thought was strengthened by the interviews that I carried out with coaches about how they use humour in their practices. I began to speculate as to how the role of humour, particularly the dark side, plays out in coaching generally. Perhaps it does not occur or is largely ignored in current coaching practices. These questions still remain with me.

HUMOUR AND ME AS A COACH

At the start of this inquiry, I was fearful that through studying humour, I would have an 'identity-quake', where my sense of identity would be 'wobbled' (Stone et al., 1999 and Ibarra, 2003) and I would lose something precious to me. My intuition was at play here, because I *have* lost something through this inquiry – the ability to hide my background from myself. I have also gained something – the potential to break old and increasingly less-effective humour habits.

Slowly, I began to see how pernicious sarcasm was in my upbringing. I admitted to myself finally and honestly that I had been schooled in sarcasm and know it well. I can parry with sarcasm and I am adept at using a mean or mocking put-down of others and of myself. Sarcasm is a defensive mechanism I take on if I am feeling tired, irritated, patronised or threatened, when the emotions involved lie in Brown's category of survival and self-preservation (Brown and Brown, 2012).

This is *not* a resourceful place to be during a coaching session for either myself or my client and I may have spent considerable energy keeping this under control in my coaching over the years. Ironically, I have used a deflective, light humour as a means to avoid using humour spitefully. When I feel the urge to use black, ironic humour, or to make a sarcastic remark that advantageously asserts my superiority, I block it by resorting to a 'performer-role', where my client becomes my audience – I fall back to entertaining rather than coaching, instead of staying honestly with the irritation, doubt or uncomfortable feelings. I observed myself doing this only last week, telling a funny story to cover up the irritation that I felt when my client arrived late *yet again* – I restrained my urge to be sarcastic and covered up the anger that was brewing in me.

I do realise that there is a need to consider whether or not to share negative reactions with clients, however when I am *not* honest and hide my reactions in this way, I limit my authentic presence in the coaching relationship. My attention shifts in those moments to an 'I – it' relationship (i.e. towards a person as an object that is separate in itself, which we either use or experience) rather than the 'I – Thou' connection that I aspire to, in which we move into existence in a relationship of deep respect and trust (Buber, 1971).

I realise that my old, hard-wired habits of humour are difficult to change, particularly in challenging situations. Thinking about this has opened up a wider, more universal perspective or truth (Silsbee, 2008), and reminded me of the enduring nature of habits, of how they serve us all so well often for a long time.... but sooner or later they need to be reviewed, kept or changed.

I have been experimenting by 'seriously' staying with and facing highly emotionally charged and difficult issues in my coaching sessions (recently this brought a breakthrough for one of my clients who had been stuck). I have begun to shift my deflective humour habit and resist the urge to deflect, even when I end up squirming on the spot. For me, somewhere hidden in this struggle, there seems to be great potential for significant learning and growth.

Through the emotional highs and lows of this inquiry, I have worked with a wider range of my own feelings, so my ability to stay with my clients when they are experiencing a range of different emotions has deepened. I believe that this inquiry has broadened my emotional holding-presence as a coach (Silsbee, 2008).

Humour will, I think, always form part of my signature presence (O'Neill, 2000) albeit *now* with a deepened awareness of how and when it emerges. It is in my 'coaching-bones'. I do realise that one of the limitations of this inquiry is that the sample of clients is only three, so exploring humour with my clients will be therefore be an on-going theme for me.

As I close this chapter I realise that I have already begun a *new* inquiry. I am drawn to exploring more of how my clients and I can chew over old, less useful habits and together develop new and more generative ones (Silsbee, 2008 and Duhigg, 2012). Starting from this unexpected and fascinating place, a *new* 'niggle' has begun to emerge and I am wondering where on earth it will lead me to *next*!

PART TWO

INQUIRING INTO THE EVOLVING COACHING RELATIONSHIP

CHAPTER 4

HOW DOES MY EXPLORATION OF EMOTIONS AFFECT MY CLIENTS' EXPERIENCE OF COACHING?

PROLOGUE

I WAS attracted by the challenge of researching and writing abou something that I have previously found difficult to express openly: feelings and emotions. In my time studying at Ashridge, in formal coaching practice sessions in pairs or small groups I have experimented with and taken the opportunity to be more open than usual in revealing my feelings, my emotions and talking about various experiences during my life that became figural during coaching from participants or during supervision. Becoming aware of a tendency to control, to ask leading questions and to become directive in coaching, I have tried to 'drop the mask' and become more open, curious, and aware of my feelings in response to and in the service of my clients. This chapter shares some of the key moments and insights from that journey and my learning experience.

INTRODUCTION

To 'check in' with the reader, I can explain that I have a lot to juggle. Like many readers, I currently combine many roles: husband, father, son, colleague, manager, coach and volunteer. I have a pattern of taking on more than is perhaps wise and yet somehow getting on with making the best of it, or coping with the consequences. I recall a teacher telling me that I had to make choices and focus my time on fewer activities, however my pattern of involvement in a wide circle of activities and volunteering for responsibility has continued!

Choosing a question in the realm of feelings and emotions resonated with that part of the learning experience at Ashridge that had engaged me and also stretched me the most. My chosen field of enquiry for this dissertation is how my clients' experience of coaching is affected by my attention to and exploration of emotions. My clients are internal, meaning that we all work for the same organisation. My attention to and exploration of emotions may occur in the moment, in relationship with the client, in my reflections and thinking about my coaching practice or reflecting upon my own affective responses to my experience of others.

EMOTIONS WITHIN ORGANISATIONS

As an internal coach I work in a particular environment which, although made up out of individuals, will have a culture or quality to its emotional life. Bruch and Ghoshal (2003) describe organisations as having intensity and quality of organisational energy. While intensity relates to strength of activity, alertness, interaction and excitement, the *quality* of organisational energy is described in terms of positive emotions (for example enthusiasm, joy, satisfaction) or negative emotions (for example fear, frustration or sorrow).

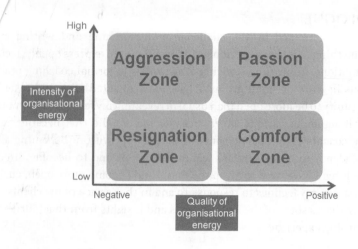

Fig 15: Organisation Energy Zones. Source: Bruch and Ghoshal, 2003.

Fig 15 shows combinations of organisational energy which create the necessary combination of cognitive, emotional and action-taking capabilities and alignment of the resulting force to achieve business goals. I like this model because it attempts to include the 'soft', human, emotional aspects of organisational life into a model of business success. The emotional life of the organisation manifested in the emotional experiences and behaviours of individuals has a material positive or negative effect upon the energy and capability of the organisation.

Parkinson (1996) argues that the dynamic of collective emotion derives from imitating and exaggerating the emotions of others. He makes the case that emotion surfaces through interaction with others and is not privately created.

Interpersonal factors are typically the main causes of emotion, and emotions lead people to engage in certain kinds of social encounter or withdraw from such interpersonal contact (Parkinson, 1996).

He makes the case that *emotions emerge in relationship with others* and summarises by saying that '...emotion is social through and through'.

The importance of emotions to coaching is hard to overstate. It can be said that emotions and feelings are right at the heart of therapy and of coaching. Rogers (1967) view is that

...the client discovers in therapy that it is possible to drop the mask he has been wearing and become more genuinely himself.

Rogers (1967) argues that clients, in expressing themselves more freely, benefit from the opportunity to express strong and persistent emotional attitudes and this provides the basis to establish real relationships based on mutual understanding.

CONSIDERING THE CHALLENGES OF INTERNAL COACHING

In my operational human resources role I seek to influence and shape our business, particularly with respect to how people are deployed, managed, rewarded and developed. In establishing my internal coaching relationships I have been very aware of the potential *role conflicts* between my role in HR and my role as a coach to an individual. I have taken great care to discuss the coaching relationship, agree the contract for the coaching relationship and refer back to this contract between us. This has been particularly important with respect to establishing confidentiality and trust. These discussions, together with the express option for the client at any stage to be assigned to an external coach have been an important part of establishing an ethical practice.

However role conflict could become a factor due to misalignment between the purpose of a Human Resources manager and the role of a relational coach. There may be certain types of 'hard HRM' (Legge, 2005) activities, implemented by an HR manager and relating to cost control and an intensification of an organisation's use of labour such as layoffs, implementation of coercive changes in organisation, systems and processes, that may be seem incompatible with that same HR manager also acting in the role of an executive coach to individuals in the organisation.

Even if the environment is more akin to the model of 'soft HR' (Legge, 2005), which seeks to increase employee commitment, flexibility, engagement, job quality and training opportunities, there may still be significant challenges in managing the potential role conflicts between the HR and the coaching roles due to the risks of an unequal power relationship between the coach and the client.

Frish documents the emergence of the internal coach, notes the potential advantages and disadvantages of internal and external coaches and makes a clear suggestion for practice:

> *Internal coaches should be outside the chain of command of those that they coach, to differentiate from the job that all effective managers do.* (Frish, 2001)

He also sets out a solution to an ethical dilemma of when an HR generalist is asked to comment on the suitability of an internal coachee for promotion or a pay rise – that the HR Generalist's safest approach is to opt out of the discussion.

Classical advice is that the coach or therapist needs to be free from factors that may hinder establishing a productive helping relationship with the client. Rogers' ten questions on creating a helping relationship (Rogers, 1967) include 'Can I be in a way which will be perceived by the other person as trustworthy, as dependable or consistent in some deep sense?' and 'Can I enter fully into the world of his feelings and personal meanings and see these as he does?' Answering these questions satisfactorily may be challenging for any self-aware coach, and given the advantages and disadvantages discussed here, perhaps more so for an internal coach.

RESEARCH CYCLE ONE – WITH CLIENTS

In my first research cycle, I attempted to be aware of and observe emotions and behaviours within the developing coaching relationships with my clients.

LAURA

Laura (not her real name) is a manager of a team of three people based in Bristol and her boss is based at our Birmingham office so she is reasonably autonomous in the way that she runs things.

The following short transcripts are representative of, and are taken from, our second coaching session. Laura wanted to talk to her manager about working part time but was concerned about the implications of having this conversation.

Laura described the conflict she was experiencing:

L: If I don't do something I will remain worried about this indefinitely. But …I'm less worried about talking to [Manager] about it than I was because like we said last time I'm just being honest. The thing is that it would change my whole way of life, maybe taking a four day week. I don't know if I can afford it?

But am I ready to talk to my manager? Am I ready to take the next step? Or should I wait for a more stable financial situation but if I do that it will be rolling on for an indefinite period. But I really want to do something about this.

Wholesale change is … [pause] … not devastating … but [I] would have to make quite a lot of adjustments and it's a big change to my whole Monday to Friday existence. I think that's it… am I ready to talk to my manager about this?

I noticed the tension here and the feelings of threat to Laura's way of life. Even though the words she used were 'not devastating' I wondered if she did see this as a potentially devastating change. I underlined this word 'devastating' in my notebook as it was such a strong phrase. Sensing a gap between the meaning conveyed by the words themselves and my bodily response to Laura's tone, intonation and body language, I was quite affected by my perception of the depth of Laura's fear and noticed my stomach knotting with tension. I wondered if I could help her avoid being 'worried about this indefinitely' and noticed that I had an impulse to be reassuring and tell her that everything would be OK. Feeling it would be unhelpful role for me to play I bracketed this impulse. It would also have been a promise upon which I could not possibly deliver.

Me: I felt concerned (pause), listening to you I felt feelings of almost like a sweat go down my spine and I thought 'Gosh…' When you talked about a big change in your lifestyle I felt tense in my tummy. And I noticed that reaction in me. I'm interested as you think about this, what emotions are you experiencing, what do you feel?

L: Well it's all about security isn't it? Safety and security. Paying the mortgage, staying in my home. OK, if I'm brutally honest, the idea of a four day week would be perfect, that would be a good balance. However my fear is that if I put that on the table [Manager] will expect me to do five days work in a four day week.

The client expressed her needs for safety and [job] security. These needs were expressed in a very prosaic, matter of fact way. The words are practical and on the surface unemotional, however the strong need to not lose what she values is expressed. However I also notice more emotional, more loaded words: 'brutally honest', 'fear' and 'expect' and I wanted to find out more about her fear.

> **Me:** So what do you need to do with that fear?
>
> **L:** I need to make an alternative suggestion, about how work could be coped with or moved around. We have a plan that could help.
>
> **Me:** So you could go to [Manager] with a proposal?
>
> **L:** OK mmm

This was a leading question and Laura backed away from the conversation and did not seem ready to move from exploring feelings to committing to actions. I attempt to return to the emotion that I had identified, but in critically reviewing this now I can see that I give advice that is dressed up as a question:

> **Me:** But notice that fear...
>
> **L:** Well potentially there could be a problem, but by the time I want to go part time, maybe in two years' time, we could have sorted something out. In two years' time I can draw a pension so I could work fewer days. Part of the fear is that if I say now that I want to reduce my hours in two years' time then [Manager] might take that as the moment to start to get someone else in and replace me.
>
> **Me:** I guess that at the moment she has no idea of what you have planned for the next few years. ... Imagine you go to her and you set out your ideal scenario... Where do you think she would go from there?
>
> **L:** Well she is looking at structure already...

Reviewing this and the session as a whole, although my intention in going into the enquiry was to be aware of emotions, I notice that my tendency is to struggle to stay with the emotions and instead I have asked leading questions and made suggestions, so I conclude that I am being very directive at times. These interventions tend to be prescriptive and have displaced opportunities for me to listen to Laura.

I notice that I am working rather hard to explore emotions and elicit emotional responses. However I did also notice that my client remained really quite practical and emotionally 'contained' throughout.

as a coach in relationship with my clients and what implications this may have for my third cycle of enquiry with my clients.

Two themes have emerged from my reflections upon my history and my current lived experience. The first theme is power and control and the second theme is reluctance to self-disclose emotions, weakness and vulnerability.

Power and control relates to my tendency to be directive, critical and challenging of authority. My perception is that when working with colleagues I am collaborative, positive, approachable and friendly and I'm told that my style tends to be logical, analytical and rational. However I'm also occasionally described by colleagues as guarded or distant and I sometimes get feedback that I can be over-critical or too much into the detail.

The following data of lived experience from earlier this year sets out a topic that I brought to a session of peer coaching at Ashridge in Workshop Two of Year Two:

> **Current lived experience:** There is pattern of behaviour within my family in which my youngest daughter may be asked by my wife to attend to some small task, such as getting dressed, making her bed or coming to eat a meal. My daughter is happily busy with her own preoccupations and ignores the request. My wife asks her repeatedly and on the third or fourth occasion raises her voice and speaks more sharply in irritation that my daughter has not come. My daughter looks angry (that she has been shouted at) and shouts 'OKaaaaY' loudly at her mother. I say 'Don't shout at your mother' and either get no response or I get shouted at by my daughter, either response resulting in me becoming more angry by the minute, angry at the initial rudeness shown to my wife and the challenge that has been made to me. These confrontations reach a verbal crescendo with my daughter and I shouting at each other. I impose a sanction for being rude such as a ban on TV and I may on occasion be criticised by my wife and daughter for over-reacting to the initial trivial issue. At some point soon after the crescendo when the anger on all sides has subsided we reconcile, my daughter is asked to say sorry to her mum and to me, I say sorry if I have become very angry and we all hug and talk about what behaviour we expect. This repeats itself from time to time.

In being coached on this issue I was able to express my doubts about how I was handling these situations and my fears of rupture with my daughter and fear of loss of one of the most treasured relationships in my life and yet I also expect reasonable standards of behaviour from my daughter – particularly that she not shout rudely at her mum. The coaching session gave me an opportunity to see that a confrontation, rupture, repair cycle was not unusual in family life and that I should continue to do my best to walk the balance between allowing licence, freedom and space to grow yet setting expectations and boundaries for my daughter. The key insights that emerged during this peer coaching session was to intervene less, to try to *role model* standards of behaviour, to try less hard to *force* my daughter to behave in the way that I wanted, to let my own moment of anger pass, to be more available to my daughter and to my wife as a whole person rather than as an authoritarian figure.

Reflecting upon this, I can see how we may be playing out roles in Karpman's Drama Triangle (Karpman, 1968, cited in Stewart and Joines, 1987) see Fig 16 below:

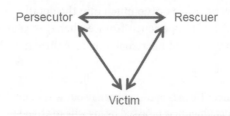

Persecutor	Victim	Rescuer
Daughter	Mother	Father
(switch)		
Father	Daughter	Mother
(switch)		
Mother and daughter	Father	
(or alternative switch)		
Daughter	Father	Mother

Fig 16: Drama Triangle (after Karpman, 1968, cited in Stewart and Joines, 1987)

I believe that I should take responsibility for escaping from this repetitive script. I am very aware of the power imbalance that there is in my household between me and my daughter and of my potential to be excessively critical or coercive. So I try to notice when these situations now arise, to be aware of my affective response when I perceive my daughter to be rude to her mother and I seek to avoid getting straight into the role of rescuer.

Through peer-coaching as part of AMEC I have been exploring and starting to experiment with greater disclosure of emotions. I took a risk and decided to talk about a traumatic experience from school. I think this event speaks to both a need to stay in control of events and discussing it a step towards overcoming a reluctance to show weakness by disclosing my emotions. The peer coaching session as part of AMEC gave me the first opportunity to speak about the event since it took place:

History: I was 16 years old and had just taken exams along with all my friends in my year. After exams we had our last day of timetabled school before the summer holidays. On this day of ending, of parting company, a mob formed and I was carried across two football fields, against my will, resisting all the way, and was thrown fully into a stagnant pond. I don't know why I was thrown in the pond. I was wet, dirty, humiliated and very confused as to why this had happened. I was upset because I could not stop it being done to me and the rupture that I felt with the close friends that I had shared the last seven years with. I remember being upset and feeling ashamed of being upset. The teachers gave me a spare pair of tracksuit trousers but I had to stay in some of my wet clothes. The day ended, the holidays started and I put it all behind me, and got on with life, not referring to it again.

Having the opportunity to disclose this shameful experience in the relative safety of peer-coaching, my coach providing encouragement and empathy, staying with the rawness of the emotion and helping me work through my shame in that coaching session. This peer-coaching experience allowed me to talk to my wife about the experience for the first time when I returned from Ashridge without being as embarrassed or upset as I had been in the peer-coaching. Today I can write about it without feeling ashamed, without resentment in my stomach and I have a greater awareness of this a possible source of my need to control what happens to me by controlling others.

Stewart and Joines (1987) define a racket feeling as a familiar emotion, learned in childhood, experienced in stress situations and maladaptive as an adult means of problem solving. Reflecting upon this experience it may be that a racket feeling was reinforced or set up. I wonder if my authentic sadness at the sudden and unresolved loss of those friendships was repressed, as sadness was not an emotion to be openly displayed at school. A possible explanation is that I set up a racket feeling of anger that replaced sadness in response to coercive control – perceiving direction, power or instruction as an external threat and responding with frustration or irritation which expresses itself as behaviour in which I critique or reject the instruction that I have received. Although credible, I hold these initial ideas quite lightly as a possible explanation based on theories of rackets and scripts and I remain open to how I might interpret these ideas. Another explanation that makes me smile is that I'm just grumpy that I got thrown in a pond! Nevertheless, I am much more aware of my anger response as a result of this introspection and reflection and am alert to choose more adult responses. My hope is that this emergent self-awareness will help me at work, as a coach and at home in my family setting.

I can see that my tendency to want to be controlling (strong and powerful in order to stay 'safe') be linked to my reluctance to expose 'weakness' (being emotionally open, communicative, vulnerable) and this is an area where I feel that I have gained some self-awareness and movement.

Considering how these issues may affect me as a coach I also turn to second person data that I have in terms of feedback from peers at Ashridge. I asked an AMEC participant for his observations of me on the course and in particular for his awareness of any aspects of emotional disclosure that I had made in the workshops. He recalled the session where I was coached on challenges at home that related to my fear of loss of relationships, yet wanting to set standards and discipline for my children:

> **AMEC Peer:** 'You became much more three-dimensional and present in
> the second workshop. I experienced you being more relaxed in the group,
> and remember you participating more in the plenary sessions. Your humour
> came through too. However, it was the video session and your willingness
> to share which made me appreciate you much more. I'm sure it was all
> there before, but it was in that moment that it registered. What made the
> connection was your willingness to share an emotional state with [peer's
> name] and I. Your vulnerability and your honesty made you human. I have
> a family, so I could absolutely recognise what you were describing. That was
> the point at which I ceased to think about you as a just some HR guy, and
> appreciated you as a fellow traveller on life's highway.'

In another AMEC workshop we coached each other in pairs on the subject of 'How are your past patterns of relating showing up in the group' and as part of the exercise we provided each other with feedback. My peer in the exercise was someone I had not worked with much before and she gave me feedback that initially, I am not an easy person to read or to know. She suggested that I could reveal more about what I am thinking, and be more emotionally open. When I have revealed more of myself and displayed my vulnerability, she experienced a warm and caring family man.

With humility and joy, I recognise the warm and caring person described by my peers. According to Joyce and Sills (2001) Perls asserted that the over-riding therapeutic need is for a real relationship, and authentic contact. My work in cycle two suggests to me that by revealing more of myself, by accessing how I feel, I might become more of 'who I really am' and I can make more authentic contact with my client.

I conclude from my enquiry in Cycle Two that it may benefit my coaching practice I were to exert less control, be less directive, allow space for my client in the room and be more vulnerable in the service of my client. I would like to practice inclusion, in particular emotional inclusion with the aim of establishing a deeper dialogue in relationship with my clients.

RESEARCH CYCLE THREE – WITH CLIENTS

In this research cycle I have tried to be less in control, less directive and more vulnerable in the service of my client. I tried to practice inclusion, in particular emotional inclusion, in dialogue with my clients.

LAURA

In my next session with Laura I worked much less hard to steer the conversation and elicit emotions than I had in cycle one. Laura spent the session reflecting on her manager's behaviours related to a major change in her department, how they affected her and the extent to which she then repeated those behaviours with her staff. My focus was more on being present and being attuned to her and attentive to whatever emerged.

I reflected upon this exchange and listen back to the recording, using Interpersonal Process Recall (Kagan, 1984) as a form of self-supervision, observing my own feelings and expression of those feelings, observing my client's language, actions, emotions and observing the interplay between us during coaching. I notice that many of my contributions to the dialogue were quite sparse (mainly mmm, yes and nods of the head) and I was calm and friendly towards Laura, reflecting back my interpretation of elements of her meaning yet letting her set the direction and pace of the conversation. I followed her tempo, pace and matched or reflected her emotional intensity with my tone of voice, volume, non-verbal responses. I encouraged her to stay with and have courage to continue with her description of worries and fears that she had about a change in her department that she was finding difficult, by recognising the difficulty, acknowledging the emotions she was experiencing and inviting her to comment further if she wanted.

L: I don't know what to do about it, I feel a bit out of my depth.

Me: Yes...I feel as though I'm a bit underwater as I hear you talk about that. Would you like to tell me more about it?

L: Yes, I'm really worried about [name] and how she will cope with the changes...

Me: mmm changes?

L: (Laura talks about the person who works for her and the affect that a change in her job might have and how worried Laura is that they might be upset and their working relationship would be affected).

Me: You really care about [the person], I really noticed that as you talked to me – I can feel a real warmth and care that you have for them. That seems really important to you?

L: (Laura opens up a conversation about her relationship with [the person] and how she wants to be trusted and liked by them and how she is worried that this may be put at risk by the changes).

This session developed very constructively, the working alliance seemed stronger. I felt pleased that I had a greater connection – I noticed that the content of the conversation seemed fuller and more tangible, substantial than previous sessions – Laura was being much more specific about naming issues and what she was prepared to do about them. Bodily, I felt solid and complete, like I was fully in the room.

In giving me feedback, Laura states that she has found the coaching helpful and comments on both rational and emotional aspects of the coaching. She has found the sessions useful as opportunities to order her thinking and try out ideas. She has also expressed some of her fears and worries and has benefited from a sense of 'being understood'.

Referring back to Rogers' (1967) ten questions on creating a helping relationship I feel that as the coaching relationship has developed I have been perceived by the other person as trustworthy and dependable and that I have only just started the process of entering into the world of her feelings and personal meanings.

Angela

I coached Angela again and she presented with a very clear issue: She wanted to work on how she could be warmer and more personable in simple social exchanges with colleagues in corridors or coffee rooms. Angela was also concerned that she may be being 'silly' in bring up such a small thing but I encouraged her that it was valid to talk about it. I let her explain the issue and after some initial clarifications and checking my understanding I asked her gently what feelings she had at the moment she went to the coffee room – Angela showed emotion as she described the fear that she was not liked and that she would be rejected by the other person if she greeted them... 'What if I am ignored...?' I acknowledged her feeling and said that I recognised the feeling she was describing, that I could feel her concern about whether she would be liked, a feeling that there was risk in making a social contact with the other person. This led to a discussion about rejection and experiences of past rejection and how Angela had felt. We had a further discussion around what was likely to happen if Angela greeted someone in the coffee room and how she might handle various outcomes. Angela resolved to experiment with being more approachable and to connect more with others in shared spaces, knowing that she had the security of her office to return to if it proved too difficult.

In this session I noticed that we were more open with each other than we had been before, it felt like less like we were acting out roles. I felt very attentive to the conversation, less aware of time and I did not feel that I had to 'perform' or arrive at any particular destination. I noticed that although Angela was emotional about the content of our coaching session she was less distracted and looked out of the window or up at the ceiling less than in previous sessions.

After the session had ended I asked Angela if she would be willing to give me feedback on the session. I asked her what she had noticed. She said 'I noticed a surprising level of emotion – a small thing is obviously a big thing. Allowing myself to say that something quite small is actually quite upsetting has been helpful'.

I asked her what had helped us to connect during the session. Angela said 'What helped was that you showed you understood me. I felt silly for raising the issue and you helped me see that it was not silly. You were more specific about your own feelings than in previous sessions and you showed me more of yourself'.

I asked Angela how I showed her that I understood. She replied 'By sharing your feelings and not pushing me too hard when I was struggling to express myself'. Finally I asked if she had noticed me showing any emotion. Angela said 'Generally you have been calm and considerate. I appreciate your understanding without you also being emotional'. I am encouraged by the feedback from Laura and Angela. It indicates to me that I am at the start of the right track, in my attempts to demonstrate inclusion in my coaching practice.

I also asked Angela about her awareness of my dual roles as coach and HR manager – who did she see coming in to the room and how had it affected the coaching? Angela smiled and spoke about how she had been very cautious initially, had been extremely careful when giving examples that involved other people in the office, taking care to only refer to people obliquely, but then still thinking 'I know that you know who I mean'. She said she was beginning to be prepared to talk about deeper issues now that we were several sessions in to the coaching. She admitted that there was a voice in her that said 'be careful around HR as they can mark your card'. When asked how this had affected that value of the coaching she said confidently 'I don't think that it has affected it at all, in a way it makes me think better about what's really going on rather than sit here and have a general moan. Actually I was surprised by how useful it has been, particularly now that I have started talking about the things that are really concerning me.'

I think that the reference to being careful around HR and being cautious about what she says in coaching sessions is a very honest appraisal from my client of the potential deficits of the combined role of coach and HR manager, deficits that I recognise from the discussion in my literature review above as having their roots in the unequal power relationship between the coach and the client. The two roles really do represent a challenging combination for the coach and the client and there may be some content, some elements of her 'whole being' necessary to speak I-Thou (Buber, 1937), that the client will never bring to a relationship with the HR manager/coach that they would perhaps be prepared to discuss or bring to contact with an external coach or therapist. For this reason the attempts by the HR manager/coach to establish a 'dialogic relationship' (Clarkson, 2002) may ultimately be frustrated by the realities of the power difference between the two.

However the feedback from Angela is that despite her initial (and on-going) caution the coaching relationship has been helpful to her and, while recognising the subjectivity of my enquiry, I'm prepared to attribute some small part of this helpfulness to my authentic attempts to communicate inclusion in the service of my client.

CONCLUSIONS FOR MY PRACTICE

> *When one enters into dialogic relation, even in the sometimes unreciprocal relationship of therapy, one experiences the release of one's own potential as well as that of the patient. The practice of the art of therapy becomes not only an expression of one's being, but a step in one's becoming.* (Jacobs, 1989)

This quotation from Jacobs resonates for me with the iterative process of learning as a coach – with small steps we learn and we become who we are in relation to others. The action research that I have conducted has helped me to reflect carefully about my coaching practice and I have reached the following conclusions which emerge from my subjective reflections on the research:

- My initial inquiry into exploration of emotions in internal coaching led me initially into trying too hard to elicit emotions or emotional responses from my client. I conclude that I serve my client better by seeking not to *elicit* emotions but to seek to engage authentically with those which are already there and are ready to be voiced and to reflect these back through by my words, gesture or tone to convey inclusion to my client.

- I was encouraged, listening to my recordings of work with my clients, to hear that I have begun to express inclusion, particularly emotional inclusion, to reflect back some sort of resonance with my client's expressed emotions, and to voice my (partial) understanding of what they are experiencing. Even if it has been imperfect, even though I could have communicated it better, even though my attempt only partly describes the complexity of the emotion being experienced by my client then for me this is a step forward towards achieving inclusion, and I intend to continue to develop this in my practice.

- I have found that peer coaching and group supervision has been a very valuable form of support for me, allowing reflection and intro-spection, particularly into how I experience authentic feelings or possibly racket feelings and how these may show up in my coaching (or at work or home) in needing to control others or feeling angry that I am being controlled. I will continue to seek an outlet through supervision for these steps of self-discovery, and to paraphrase Rogers (1967), to drop the mask I have been wearing and become more genuinely myself.

- Increasing my vulnerability and self-disclosure has helped me to make better contact with my clients. I have responded to feedback about how lack of self-disclosure has sometimes made me seem aloof and cold. I have taken encouragement from my AMEC peers to take some risks and to disclose how I feel. While this has not been easy I think it has positively influenced my coaching relationships and there is evidence from my clients that they have found it helpful when I have shared my feelings.

- I recognise that there is an unequal power relationship between me, with my combined roles as HR Manager/coach, and my internal client. The effect of this unequal power is manifested as caution from the client in what they will be prepared to bring into the coaching relationship. This may prevent a particular type of coaching relation-ship, a dialogic relationship, from fully occurring as there will be some important part of the client's self or their experience that they will not feel able to reveal in dialogue with me as coach. Although this limitation to internal coaching may exist, by naming and openly discussing this power difference and exploring the impact of my combined roles upon the relationship, my internal coaching can be of value to my clients.

CHAPTER 5

HOW DO I WORK EFFECTIVELY WITH EMOTIONS IN A CULTURAL SETTING WHERE EXPRESSING EMOTIONS IS NOT SO COMMON?

MY INQUIRY QUESTION

HOW do I work effectively with emotions in a cultural setting where expressing emotions is not common?

I was asked to become one of the coaches on an internal coaching programme just before the start of the second year of AMEC. In that programme I was going to coach groups of 4 – 5 people on General Manager level. The brief was that, as a coach, you were supposed to get the business leaders to express their emotions. I felt honoured and slightly worried. Could I really add value? Would I be accepted, being so much younger and with a different background? And most of all, how was I going to work with emotions in a company where expressing emotions is all but common?

On a personal level I was dealing with the intensely emotional process of fertility treatments. I had been trying to start a family for years and the toll it took on me and my husband was ever increasing.

Almost unwillingly so, during the assignment I found out that it is not easy for me to deal with some of my own emotions. How do you focus on being a good coach when you are in the midst of one of the most emotionally charged periods in your life – a period that contains emotions like shame, fear, joy, happiness and many others?

COACHING PROGRAMME

The internal coaching programme was a bit puzzling to me from the start because I had difficulty understanding how the group setting was related to

97

the coaching I do in a one-to-one meeting. During the inquiry I came to understand that an action-learning group (Revans, 1982) is actually a better way to describe this coaching programme. I use the term 'group coaching' as my way to describe the action learning format.

CORE INQUIRY

CYCLE ONE – WORKING WITH EMOTIONS; STARTING WITH MY OWN

What most occupied my thoughts at the start of the inquiry was how business executives in this company were expressing emotions and how I could best facilitate them. I was somewhat naïve about the impact it would have on me personally. That impact started to unfold right at the start of the programme when I experienced one of the stronger emotions in the spectrum: shame.

The kick-off event for coaches

The organisers of the Coaching programme facilitated a day to exchange ideas and to practise. A few weeks before the start of the programme I received some documentation with the company's view on coaching. One of the things that struck me was that there were a lot of tools in there – such as the GAPS and GROW models – but handling emotions was not mentioned. The GROW method is not recommended when there are emotional issues (De Haan, 2008). So how was I going to work the emotional part?

Entering the room on the coaches' introduction day I don't feel instantly welcome and try to find a way to relate to the people. I'm starting to relax when we do an introduction round and we are asked to pay attention to our feelings and emotions. The conversation feels genuine and other people also show some vulnerability. One of the coaches says that 'in this part of the company emotion is a bad thing'. I start to wonder if we all underestimate these business leaders who are going to be coached. Surely no one can function well if emotions do not play a role in one form or another?

We spend most of the day in trial coaching sessions in which one coach is coaching a group of three people. It is an excellent environment to learn and I notice that I do bring quite a bit of experience to the group.

The trouble starts when I have to be the group coach. The coachee – a woman – is being coached by two men in the group and I facilitate that process. There is one internal supervisor in the room to give feedback. At a certain point in time the woman coachee gets agitated and the two group members struggle to deal with this. First I try to deliver through them and give them tips in which direction to move. Then things get worse and the coachee almost starts to cry. I try to get her to stay with the emotion and get interrupted.

The supervisor intervenes and says: 'Stop that right now, this is not dark muddy Gestalt type of coaching'. I feel immensely exposed because Gestalt principles (Joyce and Sills, 2001) underpin my practice. This text about shame describes accurately how I felt:

> ...we feel deficient by compassion with others,
> we feel we are failures in our own and others' eyes,
> we feel so held up to critical scrutiny in our desperate misery
> that we want to sink to the ground and become invisible
> **Donna Orange (workshop on Shame with Simon Cavicchia)**

The following was going through my mind: *I don't want to be on this project, I don't want to be a coach, I don't want to work for this company'*. When we left the room after the session I climb the stairs and I almost fall flat on my face. When I calmed down a little I went up to the coachee to check if she was okay and to apologise for the way I had dealt with the situation. She said that she felt fine and that I shouldn't worry about it which made me feel slightly better.

A few days after the event I wrote in my journal:

My intervention probably wasn't the best, I can see that now. Advice I received a number of years ago comes to mind: "be careful when you are the only female in a team, you might become the emotion carrier in the group". Could it be that I was overplaying or over-compensating the emotion part? I frequently had coachees crying in my session with them, but am I qualified to deal with that? I have a sense that I can handle it respectfully and feedback from coachees is they appreciate that I'm not taken aback when strong emotions are expressed.

In the end I concluded that I hadn't done a great job but that that supervisor's intervention was not conducted in a very professional way either. It did truly taint the start of the programme for me.

Emotions in the workplace

I'm curious as to how emotions are viewed by others. There are three positions (Fineman, 2000) that could be held for the relation between rationality and emotion in the workplace:

1. Emotions interfere with rationality

2. Emotions serve rationality

3. Emotions and rationality entwine.

Personally I believe that emotions and rationality entwine (Fineman, 2000). However, if the business leaders think that emotions interfere with their rationality it might be difficult to work with those people.

My sense is that my attitude to coaching is pretty clear but I'm not always coherent in execution. Bachkirova and Cox (2007) argue that an unconscious and unexamined attitude to emotion in coaching could result in ineffective interventions and will undermine the value of coaching. I consider emotions essential for progress with business leaders but I don't always see the environment or situation fit for expressing strong emotions. Confusion in coaching might arise as a natural consequence of the contradictory views on emotions that still exist in organisations (Bachkirova and Cox, 2007). It shows me the importance of being aware of my own attitude towards working with emotions.

One of the things I want to do is to pay close attention to the relationship because in my view this contains a wealth of information. There are many ways of describing the relationship or the quality of the relationship in coaching; a relational bridge (Kaufman, 1989), the coaching dance (O'Neill, 2000), the working alliance (De Haan, 2008), etc. Many including myself believe that the relationship is one of the most important means through which change takes place (Critchley, 2010; De Haan, 2008; Bluckert, 2006).

CYCLE TWO – CAN YOU COACH WHEN YOU FEEL EMOTIONALLY FRAGILE?

In the middle of investigating emotions, I started to feel emotional turmoil myself. A number of things were going on for me. At work I had to tell the people in my team that our department had become obsolete and that they were potentially being made redundant. Personally I had to search for another job within the company as well. I noticed that I was looking after others but not so much after myself. On a private level I was going through a rough period because my first IVF treatment failed after numerous other fertility treatments in the last four years. I felt a failure and pretty alone.

I wrote the following in my journal:

> Just returned from holiday and I feel restless and stuck. What entitlement do I have to tell people how to do things? What wisdom do I bring if I struggle in my own life? And where does this feeling of needing to be 'an oracle' come from? Never been my style. Don't want to read, don't want to work. It's paralysing somehow. I have lost the overview and don't even know about the next steps. One question keeps going through my mind: can you coach when you don't feel emotionally sound yourself?

Bill Critchley talks about putting oneself at risk as a coach 'on the high road' of coaching. The high road requires the coach to be capable of self-awareness and reflexivity (Critchley, 2010). O'Neill (2000) talks about coaching with the heart. For me this type of coaching would entail making yourself vulnerable. And I am not so sure if I would be willing to do that just at this moment.

First session with Group One

I had the first coaching session with my group and although I did well, I wonder if I coached 'on the high road' (Critchley, 2010). On reflection there was not a lot of noticeable emotion in the first group which might be to do with the fact that building trust takes time.

Group One consists of four males with technical profiles, all at least ten years older than I am. During the round of introductions I invite the participants to talk a bit more about what is going on for them. I give an example by sharing that I am slightly anxious about my role because I am not used to facilitating group coaching. The introductions that follow are all highly technical and I find myself connecting to them by showing my own technical knowledge.

During the rest of the session I try to move away from business and I manage to get them to share more openly what their expectations and also their doubts are about the work that we are going to be doing together. A critical moment (De Haan, 2008) occurs when one of the participants shares the fact that he doesn't feel confident to share any issues without building a more trusted relationship first. After talking about this, I ask the group if we could simply experience what this group coaching is about and for us to reflect on the development of trust as a group during the session.

For the people in the group it seems a bit of a novelty to talk this much about their personal issues and feelings. The main skill used to understand each other is mentalising (Van de Loo, 2007); they use a cognitive skill to make inferences about the other people and their behaviour. There is a lot of intellectual understanding of each other's challenges but not so much emotional knowing. According to Van de Loo (2007) empathy is the ability subjectively to experience the world from another person's perspective. What manifested in the group session is really about what that experience would feel like for them instead of for the other person. As a result many of the questions are not truly exploratory but contain hidden suggestions of what they would do themselves in that situation. I highlight this to the group and after that I notice they do try to ask more open questions.

With hindsight I have paid less attention than I would normally do to my bodily sensations and my personal affect in the session. Was the environment not safe enough or did I indeed feel too emotionally fragile to turn my attention inwards? Or is it that my expectation of the intensity of emotions present in group coaching is too high?

Insights at Ashridge workshop

The answer to the question 'Can you coach when you feel emotionally fragile?' is getting a bit clearer after attending a workshop at Ashridge. At the moment my answer would be that it depends on the extent to which I'm feeling fragile.

In anticipation of going to a workshop at Ashridge I felt trepidation and a fear of being exposed somehow. My IVF fertility treatment failed a couple of weeks before the start of the workshop. I noticed that the combination of the IVF and the stress at work was really taking its toll and I felt that somehow I hadn't dealt with the emotional impact it had on me. In the supervision session I found that I didn't want to become active because I simply could not bear to be exposed to criticism.

A few days after the Ashridge workshop I wrote the following in my journal:

> Can you coach when you are emotionally unstable? I think it all depends. It felt really good to reconnect to people at Ashridge. There is still quite a lot of emotion – shame? – connected to admitting that I'm affected by the fertility treatments. When I'm trying to make sense of all the data and new theories for the inquiry I notice that my 'coaching voice' is missing. But that is probably because I first need to concentrate on myself.

I recalled an image of myself that I constructed a number of years ago when being coached.

At that time I saw myself as an 'adapter', I was giving other people energy but in order to do so I had to charge my own battery as well. That still resonates with me and it seems that the time has come that I need to take good care of myself *before* I can help others. I am becoming the figure instead of the ground (Joyce and Sills, 2001). I have also decided to stop coaching for a number of weeks to give myself a break. The only session I cannot cancel is the group coaching session with Group Two.

First session with Group Two

I notice I feel quite confident on the day I am scheduled to coach Group Two. Coaching of Group One has gone quite well in my view and I find myself slightly wary of meeting new people but also curious. When I enter the room – a few minutes late – everyone is already present. Right from the start I find it hard to claim presence and I sense the people in the group are not really into coaching. The room is not great either because it is too small to enable me to change the chairs into a different setting than sitting around a meeting table. And potentially as a result the meeting starts with a highly technical and not very personal introduction round. I notice I find it difficult to connect to the individuals. The group looks at me for guidance on what we are going to do. I'm trying to open them up a bit and share that I feel slightly anxious about this session. Even to myself it feels a bit superficial, it doesn't feel as vulnerable as I normally can be.

I have a slight sense of success when two of the group members share that they are not sure about this initiative. They are willing to 'give it a go' but don't really have high expectations. None of my interventions really have the desired effect. From an emotional perspective I feel quite drained at the end of the session. I am in two minds about the session; on the one hand I feel rather useless as a coach but at the other hand this might be the process for this group. On reflection the list of the things I should improve on is four times as long as the things I did well. I note the emotions that stuck to that session with me: insecure, unsafe, not wanted, and in the spotlight.

Influence of my emotional state on coachees

What do my coachees pick up from my emotions? Humans have the ability for limbic resonance, to become attuned to each other's inner states (Lewis et al., 2001). I'm not so sure if I can bracket mine sufficiently for coachees not to be impacted by them.

I believe the concept of 'emotional labour' and the price you pay for displaying the right emotional appearance (Hochschild, 1983) has a place here. Hochschild (1983) makes a difference between emotions that are really felt and those that are acted out for the benefit of others. She links this to the social context a person is in and makes a difference between emotion work and emotional labour. The emotion work is in the private sphere and the emotional labour in the public realm. The latter is about showing socially accepted emotions and that links back to the coaching I do. To me it means that I need to do my emotional work privately and be as authentic to myself as I can be in the coaching. Where does the feeling that I have to put on a brave face come from?

CYCLE THREE – STANDING OUT

A fear that continues to be with me is to stand out too much. Already from a young age I felt I was more skilled in certain areas than people around me, such as my parents – especially in comparison with my father, a blue collar worker. I remember not wanting to make him feel inferior in any way and I would try to put myself down.

Bowlby (1977) argues that we internalise our early experience with our caregivers throughout our lives. In my work this became apparent as well and the fact that I am seen by my company as a talented business person is accompanied by fear. It appears that women become anxious when success is likely or possible. This anticipation of success in competitive achievement produces the threat of social rejection and loss of femininity (Horner, 1972). This 'success anxiety' is particularly present when the success is at the expense of another's failure. Understanding this dynamic in relation to my upbringing has helped me to understand experiences of feeling isolated.

First phone meeting with other coaches on the programme
There was a call organised for the coaches on the programme. Although I knew not to expect supervision along the lines of the seven-eyed model for supervision (Hawkins and Shohet, 2006), I was hoping we would be talking openly about, and learning from, our experiences. I shared my experiences: that I had felt comfortable and knowledgeable with the first group but less uncomfortable with the second group.

The facilitator of the call said: 'it is not about *our* feelings: the focus should be on participants'.

It felt quite hurtful that we were not even able to share emotions amongst the coaches. I have come to believe that all responses you have to your client are important (Joyce and Sills, 2001). Reflecting on the working alliance (De Haan, 2008) provides important clues about the piece of coaching. I also think that my internal process – mode 4 in the seven-eyed model of supervision (Hawkins and Shohet, 2006) – provides important information. I was really disappointed at the unskilful support – I would not even call it supervision – that was offered. It led me to devalue the coaching programme I was in.

CYCLE FOUR – GETTING STUCK
Sometime during the inquiry I decided that I did not want to become a full-time coach or consultant but instead wanted to continue to pursue my business career. At that point I got well and truly stuck for a number of reasons:

- **Becoming a mother:** Another IVF attempt failed during the summer and I became increasingly mindful of the fact that we were potentially progressing towards the end of the track.

- **Career:** Although I was rationally aware that finding a new job in my own company was a temporary nuisance rather than a signal that I was not wanted anymore, the emotional experience was very different.

- **AMEC Study:** I did not have a clue as to how I was going to finish the study having decided that I did not want to become a fulltime coach.

I felt utterly lost. I decided to share my inquiry in the raw vulnerable version it was and ask for help from my supervisor and peer coaches in the inquiry group. I received an email from my tutor with feedback on my inquiry and I noticed I was anxious to read it. Was the draft so bad I would have to stop the AMEC programme? The feedback I received was difficult to take in, not because it was negative but because it was actually really positive and confrontational at the same time.

Email comments from my tutor:

> "I do hear your feelings of 'crying' and I understand your dilemma or paradox. My dilemma is that I want to let you know what good stuff it is and I suspect you won't believe me.
>
> It is not my job to persuade you to become or not to become a coach, but from both my experience of you doing the programme and also from reading this material, I know you are already a good coach and have the capacity to be an excellent coach. One of your personal patterns however, when faced with someone or some people who are not responding well to your coaching style is to default to self-denigration.
>
> You have provided some excellent reflection on how your feelings of being the brightest in your family, may have contributed to this, but it is nevertheless a painful tendency to see yourself as the problem."

A pattern of self-denigration was staring me in the face. I could not continue reading the rest of the email. I knew at the moment of reading how right he was. At first I felt pitiful that I was doing this to myself, followed by shame that I had been so vulnerable to the group to whom I sent my draft inquiry. Then I came to understand that it was this vulnerability that had helped me to this powerful learning.

Another important piece I realised is that when changing my view of self, I had woven failure into my identity. And that was spreading like an infectious disease throughout my life.

When a visiting tutor – Michael Carroll – spoke about a 'survival mode' (2009) I recognised I was in that mode for the last few months. I felt the consequences of being shut off from competences like planning, reflection, creativity, problem-solving and self-development. I was often overwhelmed by emotions and not able to learn.

> *Under stress, not only does the brain shut down and lessen our ability to function, it also loses the capability to learn* (Boyatzis and McKee, 2005)

I was wondering what had triggered my state of fight-or-flight response (LeDoux, 1998). Not becoming a parent is an existential fear to me and triggered the same neurological response as if in real danger. The loss of identity at work magnified my response. Marris (1996) suggests that dramatic change within organisations is connected with bereavement. Deciding that I did not want to be a coach, I was also mourning my identity as a coach. The theme of mourning occurred in major parts of my life.

Reaching out for help

What made the difference to me was reaching out to others for help. I have come to understand that female responses to stress– although primary physiologically the same as male – differ in an important way (Taylor et al., 2000). In a typically female 'tend-and-befriend' way I started connecting to people. Relationships have the power to stabilise (Lewis et al., 2001) and that happened for me through connecting again to people.

The insight of the pattern of self-denigration and understanding my feeling of failure felt cathartic (Heron, 1975). Within a few days I could read again for my inquiry, apply theories, think about new jobs in my company, and I felt more emotionally sound.

CYCLE FIVE – HOW I THOUGHT THAT HANDLING EMOTIONS HAD NOTHING TO DO WITH THINKING

Feedback by coachees

To get a better view on how my handling of emotions was perceived I asked feedback from a number of people I was coaching internally and externally. When I was analysing the feedback I divided comments into two categories: thinking and emotions. In doing so I became aware of an assumption that dealing with emotions is something that does not require any of my cognitive skills. Did I really assume that handling emotions is a non-cognitive skill?

The co-inquiry with one coachee was interesting because our sessions have been quite emotional at times. It appeared that my cognitive interventions (e.g. probing, getting to the heart of the matter) were things he had really valued.

Feedback by peer students at Ashridge

In the last workshop we were asked to create a poster of the type of coaches we were becoming. The posters were hung around the room and everyone was able to put Post-its on the posters with feedback on the coach. I noticed strong feelings during the process; it was very pleasant and at the same time I had an image of a funeral. It was almost physically impossible for me to walk to my own poster and read what other people had written about me. When I did this, I was overwhelmed by emotion and felt physically full (I couldn't even eat one of those Ashridge scones). What I gained from the feedback is that I really make an impact on people.

A few comments that stood out for me:
- Insightful and special wherever you tread.

- I am inspired by your vulnerability and at the same time by your strength. You display both with humble balance.

- Extraordinary emotional maturity

- I admire your inner strengths and your ability for insight.

- You are more powerful than you know and can achieve what you want.

Again there is a nice combination of feedback on both my cognitive and emotional ability. It amazes me how much I have already become the coach (and person) I aspire to be.

Cycle Six – Benefits of the inquiry start to become apparent

The effect of the action inquiry is apparent also outside the coaching context. My pattern of self-denigration showed up when I attended a global leadership conference for 950 women from all over the world. Several women spoke about how they added value to this world. I felt my work was really insignificant and this left me feeling really small.

I decided actively to practice 'befriending' (Taylor et al., 2000) to address my pattern of self-denigration. I started sharing my experiences with other attendees and found out that quite a few people had a similar feeling. Not only did I feel less alone in my feeling, I also received tips on how to deal with this.

In one of the workshops at the conference we were asked to write down an important achievement in our lives. The facilitator pointed out that women often undersell themselves. I had written down a lesser achievement because I was afraid that I had to read it out to others and would feel exposed. The pattern of not wanting to stand out stared me in the face. I realised that I did not own up to my achievements because of the success anxiety (Horner, 1972) that I spoke about earlier in this inquiry.

These two experiences showed me that I haven't just become better at recognising my own patterns but I am also becoming successful at addressing them.

CYCLE SEVEN – THE VALUE OF MERGING EMOTIONS AND THINKING

It is all well and good to have the insight that I needed to connect my cognitive skills and emotional skills better, but how do you do that in practice? There were three interesting pieces in which I had the opportunity to practice.

1. Withdrawal as a coach for Group Two

The first session with Group Two did not go well. The leader of the coaching programme shared with me that one person in the group had asked him for a new coach. I said to him that I might not be the correct coach for this group. If you don't click, you have to find a replacement coach (De Haan, 2008). When he mentioned the name of the coachee I said I was not surprised and I found myself trying to explain some of that person's behaviour in the group. All of a sudden I was aware that I was breaching confidentiality by doing so and I stopped sharing.

I realised the programme was not up to my standards of coaching and decided to stop coaching Group Two. The organisers of the programme were not qualified in coaching, the confidentially was blurred, and coaches were not supported by proper supervision. In my view good supervisors have some sort of qualification and are preferably from outside the company. I decided to continue with my other two groups, but to position it clearly as action learning (Revans, 1982) instead of coaching.

2. First session with Group Three

I had my first session with Group Three and the session went really well. At the introduction I started out with sharing something personal and the impact it had had on my career. Another person in the group built on that experience and shared an accident at the company's facilities. Although it was nearly 25 years ago, he said it was making him emotional even thinking about it now and I could see his eyes were moist. I noticed that I felt touched. The rapport in the group deepened and consequently we had a good conversation about what we wanted to achieve together.

I do think that I had too high expectations of the intensity of emotions present in a group coaching setting when I started out. More so, I overvalued emotions at the expense of cognitive thinking. Balancing myself is helping me to be a better coach.

3.   Second phone meeting with internal peer coaches

There was another meeting with peer coaches facilitated by the same person as the first meeting. We talked about experiences we had in the past few months. Another coach shared that he had had a difficult first session with one of his groups. After he explained this in more detail he was asked the question by the facilitator: 'So it didn't work for you, but did it work for them?' This question highlighted her view on coaching to which I so objected in the first call. Instead of triggering a similar response, I said to myself that it is actually okay for her to think that. I still believe that she could learn more about coaching but I am also okay that there are multiple realities around.

PERSONAL CHANGE AND LEARNING

The good thing is that my 'self-denigration radar' works well now beyond the realm of coaching.

I wrote the following in my journal:

> Reading my inquiry so far I feel a bit silly that one of the main conclusions is that my emotional and cognitive self are more integrated. It is so obvious that surely I cannot have thought that they were disconnected. And how is this blatantly obvious knowledge going to make any difference to other coaches?

Before I started with AMEC I viewed my emotional capabilities at the work place as a real strength. Probably I even thought it was compensating for my weaker cognitive ability. On a very regular basis I felt 'outsmarted' by colleagues. It is only through this inquiry I have really acknowledged my cognitive abilities. Goleman (1998) says that emotional intelligence (EQ) is a different way of being smart. I now see that pre-AMEC I felt that EQ was my main way of being smart. I did not really acknowledge my capacity in the thinking space. Perhaps that is the crux! By doing this degree and this inquiry, I have come to understand and value my cognitive strengths and as such I have increased my emotional abilities as well. That is actually not a small thing at all. Writing this I suddenly start crying and I am truly moved. Tears of insight, tears of joy, tears of compassion for myself?

NO REWARDS IN UPBRINGING FOR COGNITION

Inquiring into the lack of acknowledgement for my cognitive skills with my psychotherapist brought another interesting view. I grew up in a family where cognitive skills were not necessarily recognised and as such not rewarded. Schmidt (1982) argues that girls are treated differently in classrooms in elementary and secondary schools. Bright females with many questions and ideas suffer perhaps more than any other group in the mixed messages they receive from parents, teachers and peers. The following anecdote is an example. At the end of the elementary school I had to make the choice which high school to go to. Although my test scores were top of the class, the headmaster refused to give me a recommendation for a more elitist school because according to him I would not fit there. Two of my friends – with lower test scores but with fathers that had high-standing employment – did receive the recommendation. My parents did manage to get me into the more elitist school in the end. When I achieve something important in my life I sometimes think about the headmaster and I notice a desire to prove him wrong.

AWARENESS PROVIDES OPPORTUNITY FOR CHANGE
Being aware of my patterns enables me to also counter the 'Great Imposter Syndrome' (Clance, 1985; Machlowitz, 1982) of viewing my status of a bright achiever as being undeserved or accidental.

This syndrome occurs when high levels of success have been achieved by females which lead to a low sense of self-esteem when females attribute their success to factors other than their own efforts (Reims, 1987).

During my AMEC accreditation coaching session I was able to catch a feeling of failure and turn it into something useful. Halfway into the coaching I felt completely useless and I even sensed hostility from the coachee towards me. My attempts jointly to decide how to proceed were met with a response that I was the coach and thus I should know. Instead of trying further I inquired into the relation between us and I admitted that I was at a loss. The coachee was then able to speak her mind and share her frustration with me. This allowed us to work more collaboratively for the remainder of the session.

Feedback from the accreditors on my live coaching session:

> Initially building rapport was not easy as the coachee did not feel safe at the start, but the coach resisted the temptation to keep trying harder. She stopped and reconnected. This was very skilful coaching.

Because of the inquiry I have been able to increase my self-awareness and as such I have created more options. Cognition contributes to emotion by giving the ability to make decisions about what kind of action should occur next (LeDoux, 1998). I believe I am now better equipped to handle coaching conversations, and to be more compassionate to myself afterwards. Perhaps the biggest change though is that as a person – not only as a coach – I am better aware of my strengths and patterns.

CHANGE ON A PERSONAL LEVEL

We were undergoing another fertility treatment. We had one frozen embryo left that was supposed to be implanted back. The day of implantation we were notified that it had not survived the defrosting. The news was a real blow to the both of us. The reason I mention it is that this type of news would have previously knocked me out for quite some time.

After hearing the news there was still the moment of deep despair. Almost manically I decided that I did not want the news to spoil my Saturday and we filled the day with all sorts of nice activities. When I woke up the next morning I noticed that the news had really impacted me and it was hard to get up. My normal pattern would have been to stay at home and deal with this myself. I would not have been able to do much – certainly not the studying I was planning to do on a normal Sunday – and the mood would have continued for weeks to come. Knowing how to counter my stress better, I reached out to a friend for help and asked her to go for a walk. We talked, cried, and gradually our conversation changed from the sad personal news to my positive experiences in my new job. When I went back home again I felt a lot better and I studied for most of the afternoon. I am not pretending in any way or form that I have found a miracle cure but I do think that I have become better at dealing with some of the difficult emotions.

PERSONAL CONCLUSION

My inquiry has been a difficult journey with many parts of my life at a cross-roads. According to Shaw (2002) anxiety is a necessary and inevitable part of all change processes. I have experienced plenty of that anxiety and perhaps as a result I have become more confident as a coach especially in the way I handle emotions and choose interventions.

I have come to believe there is limited value and even potential damage with internal group coaching programmes if they are not set up well. One-to-one coaching certainly has my preference although I have learned a lot from the group coaching.

I have doubted whether my experience was relevant at all to other coaches. Mine is a story of looking at oneself differently – through having 'new eyes'.

The real voyage of discovery consists not in seeking new landscapes, but in having new eyes (Marcel Proust)

CHAPTER 5

Testing your assumptions and way of thinking is valuable for any coach. Many coaches deal with emotions and go through emotional turmoil at some point in time. Being aware of the effect which that can have on coaching and of the possible coping strategies might prove a powerful ally in difficult times.

CHAPTER 6

HOW DO POWER AND CONTROL MANIFEST THEMSELVES IN MY COACHING PRACTICE AND WHAT IMPACT DO THEY HAVE ON THE COACHING FOR THE CLIENT AND FOR ME?

MY INQUIRY QUESTION

H OW do power and control manifest themselves in my coaching practice and what impact do they have on the coaching for the client and for me?

I am very interested in the issue of power and control in coaching. Who holds these elements, do they move between client and coach during the sessions, and what impact do the ownership of these elements have on the coaching?

MY OWN HISTORY WITH THE INQUIRY QUESTION

My relationship with these questions arises from my change of career from a senior director role, where I was used to leading, to being an executive coach. My journey has been about letting go of the power and control. Well, this is what I thought until my early work on the Ashridge course. I was startled to note that my espoused theory and theory-in-use (Argyris, 1991) differed widely. I thought I was giving my clients the space to hear themselves speak when in fact I noticed a leaning towards controlling, supplying solutions and driving action plans.

CORE INQUIRY

I contacted a number clients with whom I had worked within the previous two months and asked them to complete a short questionnaire about how they experienced power and control in our coaching sessions and the impact, positive and negative that it had on them. The themes that emerged were:

- I thought I contracted well with my clients – but I discovered I have not contracted about our relationship or inquired into how they would like power and control to manifest themselves in our coaching; how would they like the sessions to be conducted. These aspects have sometimes been expressed but more by luck – never through overt discussions.

- As I read the responses, although often supportive of my approach (but it is my approach not a mutually brokered approach), it feels like I've been cajoling my clients along, been pushing them towards actions and solutions. I'm not a coach at all. I'm still the old-style director I was – benevolent maybe – but a director nevertheless.

I also took note of the feedback from the Ashridge Accreditation process relevant to my reflective inquiry which was that:

- I was not sharing my approach or line of questions with my clients

- I focus on seeking the 'killer question'

- I ask probing and provocative questions which do make my clients think hard, but that there were times that I needed to pick up on the responses I was getting rather than thinking about the next question I might ask

- They observed a professional front to my coaching style, which could come across as a bit abrupt and challenging and they wondered if I may need actively to flex my style to become warmer and more empathic.

Am I prepared to make the significant changes it will take to move from my style (that the feedback tells is more about control) to relationship-based? Have I got the personality for it?

And yet, is it really so hard for me to have an open conversation with each of my clients about how we conduct our sessions?

I reconsider Chris Argyris's article, *Teaching smart people how to learn*, (Argyris, 1991). It's interesting that I seem to have been looking outside for solutions to the issues I've been facing, and been less curious about my own contribution to the session. I'm perplexed about why I appear to embrace change, and help my clients to change, yet I don't appear to be changing very much myself as a coach. There is perhaps a fear of failure. I consider how it would be to be told that my coaching with a client was not valuable. This is a frightening thought for me. And yet my reading has shown me how many gifted and highly experienced coaches and researchers openly explore work that has failed. Do I lack courage? Do I lack humility? Be Perfect comes into my mind (Stewart and Joines, 1987). And yet to Be Perfect it is entirely necessary to learn. Maybe I just want to think I'm perfect and don't want to learn otherwise.

Even my precious notes for clients, which I have always been so proud of, were controlling too, as I have never, as one client has commented, thought about them as a collaborative matter; never sent them as a draft for the client's responses. I've rarely given the client the option of not having notes.

I completed five research inquiries for my dissertation:

- The impact of explaining the purpose and path of my questions, and allowing my client to explore 'light bulb' moments

- The impact of having a more approachable style from the beginning of my relationship with my client (whilst continuing to be alert to my behaviour generally in terms of power and control)

- Ceding all power and control

- Engaging in a stronger emotional way with my clients

- Managing power and control when my roles are as challenger and as an experienced person.

MY FIRST RESEARCH INQUIRY – IMPACT OF EXPLAINING THE PURPOSE AND PATH OF MY QUESTIONS, AND ALLOWING MY CLIENT TO EXPLORE 'LIGHT BULB' MOMENTS

The first strand I choose to consider is that of the power I exert by not explaining the purpose and path of the questions I ask the coachee, which was raised both at my Ashridge Accreditation and in the questionnaire feedback from clients.

I also decided to couple with this ensuring that I do stay with the client and don't move on before finding out if they have completed their thinking when important revelations emerge.

I know I focus keenly on what the client is saying and doing, and create suitable questions to assist the client find their own solutions. It had never occurred to me to explain the reasons for or style of my questions. Yet thinking about it now, I can imagine how powerless someone might feel on the receiving end of a series of questions the purpose of which they may not understand, and certainly where I had never given them the chance to agree or otherwise to a line of questioning from me.

What do I know about the theory of questions rather than simply relying on my intuitive approach that the right question will present itself to me? From John Heron's work:

> *The skilled practitioner is, in the ideal case, someone who is equally proficient in a wide range of interventions in each of the categories ... has a creative balance between power over the client, power shared by the client, and the facilitation of power within the client.* (Heron, 2001)

I could discuss with my clients this latter point from the quote above. We could consider between us the question of power and where it resides.

I completed a piece of research of my own work using Heron's six categories as adapted by Erik de Haan.

This indicated that primarily I used 'Discovering' and 'Supporting' interventions with rather less use of 'Prescribing', 'Challenging' and 'Informing'. I could perhaps share this model with the client, so he/she could be clearer about where my questions might be coming from.

How might the dialogue with the client be framed in the context of questions being proposed by me? Perhaps by drawing on 'the working alliance based on trust, clarity and commitment' (Joyce and Sills, 2001). I believe my coaching relationships have these elements. And later I find in the same book a specific reference to 'making an explicit verbal contract' when the therapist is considering exploring something new where it is made clear that the client has the power to refuse. So perhaps that is a model I can use.

> *For my session with my client, I set out to ensure that I explain any line of questions, and that I understand the impact of that approach on me and on the client. The client wanted to consider why he got nervous in front of large groups and how to project seniority with his peers and in his networking. I explained to the client that in response to his stated outcomes for the session, I proposed to raise a number of questions to help him find out more about these issues and to discover the times when he did and didn't have these problems. I asked him if he was happy about this approach, which he was.*
>
> *The client explored his nervousness in this way and I collected his responses on flip charts listing when these problems showed up and when they didn't. I then invited the client to review his responses and to note what thoughts emerged for him. From this work I invited him to consider what tactics might help him to overcome his nervousness.*

I noticed that two clear areas had emerged from this work. Before my Inquiry work, I would have chosen for the client that we explore further the first theme, as we only had a short amount of time left, and he had already done a lot of work on the first theme, but little on the second. However, now being more alert to the way I exerted power in the coaching room without the client's permission, I asked the client what he would like to pursue in the time available and he chose the second theme. The client then chose to reflect on this work before our next meeting.

I explained my dissertation topic to my client and asked for his feedback on how he felt power and control emerged in the coaching room. He commented that he thought I did give him certain power to choose the way forward. However, he said that he saw me as an expert whom he expected to be there to help him and to pass on my experience.

Reflecting on this session, I was first of all struck by how simple it was to explain a proposed line of questioning in advance to the client and to ask permission to pursue it. So why hadn't I done this before? It hadn't occurred to me.

Historically I had failed to consider what it must be like for a client to be coached. So without my explanation about the line I was suggesting pursuing, and without asking his permission to do that, he would have found himself on the receiving end of my questions without being offered any power from me over the way the coaching was conducted.

I realised I had been relying on my professional approach, my guarantee of confidentiality, and my integrity to support the client relationship. But I had not normally contracted about power and control either broadly, or in detail, for example, about the direction of questions.

I also noticed how odd it was for me to be observing myself – something that I reflected I hadn't been doing for some time. This coaching space was supposed to be for my client, yet here I was concerning myself about me – and that didn't seem right. I was content to observe my client and his spoken and other responses, and to take work into supervision to consider my coaching issues, but not to observe myself in the coaching room.

I reflect on these observations above as I write them up and notice how much control I was still applying to this coaching session. I concluded on the two main themes that had emerged, rather than ask my client what he noticed, or simply what was he was drawn to by the work we had done together. I also noted the control I had in putting material on flip charts without asking the client whether that suited him, and even if it did, would he prefer to write up the charts himself. Historically clients had commented on the usefulness of such charts and I realised I had got into the habit of using them without considering each individual's wishes.

And from the client another thread has emerged, and that is the power of the coach's experience in the client's world and perhaps unspoken expectation on the client's and my part that I have wisdom to impart. And if I do, is this coaching or is it something else?

This was a powerful learning session for me; the contrast of my espoused theory of allowing the client to consider their thoughts, against my clear practice of taking a lot of control. I smile as I hear the echo of my espoused theory about my coaching. 'At its most elegant coaching creates a space for my clients to hear themselves think.' Yes, but only in the context and structure that I have been determining.

My major learning through this first enquiry has been that I can cede some control to the client and the world doesn't fall apart, the client isn't dissatisfied (indeed the reverse) and that I don't have to be in control in the way I have in the past in order to be respected and valued as a coach.

I also appreciate the need to be observing myself as I work, and to be much more alert to my tendency to take/hold power and control, even as in this example, my intention was not to do so!

To be conscious that you are ignorant is a great step to knowledge
(Benjamin Disraeli, Source: *The Times*, 2009)

MY SECOND RESEARCH INQUIRY – THE IMPACT OF HAVING A MORE APPROACHABLE STYLE FROM THE BEGINNING OF MY RELATIONSHIP WITH MY CLIENT (WHILST CONTINUING TO BE ALERT TO MY BEHAVIOUR GENERALLY IN TERMS OF POWER AND CONTROL)

I decide to continue to be alert to the way I conduct myself during coaching: ensuring that the client is given the power and control over the type of approach I take, questions and so on; to watch for where I am tempted to make decisions for the client and to avoid doing so. However my next main curiosity is around the challenge of creating a more approachable style.

In the absence of such a style I may have been taking power from my client by being the implied controller in charge of the coaching. How intimidating may I be to my clients? How much would my style impede my client's journey?

This links with feedback I'd forgotten about from a gestalt course some years ago. A delegate who had got to know me commented, after a short coaching exercise with me, that I had disappeared and that I presented as a neutral person without my warmth. So perhaps a number of clients on first meeting with me may find me very daunting and powerful. Yet the irony is my intention has been to be neutral, not to get in the way of the client. And I note a jarring of the above feedback with the testimonials from clients and the warm relationships I have with many clients.

I think that I start in a reserved way but as the client and I get to know each other I am more open and warmer – hence testimonials at the end of six or more sessions which include a warm personal regard for me.

However, does it really matter whether I am warmer and more empathic? And I'm wondering if I even understand what 'relationship' means in the context of coaching. I return to Erik de Haan's work (De Haan, 2008). He refers to the 'quality of relationship ... closely related to the success of the therapy'. Quoting from Wampold (2001) he lists 'affectionate relationship... client's motivation to work with therapist ... therapists' empathic responding... agreement on goals.'

Carl Rogers' review of research and his own experience (Rogers, 1961) led him to suggest a number of questions that those of us hoping to create helping relationships might consider. I'm drawn by his questions around the ability of the therapist to communicate unambiguously what he is (and here's the sting – to be able to communicate this to oneself), and being able to remain separate. This feels really uncomfortable. I seem to be very wary of getting sucked into the other person and their life. This could be an issue of boundaries for me. And finally Rogers asks us to question our ability to enter the client's world – feelings and meanings.

I become aware that I haven't given time to finding out what sort of coaching relationship and approach would suit each client. Their different needs, experiences and stances ring out from their responses to my question-naire, yet I seem to have been offering only one type of approach and relationship – especially in the early meetings.

My challenge to myself is whether I could create a strong coaching relationship, tailored to the client, right from the beginning of working with that client. I have an imminent chemistry meeting of one hour with a potential client. I've decided to use this opportunity to attempt to achieve this strong coaching relationship.

The client is in a business which is in the middle of major restructuring and the environment and the client seemed under great stress.

My approach normally in chemistry meetings would be to progress quickly to my agenda of explaining what coaching is, exploring the client's coaching needs, and to demonstrate a short example of my coaching – all conducted in a professional business meeting way, which for me meant minimum self disclosure and maximum getting through my list of tasks.

I commented on how difficult the last year must have been for those in his industry and he responded openly about his and his colleagues' challenges and discomfort. I shared a number of difficult times I had lived through in my previous business roles. As we continued, he explained further about the many questions he had about his career. He had also been discussing with his wife what was important to them both for the future. I asked him more about their future and he added more personal disclosure about his current thoughts and options.

I asked him what it would be useful for him to know about me, and what he wanted to explore through coaching and during this meeting. My client had had to combat many changes in a short period of time and was struggling with managing a large group of people for the first time. He asked me a number of questions and I gave him unguarded responses.

My client allowed the meeting to continue after its allocated time and thanked me for my time, saying how useful it had been to him. I have heard subsequently that the client chose another coach because that other coach had 'more experience of his industry' but that I was being considered as a coach for future clients from that business, which is encouraging.

I reflected with pleasure on the degree of personal disclosure that the potential client offered in contrast to other first meetings, which surprised me. I believe that this was because of the changes I had made in my behaviour. My previous model would have been almost entirely to aim to win work through presenting myself as a professional business person at a business meeting.

I found it uncomfortable to work without my trusted agenda and to offer personal disclosures so early in a relationship. This holding back approach echoes my approach in my personal life. I rarely offer much information about myself and even when asked I often deflect or suppress much real openness. I'm aware of feeling very vulnerable – but to what I'm not sure. Yet in terms of my inquiry into power and control, I felt that the client was given more power and control than I had perhaps ever given in the past. And although it was different and difficult for me, it also seemed alright. Somehow more me, more relaxed, more authentic.

I'm also becoming aware that maybe the attraction of coaching, or rather the coaching model I have pursued, is that it allowed me to work with people whilst still keeping myself behind a screen. I explored my preference for wearing what I describe as the armour of professionalism; the way it has manifested itself in terms of my clothing (business suited), keeping control of encounters, my preference for meeting in professional spaces and following a business meeting style of encounter. Without these containments, I seem to fear that work (and life) will be messy and out of my control.

MY THIRD RESEARCH INQUIRY – CEDING ALL POWER AND CONTROL

I reconsider the journey which I'm on of creating a warm and empathetic relationship with my clients, together with the work I've done (above) in beginning to give my clients increasing amounts of power and control over their coaching; for example offering approaches for them to choose, explaining my lines of questioning and asking for their permission to follow those. What happens, I wondered, if I cede all my power and control in coaching situations, whilst continuing to aim to improve the coaching relationship to a more open, less guarded approach?

The client I choose for this research is a bright man who is also very open to giving feedback. From his feedback to my questionnaire he seemed quite relaxed about power and control, yet I was aware that I could alter significantly my behaviour at what would be our second session, compared to our first. I chose this client for this experiment because I would have felt nervous practising on a less robust and confident client. Why? Because in trying something new I fear confidence may drain from me, causing worry or confusion for the client. I suspected that if the session wobbled I would dash back to my old model. With a more robust client, I believe I will be more ready to stay with the experiment.

I appreciate how subjective are not only the lines of inquiry in my work, but the way I make choices about the clients on which to practise what.

What would it take to cede power and control? It seems to me that, above all, the important thing is to give the client choice in all matters; to watch carefully my tendency to take power and control without thinking, as illustrated in my first inquiry above, and to stop myself doing so. The really scary thing for me was the dawning realisation that, with these behaviours, I would not be able to step in and ensure the client saw the session as a success. So what was all that about? I believe I have a salesperson's ability to spot ways of persuading people that things have gone well, for example by highlighting something that arises in a session that is obviously very important to the client.

Supposing the client made all the choices they wanted, but it didn't lead to a satisfactory place for them? Well then I'd have to change my behaviour even more, and instead of rushing in to 'repair' the 'problem', I'd need to see if the client wanted to explore why the session wasn't of help to them. This is beginning to take me to what I am guessing is more sophisticated coaching. I'm beginning to think that my ability and drive to be neat and tidy, and at the very least encourage clients to solutions, has enabled me to avoid a deeper and more meaningful level of coaching. Maybe I was aiming just to 'fix' clients, rather than truly helping them to explore what their deep issues were and why, and whether they wanted to do anything about those, and if so what.

> At the beginning of the session I asked the client about what he wanted from the session, and he explained he wanted to get input from my experience about his issues and any other learning.
>
> I let him be the guide to the session and I didn't impose my structure on it or otherwise take the journey into my hands. I found this extraordinarily difficult and felt at sea during the session. Also it still seemed very unnatural to be observing myself so intensely, and I was worried that my ability to be present for my client was being undermined.
>
> Nevertheless I stuck to my project, checking regularly about what the client wanted to happen next, whether the work was meeting his needs, and whether he wanted anything different. I noticed that even where he sought my experience and learning, the power was with him to continue or stop that course. And I abstained from commanding the space with a long list of my observations about his issues, but spent time inquiring into his experience of the same areas. During the session the client changed considerably the outcome he sought. I wonder if I had been 'in charge' I would have focused the client on his original outcome, never allowing the space for him to reframe his outcome.
>
> The client produced two pages of notes of things that occurred to him and that he wanted to consider or apply as a result of our coaching session. He declined any notes from me as he had the essence of what he wanted in his own notes. He later e-mailed them to me. This was a complete reversal of my normal pattern of writing up and sending the notes to the client.

> *I checked if his needs had been met and he confirmed that they had been. I asked for his feedback about the session and he was very positive about it. 'Extremely enlightening'. He felt that he had control about what lines to pursue and that I had only put in my thoughts and ideas when he had specifically asked for them. He appeared to be in charge. I had stopped myself at least half a dozen times from taking the power by steering the client towards what I might see as a useful destination.*

So here was I, cast adrift without my usual tactics, feeling uncomfortable observing myself – and without the client wanting any notes from me – yet here was a very satisfied client in terms of his journey. I note a feeling of being less worthy of the client's respect and less worthy of my fee. Am I doing anything at all? I'm feeling lost.

However, I had been working in the service of the client. He had been in charge of the process and his lines of inquiry throughout.

Mick Cope refers to collaborative coaching 'giving both client and coach the shared language by which they can agree the journey to be taken' (Cope, 2004). I am attracted to the model of a companion on the client's journey.

The 'designed alliance' (Whitworth et al., 1998) refers to a 'customised relationship where the client grants power to the relationship, not the coach'. I consider this as a great way of introducing coaching to clients. And to make clear to the client that it is they who do the customising.

MY FOURTH RESEARCH INQUIRY – ENGAGING IN A STRONGER EMOTIONAL WAY WITH MY CLIENTS

Since my second research inquiry I have been practising being warmer and more approachable, but I haven't let the client know much about me. Could I engage in a stronger personal and emotional way with my clients? What would be the impact?

I believe my preference for not only keeping my distance but also taking so much power and control was my attempt to package life neatly, as if I could control the messiness of life as it is really lived (Higgins, 2009). I now appreciate my lack of confidence in dealing with personal disclosure and emotions.

These types of feelings are so uncomfortable for me. They take over my life – they're not neat and ordered in the way I like to run things. A poem I have written recently, entitled *I Wouldn't Have Missed It For the World*, acknowledges that love and pain are at the heart of a life lived. And I have a better understanding about the emotional turmoil that clients may be going through. I and they are not contained within business agendas. If I am willing to engage at this deeper level, maybe it will provide a space for my clients to do so also.

John Heron highlights the importance of emotional competence and the ranges amongst the helping professions from those always being contaminated by 'hidden, distorted emotion' to those who slip rarely and are aware when then do (Heron, 2001). My lack of confidence in handling emotions has blinded me to the more subtle ways a client may have expressed their emotional responses.

> *I have a new client. I have had one chemistry meeting with her, which seemed rather stilted and uncomfortable. It was held, by her choice, in a coffee shop, which I noted irritated me. I could not discuss her issues in a private space and I felt unable to demonstrate my coaching. I also noted I found it uncomfortable as it was rather informal – this is me clinging to my professional office model again. Yet it was the client's choice. I was surprised when she chose me as her coach as the client hadn't asked me any questions or raised anything about her issues.*

> *I chose to be focused on creating a strong, emotionally engaged relationship with her, whilst still ensuring that I did not take over the power and control for the session. The latter was a particularly difficult challenge for me, as at the chemistry meeting the client didn't appear to have a strong agenda for her new role, and my instinct was to help her draw that up!*

> *At our first formal session she did not engage in my attempts to set up a coaching contract about how we worked together or what sort of style of coaching she wanted. All I managed to discover was that she wanted to talk about a few things and for me to be a sounding board.*

> *We considered how she felt about the issues and what felt right for her. With a couple of exceptions I avoided giving advice. I remained connected as a friend might, rather than move quickly into rational, problem solving mode, to which these types of issues would normally take me. In contrast to our chemistry meeting, this session was warm, with lots of humour, despite the seriousness of the issues. I was much more the whole me my friends meet, rather less the neutral professional. And the actions she decided to take were truly hers. The client's feedback at the end of the session was that it had been very helpful, and she felt confident about how she would tackle her issues. She didn't want any notes as she had taken down 'all the points I need'. Once again my client is able to cope without my notes.*

> *At a recent second session with this client she disclosed a series of insecurities she had on which we worked. She seemed relaxed about discussing these openly with me. I was very surprised about the amount of intimacy at this early stage in our relationship.*

So I have discovered that I can cede my armour of power and control and I can let my guard down and through both these changes my clients seem to be more empowered, even though I am uncomfortable as I have no idea where the session will go, or the outcomes, if any, that will be achieved. Maybe I am finding a place 'to be comfortably open' (Higgins, 2009).

I'm still astonished from this research that I could carry for so long my belief that I don't control my clients – yet discover that I have done just that in many large and small ways. I have been operating on the surface, and not challenging why I do what I do and whether I could do better. I wonder why I have chosen to remain ignorant and self-satisfied.

I'm also drawn to thinking more about what has to happen for me to change. What will create second order change? (Watzlawick et al., 1974).

Learning without thought is labour lost; thought without learning is perilous. (Confucius, Source: *The Times* 2009)

MY FIFTH RESEARCH INQUIRY – MANAGING POWER AND CONTROL WHEN MY ROLE IS CHALLENGER AND EXPERIENCED PERSON

During my third research inquiry I practised ceding all power as an experiment. That set me wondering about how to apply ceding power when a client has specifically chosen me for my experience and as a challenger. Can I do both at the same time or, in a role as an experienced person, do I cease to be a coach?

I have a new coaching client who chose me particularly because of my understanding of his sort of business. In my initial chemistry meeting with him, I had asked him specifically what style of approach he wanted from a coach, and top of the list was someone to challenge his thinking and approaches.

So my next line of inquiry is about how to manage the power and control in the coaching room to the client's satisfaction when the role I am being asked to take is as challenger.

I realise also that I have a skewed attitude to the different styles of intervention, thinking that some approaches require the coach to take the power and others not. Therefore historically I have believed that I used open questions that allowed the client to determine their thoughts.

Yet feedback and my research have shown that I can take a lot of control and power into my own hands, even when I use open questions.

However, it would appear that it is up to the skill of the coach who is both aware of where the power is at any time in the coaching relationship, 'knows when to lead and when to follow, ... and has a creative balance between power over the client, power shared with the client and the facilitation of power within the client'. (Heron, 2001)

Also I wanted to practise the 'designed alliance' (Whitworth et al., 1998) the 'customised relationship where the client grants power to the relationship, not the coach'.

> *I have now had my first and second sessions with this client. Our relationship from the beginning was warm and mutually accepting.*
>
> *At the first session he explained that he wanted challenge from me and any ideas about his plans and issues I had from my experience. I explained that I proposed for us to both challenge his ideas together. I wanted to avoid any sense that he was under attack from me; rather we were both together taking a critical look at the ideas. I suggested we kick the ideas about and check how robust they were, if he was happy with that approach. I also explained that when I raised a challenge it wasn't from a place of disagreement, but from curiosity. I mentioned that I would also chip in thoughts from my experience but as ideas he might want to consider rather than directions. He agreed with this approach.*
>
> *I checked in regularly during the session that our work was meeting his needs and he confirmed that it was. He also asked for a short summary of the notes I was taking. So here is an example of the client choosing to have notes from me, not me insisting. When I sent them, I offered them as a draft for him to amend as he wished.*

My reflections are that, provided the client is given and retains the power about how the coaching session should be conducted, the content of the contributions from the coach do not in themselves take the power from the client. So a coach can be challenging, can offer ideas, and can discuss the coach's own experience, providing the interventions meet the client's stated wishes as contracted for overtly, and that this status is checked regularly.

However, without the warm coaching relationship it would be less likely that the client would be able to be open about their deeper issues.

PERSONAL CHANGE AND LEARNING – LESSONS FOR MY PRACTICE

When I set out on this work, I expected it to be more about an inquiry into my behaviours and about changing those behaviours, those actions. I have actually discovered more fundamental issues:

- Some of my reasons for using control and power (whether consciously or not)

- Some of my reasons for suppressing myself in coaching encounters, yet the importance of openness and vulnerability

- Hiding my emotions lest I lose control and lose my boundaries and now realising that life is messy and confusing and there are no neat packages into which it can be put

- My misunderstanding that power moved with the type of questions being asked, rather than the client having the power to choose the coaching approach

- My deeper thinking about why historically I have learned new ways of working, yet resisted applying many of them, resisted actually changing

- I have become aware of:

  - My fear of letting go of my coaching models

  - My fear about being found wanting

  - The predominance of my 'Be Perfect' driver, with a strong dash of 'Be Strong'

- I'm delighted to discover that being more relaxed and more the whole me – more open, and less in control – results in the client's willingness to be more open and, I believe, increases the usefulness of the coaching to them

- I feel as though I have only covered a few of the many behaviours and interactions with clients that may impact on power and control. For example with my supervisor we noted that his use of certain technical language, which was outside my knowledge, could be considered a power-taking activity (even though done unconsciously)

- So, for me, continuing to being alert to power and control (whatever their disguises) is very important

- As mentioned by the Ashridge assessors of my dissertation, an outstanding question is 'what is the proper power that a coach needs to exercise?'

Carl Rogers arrives at the end of this piece of work, better understood by me than ever before. His movement from his early approach: 'how can I treat, or cure or change this person' – to 'how can I provide a relationship which this person may use for his own personal growth?' (Rogers, 1961).

- My personal life has become enriched by letting down my guard, and so I'm beginning to learn, will my coaching life

- My second order change has been that what I have often be doing in my style of coaching is believing that my methods were in the service of the client, when many of them have been entirely in my service, protecting me from facing up to and dealing with my emotions (Watzlawick et al., 1974)

- And I feel a huge release by accepting that life and emotions and relationships and performance are messy, cannot be fully 'controlled', that there are no perfect answers, and that's OK

- My new sensitivity to power and control has allowed me to become more aware of my impact on many different types of people, and the choices I have in adapting myself for their benefit

- This inquiry has made me much more curious about relationships, whether professional or personal, and the many and subtle ways in which relationships can blossom or flounder. I realise that the few aspects on which I have focussed are just examples of the enormous complexity of human connectivity

- Above all, I have an enhanced understanding that whether intended or not everything I am and do impacts on others, as they do on me. There is no neutral or shielded place for me to be.

CHAPTER 7

HOW DO I CREATE A SECURE BASE IN THE COACHING RELATIONSHIP?

MY INQUIRY QUESTION

We must not cease from exploration and the end of all our exploring will be to arrive where we began and to know the place for the first time. (T.S. Eliot)

W H A T impact does the history of the coach have on her coaching capabilities? How important is safety in the coaching relationship for both the coachee and the coach? And, what are the conditions that need to be in place for the coach to feel at her best in coaching?

These are the key questions I dealt with as part of my action inquiry (Reason and Bradbury, 2001). It's a journey of exploration which unexpectedly turned into a very personal quest into my past and helped me understand how my history influences my capabilities as an executive coach in the here and now (Joyce and Sills, 2010).

This journey brought me back to myself in cycles. Every time I arrived at the end of one cycle, I saw myself in a different light. Like an onion, I peeled layer after layer to discover new things about me and my coaching practice, and I experimented with adding layers back on, but in a different way.

This inquiry has been conducted and written over a period of nine months, between March and November 2011, and is structured in four action inquiry cycles.

My journey started by exploring how I deal with emotions in the coaching relationship. In this first inquiry cycle I explored the impact my history has on my capabilities as a coach. This also helped me to identify the core essence of my inquiry: Psychological safety and creating a secure base for myself and my clients (Bowlby, 1988).

The second and third inquiry cycles focus on the journey with my clients and the changes I made to my coaching practice as part of this.

During the fourth and last inquiry cycle I reached out to a wider audience in and outside of Ashridge. Through an online survey I inquired into when coaches feel at their best in coaching in order to validate my own findings and identify areas upon which I could improve further.

Please join me now on my journey, exploring how to create a secure base in coaching.

MY OWN HISTORY WITH THE INQUIRY QUESTION

CYCLE ONE: SELF-DOUBT AND MY NEED TO ADD VALUE

When we were first asked to think of a research topic for our dissertation, it was clear to me that I wanted to write about emotions. During my first year at Ashridge I learned that I connect easily with my client's emotions and quickly gain deep insights. I also learned that strong emotions experienced by my client and/or me can lead to 'being stuck' in my coaching engagements, and that I need to be aware of the boundaries between coaching and psychotherapy. I was fascinated and drawn to this topic. I was curious to explore and reflect on my own responses, biases and limitations when dealing with emotions in the coaching relationship.

Reflections on my practice quickly revealed that emotions were mainly the outer layer of the onion that I had started to peel. During the peeling process, I discovered four interconnected themes that influence my coaching practice:

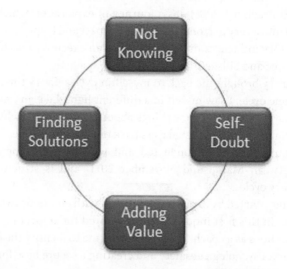

Through exploration in group and individual supervision I realised that in situations of uncertainty, situations when I don't know how to proceed with the client, I tend to self-doubt my coaching capabilities and start trying very hard to find a solution for my client.

In further discussions with my Dissertation Supervision Group I realised that this behaviour of mine, trying hard to find a solution for my client, is built on my need to add value. I learned that I am not listening and am not present in the moment, when I question whether I add value to the client. The need to add value seems to impact on my effectiveness as a coach in that context.

At this point my tutor reflected back to me that she saw my dissertation topic related to the theme of 'safety'. How can I create safety for myself in the coaching relationship? I remember thinking: 'But I want to write about emotions – what does safety have to do with it?' But as it turns out, she had seen a connection that I was not able to make at that point.

A workshop at Ashridge provided me with additional insights on this topic. I became aware that my behavioural drivers – 'please others' and 'be perfect' – influence my need to add value to the coaching experience of my clients (Kahler, 1975).

But what causes moments of self-doubt for me, which then drives my need to add value by pushing for solutions?

In order to answer this question I decided to take a closer look at my own past and how it influences my behaviour today. According to Drake

> *coaches routinely encounter vestiges of long-held patterns that continue to echo across their client's stories and lives. In tracking these patterns, coaches are looking for the ways in which clients are living the same 'story' over and over again.* (Drake, 2009)

This might be something that applies equally to the coach as well as to the client, and I was curious to explore the patterns of my own story.

The two areas most relevant to my story are the fact that I am adopted as well as the impact that my adoptive parents' life scripts had on my own development. Using 'The comparative script system' (Lapworth, Sills and Fish, 2001) as the basis, I created an overview of my life script:

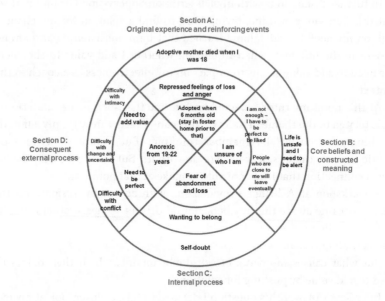

This life script focuses on the impact that my adoption had on my life and meaning-making. The core beliefs influencing my story can be summarised as:

- I am unsure of who I am

- I am not enough – I have to be perfect to be liked

- People who are close to me will leave me eventually

- Life is unsafe and I need to be alert.

Looking at the above, my behavioural drivers seem to make a lot of sense. I please others to avoid them abandoning me, and I aim to be perfect in order to overcome my feeling of incompleteness.

Where is the feeling of incompleteness coming from? When reading relevant literature, I came across the topic of shame and how adoptees are ashamed of their core essence of being (Newton Verrier, 1993).

> *Adoptees are quite familiar with this feeling. It is the feeling of being the*
> *'bad baby', the baby who wasn't good enough to keep. [...] Part of this feeling*
> *of shame has to do with the feeling of incompleteness which follows the*

premature separation from the birthmother. Something is missing. There is
a feeling that he is disabled or handicapped. He is not whole or wholesome.
(Newton Verrier, 1993)

Upon reflection, I do not think that shame is the key topic for me. I cannot remember any conscious feelings of being the baby that was not good enough to keep, however the feeling of incompleteness resonates strongly with me. Throughout my life I have been looking for something that would allow me to stop and feel happy and whole. I believe that this 'quest' has been a contributing piece to my professional success – I have always been driven to achieve more and to move on to the next thing.

I also believe that the feeling of being incomplete has been a driving factor for my need to add value. It is as if I have to overcompensate for my incompleteness by performing really well in everything I do.

Newton Verrier describes adoptees who want to please everyone and perform well in everything they do as the 'walking-on-eggshells' type adoptees, who are overly responsible. She says:

[...] this overly responsible behaviour may be a response to anxiety. It may
be due to the feeling that the original cause of their abandonment was that
they were defective, so that in effect they now have to be perfect.
(Newton Verrier, 1993)

This feeling of anxiety is a familiar one to me and one that I also experience in coaching sessions. When looking through my reflective coaching journal, I was able to see a pattern. I seem to experience anxiety in situations during which I am unsure of how to proceed with the session.

One way of addressing the anxiety in my life has been to organise and structure the world around me in order to make it more predictable and feel safer. This could be seen as an attempt to control my life and not be at the mercy of others.

So after peeling layer after layer of my onion, the key issue for me seems to be safety – as my tutor had already mentioned previously.

I believe, however, that it was not only my adoption, but also my parent's script system which influenced my need for safety and my unsure sense of self. Alice Miller's The Drama of the Gifted Child (2008) really resonated with me in that context. Miller argues that children can sense their parents' needs and take up a specific role to please an emotionally insecure mother to secure love for themselves.

My assumption is that my adoptive mother might have been emotionally insecure because she was not able to bear children. One of my roles might have been to enable her to prove that she was a good mother. In addition to this, both my mother and father grew up during World War II and experienced their childhood as refugees. This might explain additional anxieties my mother had throughout her life, as well as a sense of not belonging that both my parents experienced.

Implications for my practice

Upon reflection, my adoption has left me with a sense of incompleteness, anxiety of abandonment and a sense of not knowing who I am. In addition to this, I may have unconsciously fulfilled the needs of my parents and played a role which secured love and existential security as a child. Both aspects have driven me further away from understanding who I really am. There seems to be an ideal image that I have been trying to live up to. It is my assumption that this ideal image is reflected in my 'please others' and 'be perfect' drivers. If I fail to live up to those, I experience self-doubt which in turn influences my effectiveness as a coach.

In moments of uncertainty I experience 'anxiety of not being perfect', 'anxiety about the unknown' and subsequently 'fear of losing the client'. In those situations my coaching style becomes more directive (in contrast to my natural coaching style, which is person focused and facilitative) and I start working very hard to solve my client's problem. Feedback I received during the Ashridge coach accreditation process summarises clearly how my effectiveness as a coach is impacted in those situations:

- I do not fully listen to my client in situations when I want to add value. I am not fully present in these moments and my mind is occupied with thoughts on what I could do next with this client. My 'not listening' is demonstrated by:

- Me interrupting the client

- Very short 'latency times' between me and the client:

- I use 'closed' questions, or questions that start out 'open', but are quickly closed down through subsequent follow-up questions.

Core inquiry

Cycle Two: Reframing and reflecting

After focusing on the history of my inquiry question in my first inquiry cycle, I conducted a second inquiry cycle to illustrate the impact on my practice by looking at selected critical moments with two of my clients. As part of this I experimented with the following:

- Longer latency times

- Avoiding interrupting the client

- Avoiding leading questions

- Focusing on active listening and being fully present.

CASE STUDY 1: HELEN

Helen is a senior finance manager in a global multi-national corporation and we contracted for 12 sessions. The coaching took place via video conference. I chose to include Helen in my action inquiry, because we had one critical moment (De Haan, 2008) that impacted both of us significantly. This critical moment provided me with relevant learning for my inquiry.

The critical moment happened during our sixth session. Previously we had explored how she could be less controlling and hands-on in her role as manager in order to enable her to be more strategic and achieve a promotion to director.

I felt that we were stuck; my impression was that Helen did not want to change. We discussed different ways for her to be less involved in the detail and less controlling, but she always found reasons why change would not work for her. I started to get frustrated with the lack of our progress and brought this case to supervision.

Supervision helped me to realise that I was working very hard to find a solution for Helen. This situation is one that illustrates how my need to add value contributed to being stuck with a client. Looking at Karpman's (1968) drama triangle, I was taking up the role of 'rescuer' and Helen was the 'victim'.

In the sixth session I listened to another story about why Helen would not be able to do a specific strategic task which her manager had asked her to do. At this point I noticed that I started to sympathise with her manager. I decided to take a risk and use an intervention taught to us at Ashridge: using the relationship between the coach and the client as an indicator for the client's functioning in the organisation (relational coaching; De Haan, 2008). The behaviours the client demonstrates in the relationship with the coach can provide the coach with insights into how the client might behave in the organisation. O'Neill (2007) describes this as follows:

> *Find a time early in your relationship to give your own feedback and observations to the client. Even if you have just met, you have your own experience of her up to this point. From a systems view, this brief experience with her gives you a picture of her functioning in the organisation with regard to the issue.*

I reflected back to Helen that I had been experiencing her as negative – she seemed to focus on why something would not work instead of looking for solutions (focus on the problem instead of the solution; Rock, 2006). After I said this, I could see in her face that Helen was shocked. She started crying and said that she did not want to come across in that way.

After this session I wrote the following into my reflective journal:

> *I felt very sorry in that moment – sorry that I had given her that feedback and maybe hurt her by doing so. I was wondering, if I had done the right thing or if I should not have told her. Maybe I was wrong with my perception? I was worried that she would not like me anymore and that our relationship might be jeopardised.*

I remember that shortly before the intervention I questioned whether I should do it, as it could have harmed my relationship with Helen. So what enabled me to take this risk? Because of my 'please others' driver I like to help and support my clients, rather than challenge them. Challenging is not really helping, is it? However, in order to help Helen I needed to take a different approach. I told myself that helping in this situation is to challenge Helen and share how I perceive her. Reframing my definition of help/support was a key enabler here.

In addition to that, I believe that another important factor that enabled me to challenge Helen, but also enabled Helen to accept the challenge, is a sense of security that we had established in our coaching sessions prior to this. Drake explains this as follows:

> *Provide clients with a sense that the coaching sessions are like a safe haven and a secure base [...]. Use the rapport that is gained to help leaders take a good look at how they currently relate to others [...]. (Drake, 2009)*

Reflecting on this, I believe that this secure base was important for Helen as well as for me.

During an interview I conducted with Helen as part of the action inquiry I asked her if she had experienced any moment of discomfort in our work together. She said: 'When you told me that I might come across as negative. This was the hardest thing to hear from you.' She said that she did not expect it and that she was upset at first. However, upon reflection she realised that what I said was true. She said that this insight made her want to change and if I had not said it as directly as I did, she probably would not have accepted it. In addition to that, Helen told me that I could have been more encouraging after the intervention. I could have given her hope by mentioning that there is a solution and that we can work on it. She experienced me as not supportive in that moment.

Case Study 2: Anna

Anna is a communications and marketing manager in the financial sector and we contracted for six sessions. I chose Anna for this case study because my work with her demonstrates some of the changes I have been able to make to my practice.

My work with Anna started when I was already mid-way through my action inquiry cycle. This means that I was able actively to experiment with improving my practice in the following areas right from the beginning of my work with her:

- Longer latency times

- Avoiding interrupting the client

- Avoiding leading questions

- Focusing on active listening and being fully present

- Being conscious of situations when I direct the session, because I want to add value

- Being more supportive (based on Helen's feedback).

From the beginning I was aware consciously of my need to add value, and I deliberately rephrased what 'adding value' meant to me. I rephrased it into: 'Adding value is providing 'containment' and a 'secure base' for my clients' (Drake, 2009)' based on the insights I gained from my work with Helen.

My awareness of what influences my need to add value and my reframing of value-add has helped me to make progress in addressing it. Looking through my reflective journal on my sessions with Anna, I found evidence for this in a quote following our third session:

> *When we discussed her plan to get a new job, I was impressed with the amount of thought she had put into it. I praised her for that – being conscious that I sometimes should be a bit more supportive. Anna mentioned that it really helps her to have the time with me to reflect on her thoughts and to have a commitment to do work until we meet next. I thought that it was amazing that you can be adding value as a coach by 'just' providing the space for reflection and by adding some rigor to it in form of actions. I was also very aware not to drive the session, but instead to hold the space for the client.*

In the same way as with Helen, I conducted an interview with Anna that gave me an indication of potential progress I was making against some of the areas I had wanted to improve. She mentioned: 'The way that you present yourself in coaching has been a key success factor. You are present, but without being the energy in the room.' In addition to this, she also mentioned: 'What has been good is that you did not ask question after question, but instead you hold your question and let the person keep talking.'

In addition to this, there was one critical moment that was a breakthrough in understanding Anna's behaviour. Throughout our time together Anna came across as very focused on being the best at everything she does. She said herself that success and money are most important to her in life. We were able to identify that money is important to her, because she grew up in poor circumstances and never wanted to live this way again. Her need to succeed and be perfect, however, was a mystery to me.

The critical moment happened during our fifth session. Anna appeared very nervous throughout the session; she was fidgety and did not sit still. We explored her anxiety in regard to a potential job that she had been offered, but the session did not seem to go anywhere and I was unsure how to proceed. A combination of leaving long latency time and following my 'gut' instinct provided a completely unexpected new insight. I felt slightly uncomfortable, because I wanted to add value in this session and wanted Anna to have a breakthrough, but I was conscious of it and did not act on it. Instead, I left extra-long pauses between my questions. I also got a hunch that the ego states from Transactional Analysis (Stewart and Joines, 1987) might be useful to Anna and explained the parent, adult and child ego state to her. When the session was nearly finished, I asked her if the worry and fear she was experiencing when thinking about the new job comes from the child ego state. This seemed to resonate with her and she told me a story from her childhood. When she was eight years old she was still not able to read or write and she had to ask the principal of her school for help. She told me that by performing really well and being perfect in the present, she is trying to compensate for this 'shortcoming' in the past.

I was amazed by the impact of this story. It seems that my ability to stay with the 'not knowing' and withholding from finding solutions helped me to be present and act on my instincts. I remember thinking that it might be a long shot to bring in the ego states, but I took the risk. Leaving extra-long (as I perceived them) latency times enabled Anna to make the connection with her child ego state and link her present feelings to this significant incident in her childhood.

Newton and Napper (2010) say that 'alert coaches will be constantly mapping the flow of energy between ego states through use of language, voice tone or body language – and checking out hunches'. It seems that my 'hunch' was a very productive one.

IMPLICATIONS FOR MY PRACTICE

Reflecting on my work with Helen and Anna as part of the second inquiry cycle, I learned the following about my practice:

- Re-phrasing 'value add' into 'Adding value is providing 'containment' and a 'secure base' for my clients' (Drake, 2009) has been very helpful for me in dealing with my need to find solutions

- Giving feedback to the client on how I perceive him/her is a very powerful and effective coaching tool that I should use more often. This technique can be challenging for the client and I need to be conscious about supporting the client through this process. Reframing that to challenge can mean to help the client has enabled me to use this approach

- Being able to stay with being stuck and actively working with it does not mean that I am a bad coach. On the contrary, it can be a very skilful and effective technique which helps to get 'un-stuck'

- Actively observing and ensuring long latency times between the coach and the client enables me to listen more actively, be more present and it provides the client with additional space for reflection.

CYCLE THREE: HOLDING THE SPACE

The aim for my third inquiry cycle with this next client was to further strengthen my ability to reframe 'value-add', to reflect how the client comes across (relational; De Haan, 2008) and to stay with being stuck.

CASE STUDY 3: THOMAS

Thomas is a senior sales manager in a global multi-national corporation and we contracted for six sessions. I chose to include Thomas in my action inquiry, because I was able to deepen my learning from the second inquiry cycle through my work with him.

Thomas had joined the company only eight months previously and he was struggling to adapt to the corporate culture. We had agreed that I would help him to increase his self-awareness, but instead of reflecting outside of our sessions, he seemed to prefer to work through issues during our sessions. Initially this caused self-doubt in regard to my value-add. After our second session I wrote the following in my reflective journal:

> *I was not sure how to proceed, so I asked him what would be most helpful for him and what he would want to use our sessions for. He said that it would be helpful to review the corporate culture of X and compare it with his own personality and values. I asked him if he would prefer to talk about it or paint a picture. Thomas reminded me of another client who also did not like exercises in-between our sessions, but instead preferred working on the whiteboard. He chose to use the whiteboard and created a mind map. I was wondering where I was adding value, because he seemed to be doing all the work, but I decided to trust in my abilities.*

As you can see in my journal entry, I was wondering where I am adding value, but this time, I did not move into finding a solution for Thomas. I used my learning from the second inquiry cycle and deliberately rephrased 'adding value' into providing 'containment' and 'holding the space' for my client. Reflecting on what I wrote, it seems to me that I did not only hold the space and containment for my client, but also for myself. I created a 'holding environment' for myself and Thomas (Bluckert, 2006). It seems to work both ways!

In addition to this, I was able to further practice the relational coaching approach with Thomas (De Haan, 2008). I reflected on it after our third session:

> *In the same way as during our last session, Thomas was talking a lot in the beginning and he came across as overly confident and dominant in his way of speaking. His voice was loud and he spoke very succinctly. I offered him the suggestion that we could use the relationship between him and me as a testing ground for him to get feedback on how his communication style is perceived. I experienced him as confident with loud voice and dominant body language and posture. I also experienced him as not listening. He has a tendency to cut me short and talk a lot. The listening bit especially resonated with him and he seemed to become quieter after I reflected this back to him. He became more reflective and we were able to identify steps that might help him to change.*

Previously, I would not have had the courage to challenge Thomas in the same way The second inquiry cycle has helped me to understand that to challenge can mean to help the client and this has enabled me to use this approach. In addition to this, I can see as an outcome of going through the inquiry cycles an increased trust in my own abilities.

Implications for my practice

Taking and applying the learnings from the second inquiry cycle with Helen and Anna has helped me to increase my self-confidence as a coach in the third inquiry cycle with Thomas. It seems that this self-confidence or trust in my abilities has helped me to create a 'holding environment' for my clients as well as for me (Bluckert, 2006).

Cycle 4: Meaning making for and with professional coaches

My aim for this fourth and last inquiry cycle was to understand what other coaches do in order to feel at their best in coaching. The objective was to validate my learning to date and to understand what additional changes I could make to my coaching practice to further improve my capabilities as a coach.

I conducted an online survey to inquire when coaches are at their best in coaching and what influences this state. The survey included five open and closed questions and was sent out to 82 coaches. I received 34 responses, a response rate of 41%.

Looking at the results, there are four key things that need to be in place for the coach to feel at his/her best:

- Being present in the moment

- Finding new solutions, perspectives and insights with the client

- Being in rapport with the client

- Being physically and emotionally well.

Overall, it seems that the insights from my action inquiry have helped me to improve in the first three areas above. The area where I see further room for improvement is looking after myself emotionally.

When reading relevant literature on attachment trauma the following statement by Solomon strongly resonated with me:

Focusing too much on childhood traumas can reinforce externalisation, and cause projection and a sense of victimisation. An adult may have been victimised as a child, but the way the person deals with his or her feelings about these issues in the here-and-now is their responsibility. (Solomon, 2003)

This reminded me of Drake's (2009) point about helping clients to get unstuck with regard to 'long-held patterns that continue to echo across their [...] stories and lives'. The key focus seems to be about taking responsibility for your life story in the here and now – which could be a part of looking after yourself emotionally.

Looking at the work I have done as part of this dissertation and my time at Ashridge, you could argue that this equates to 'looking after myself emotionally'. A lot of the work at Ashridge focused on reflecting on yourself and your work as a coach. This reminds me of a person's ability for reflective-self function which De Haan (2012) describes as 'being aware of what is going on in the minds of self and others, in the present moment.' This awareness has helped me to identify and change 'long-held patterns and stories of my life' and become emotionally more secure.

PERSONAL CHANGE AND LEARNING – CREATING A SECURE BASE

Those who do not have power
over the story that dominates their lives,
power to retell it,
deconstruct it,
joke about it,
and change it as time changes,
truly are powerless,
because they cannot think new thoughts.
(Salman Rushdie)

I chose to include this quote by Salman Rushdie, because it describes the journey I have started with this dissertation. In my introduction I used the metaphor of an onion to describe what I was about to do with my action inquiry. Using this image again, it feels like I have peeled the onion layer by layer, and put it back together, but in a slightly different way. I then peeled it again and put it back together, but again slightly differently. By understanding my life script and how it influences my behaviour I have been able to deconstruct and rebuild it. This work has not only helped me to become a better coach, but it also helped me to become more authentic as a person.

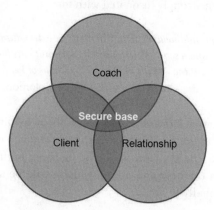

My inquiry started out by exploring how I deal with emotions in my coaching relationships and developed into a study of what helps me to create a secure base for myself and my clients. Looking at my findings over the last nine months, I see safety and a secure base in coaching at the centre of three interrelated areas:

As part of this dissertation I was able to identify conditions and enablers that need to be in place to create safety in my coaching relationships. The enablers might differ from coach to coach as they are very personal, but I believe that the conditions can be applied universally. A summary of my learnings follows:

Area	Conditions	Enablers
Coach	• Fully present • Calm and self-confident • Physically and emotionally well • Authentic => builds connection	• Building the ability of reflective self-function (De Haan, 2012) • Ensuring long latency times between the coach and the client • Rephrasing 'value-add' into: Adding value is providing 'containment' and a 'secure base' for my clients • Reframing that to challenge can mean to help the client • Being able to stay with stuckness
Client	• Feels accepted and supported as a whole person and trusted • Develops self-awareness • Builds resilience	• Unconditional positive regard • Give the client an overview on what will be covered => sense of security • Explore values and beliefs • Explore life script • Relational coaching approach
Relationship	• Trust and rapport	• Unconditional positive regard

Looking at the conditions I listed, which are required for the client to feel safe, I believe that Ashridge and this dissertation have provided exactly those conditions for me. At Ashridge I felt accepted and supported as a whole person. I did not have to play a role, but could be myself. The reflection and learning during the two years at Ashridge has helped me to develop the ability to reflective-self function (De Haan, 2012), gain greater self-awareness and become more authentic as a result. According to Fonagy et al. (1991) 'the capacity to reflect on the mental world of others and self assumes that the individual perceives the world of intentions, feelings, and beliefs to be a safe environment for exploration. 'Building this capacity has helped me to build a secure base and safety for myself.

Using Critchley's (2010) words I believe I have started 'taking the coaching high road':

> *The high road requires the coach to be capable of self-awareness and reflexivity, to allow themselves to be subject to the process of relating rather than to be in control of it and hence to be open to being changed by the interaction.*

By creating a secure base for myself and my clients I have been able to build the foundations to take the coaching high road. Making those foundations more solid will be the continuation of my journey.

MY PERSONAL CONCLUSION

> *We must not cease from exploration and the end of all our exploring will be to arrive where we began and to know the place for the first time.*
> (T.S. Eliot)

I started my inquiry with this quote from T.S. Eliot and, having arrived at the end of this dissertation, I realise that I came back to a few familiar topics. As Eliot is saying, at the end of all our exploring we will arrive where we began and know the place for the first time. This is exactly how I felt when reviewing my final dissertation. With the help of my tutor and peers I became aware of arriving back at two familiar themes:

- My behavioural drivers: 'Be Perfect' and 'Please Others' (Kahler, 1975)

- Safety.

I realised that I was handing in a perfect paper more than one month in advance of the deadline. Is this based on my need to be perfect? Or am I trying to please anyone?

I also learned that I have written a very safe dissertation. I am saying what the markers want to hear. However, I stayed away from potential controversy or personal struggle. My inquiry seems rebellion-free. Upon reflection, there have been two situations of personal struggle in my two years at Ashridge that have significantly influenced my learning. I had decided to not include them in the main body of text due to word count restrictions, which seems interesting now. Did I leave them out to be safe?

In the first instance I volunteered to be coached by the program director in front of the AMEC group. The topic was a decision I had to make between two different jobs. Towards the end of the coaching the coach challenged me by reflecting back that I appeared to him as taking myself too seriously. It seemed that I fed on being different, because I am adopted, and that I wanted to be special. He also said to me that he felt pushed into the parent ego state (Stewart and Joines, 1987). Do I really want to be special? Special in order for me to be loved and not given away? In my opinion, this intervention was quite harsh, but it did make me aware that I was acting out of the child ego state (Stewart and Joines, 1987), and it enabled me to look at my behaviour from an adult point of view.

The second instance happened during a performance evaluation at work where I received feedback that I had come across as too emotional. It was suggested to me to take acting lessons to learn how to appear differently and not show my emotions. This happened at a time during which I experimented with showing more of myself at Ashridge, and this might have translated into work as well. My take away was that my authentic self does not seem to be wanted at work. This was a very hard time for me to go through and it impacted my self-confidence.

Upon reflection, those two situations challenged my emotional reality. Why did I not include this personal struggle in my dissertation? Did I want to be the compliant child? With the knowledge I have now, I know that I acted out of child mode (Stewart and Joines, 1987). In both situations a person of authority challenged my emotional reality, but instead of reflecting on it and challenging the authority figure back, I complied and looked for the fault on my side.

In summary, safety seems to continue to be an important topic for me. Maybe I could be more rebellious (in form of standing up for my authentic self in the adult ego state) and be less perfect as an experiment. This could be my next action learning cycle after the dissertation – potentially leading into another paper.

PART THREE

INQUIRING INTO SPECIFIC CHALLENGES FOR THE COACHING RELATIONSHIP

CHAPTER 8

DEVELOPING AWARENESS: THE ROLE OF SOMATIC EXPERIENCE IN BUILDING CLIENT AWARENESS

MUCH has been written about the role of attention and awareness in coaching, but attention to and awareness of *what* is often unclear or narrowly defined. The emphasis on cognitive skills in problem solving – the dominant mode of thought in most organizations – leads to a focus on conscious thought and language as the main signifiers of being. This case study highlights the oft-forgotten aspects of somatic experience, and how increasing awareness of what the body communicates to both coach and coachee can have a profound impact on both the participants in a coaching relationship.

FOREWORD

There's a clock ticking in the corner of the room.

The door is ajar; I can hear water running in the kitchen.

My pencil dots the end of the sentence then scratches the marks of the next word, catching an invisible hiccup in the paper. I have a slight ache in my left arm (resting my notebook on a raised knee). I take a deep breath to compensate for holding the previous one while writing about my arm. My neck aches, also: too much gardening or a sign of age?

Such is the nature of my physical being as I re-write the opening paragraph, directing my attention to the here-and-now. Some call it mindfulness, others phenomenological inquiry. I think of it as being present.

That presence was the focus on my inquiry: its nature and its impact.

However, as my Inquiry progressed, the central theme morphed, and the work became about personal transition. The learning changed more than just my technical approach to coaching; it changed something much deeper in the experience of being me.

Unsurprisingly, the clock is still ticking. My arm also still aches – although on closer inspection the pain is more specific, located where my triceps meets my humerus, and is affected by the angle at which I rest it on the chair.

The experience is the same, and yet it is different.

WHY 'PRESENCE'? (*AKA* WHY COACH?)

In his book *Between Person and Person*, Richard Hycner writes:

...it is so difficult to discuss this essential concept of presence because it does not lend itself to any objective understanding or clear description.
(Hycner, 1993)

Similarly, Peter Senge et al. (2005) – after defining Presence as 'waking up to who we are' – go on to suggest that 'in the end, it may be impossible to give a very complete explanation of it.'

So why chose it as my topic? Why not something more concrete, more easily defined?

At the end of one particularly in-depth coaching session, a client asked me: 'Why do you do this? Why do you coach?' After a long pause I said:

Because when it goes well, when I really connect, something very powerful happens for me. It's a stillness, a calm, when the 'chattering monkeys' of the mind switch off, and all I experience is a Presence to what's happening immediately in front of me.

So in this inquiry I want to explore what happens and how it happens.

PURSUING THE PRESENT

I have been chasing the present moment for almost 30 years. I started at university, attending philosophy and meditation classes, discovering the virtues of 'falling still'. This became an interest in Buddhism and lay membership of a Sangha (community) studying the Tibetan Mahayana tradition. I went on retreats, took part in festivals, attended chanting rituals and eventually taught beginner classes.

After six years, I stepped back from it, deciding that I wanted Buddhism in my life, rather than putting my life into Buddhism.

There have been many occasions during Ashridge workshops and studies when I have heard the echo of Buddhist thought; Gestalt's focus on here-and-now (Buddha's present moment), the immediacy of phenomenological inquiry (concentration), the unconditional positive regard of Person-Centred Therapy (compassion).

In coaching moments like the one described above, my mental habits, my anxieties, and my desire to problem-solve all dissipate. The quality of engagement shifts and the essence of the relationship changes.

PART OF THE COACHING PROMISE

For me, the essence of Relational Coaching is that it is done *with* the client not *to* the client. Gone are my early conceptions of expertise, authority and being the person with all the answers. While many of my clients retain me because of my business background, that has become a calling card to give initial reassurance; it is no longer the content of my practice.

At least, that's what I attempt. In truth, the desire to provide solutions still arises, and too often I pursue that well-worn path, at which point I know that my presence with and for the client has diminished.

> Presence is the state that allows us to be the most resourceful, resilient and self-generative person we can be, and this is, in fact, part of the promise of coaching. (Silsbee, 2010)

I am unsure that it's a promise I fulfil.

So I hope to develop a deeper understanding of what's happening during presence and, just as important, what it is that 'breaks the spell' – the 'aspects of relational coaching work(ing) together to make the coachee and the coaching relationship *from moment to moment as central as possible to the coaching conversations.*' (italics added; De Haan, 2008b).

THE CORE INQUIRY

My approach consisted of three cycles of inquiry:

- *Cycle One*: Reviewing recently recorded coaching sessions in which I sense I have lost my presence

- *Cycle Two*: Revisiting the clients from Cycle One to put the learning from Cycle One of inquiry into use

- *Cycle Three*: Use further learning from Cycle Two with new clients with whom I have no previous relationship.

CYCLE ONE – LOSING PRESENCE

Michael's Work: Michael and I have been meeting monthly for just under a year; when we started he had been ousted from his start-up company by investors. Much of our early work was in support of him rebuilding his confidence and exploring what he wanted from his career.

At session nine he says he is feeling more settled now; not as ambitious as he used to be. The past few months have been a voyage of discovery, and he wants to reconsider what work is really about: 'Being ambitious to impress other people doesn't matter anymore.'

As he speaks, I notice that his posture changes; he sits slightly more upright. He says: 'I want to teach and consult.' Michael's field of expertise is sustainable energy. 'The energy transition we face over the next few decades is so important. I want to educate people about that.' He becomes animated. 'I have a contact at a couple of Universities. I'm speaking to them about lecturing and tutoring. There are also the XYZ people; they still want to talk about some consulting work.'

I mention that his voice quietens when he names the consultancy...

Not for the first time, I experience a twinge of frustration with Michael. During the early sessions, I had great empathy for his position (I have been on the receiving end of investor downsizing in my career); however, during our past couple of meetings, I have wondered if he has been 'milking' this somewhat.

I find myself switching into pep-talk mode, reminding him about his capabilities. In that moment I see it as my responsibility to step-in and solve his problems for him. I speak for too long, using 20 words when five would do, offering him advice on working as a freelancer, and the expectations he should set.

Actually, listening again, I don't *offer* him anything; I prescribe. Later, I note in my journal:

> *Evidence of slipping into an old habit: After two decades in corporate life, driving myself and others to pre-defined objectives, my preferred interventions were Prescriptive and Informative. After much practice with the other categories, and a self-belief that I am balanced across all six (Heron, 2001), it is a shock to hear me revert to type.*

> *In playback, I hear myself starting to build a business plan and strategy for him, and generating ideas of how he might price himself in the business – work I had done for myself a few months before.*

I noticed how my attention is distracted when the client triggers a memory of a previous experience, especially an emotional one. I later note:

As in concentration meditation (on the breath, an external object or an idea/mantra), when I notice this loss of focus I must bring my attention back to what happens in the moment. For me, that is the foundation for true presence with the client.

During one AMEC Workshop, I find a particular technique especially helpful in bringing me back to the present: phenomenological observation.

We were asked 'What is Ashridge Business School?' Walking around the buildings and gardens, noting anything and everything that my attention fell upon – from sunlight on polished brass to scuff marks on a skirting board – the 'idea' of Ashridge began to disaggregate, and I became aware of the nature of the physical components – the bricks, the flagstones, the paintwork.

And everything seemed so much more *real*. I was genuinely 'alarmed at the marvel of it all' (van Deurzen, 2010).

We returned to the classroom and huddled in our work groups. The first person who spoke read their description of the chapel; the second painted a verbal picture of the gardens. They were articulate and clever; it was the approach I would normally take. So I wondered about my list: had a missed the point? Did I have the right answer and what I needed to do to keep up with the others? But as I had no other material, I read my shopping list of things I had observed, including gardeners, cooks and porters going about their tasks.

The response was intense; one of my colleagues wept 'at its beauty', another said 'I'm ashamed to admit that I didn't notice any of the people.'

It was a personal critical moment. I grasped the real meaning of phenomenology – "reduction' as a special shift in attitude' (Husserl, quoted in Finlay, 2011).

So, going forward I resolve to retain a phenomenological viewpoint, trying to connect with only that which is present with my client. It brings me back to my Buddhist 'bare attention' (Naranjo, 1970; Epstein, 1995), watching calmly and without attachment.

It's not easy; there are years of bad habits to unlearn. But when it happens, especially in the coaching room, that sense of *real* arises, and the quality of connection becomes tangible.

From Cycle One into Cycle Two...

Focus **attention** through phenomenological inquiry

CHAPTER 8

CYCLE TWO – FINDING PRESENCE

Michael Revisited: While waiting for Michael to arrive this time, I realise that I am prejudging the outcome; reflecting on my past feelings of both frustration and empathy, I wonder what today will be like. I bracket my expectations, in the hope that 'my reactions to the experience of meeting the (client) will not be coloured by (my) past experience of the world' (Mann, 2010).

He arrives looking buoyant, which immediately has me thinking 'oh, this is going to be an upbeat session,' then check myself again, aware of my hopes for a more positive 90 minutes and focus my attention on contracting with him.

He wants to talk about some writing he's doing, and how he might maintain his enthusiasm for this project. I reflect back the energy he's currently displaying. He tells me about the blog he's started, the response he's getting, and how another, more established site, has shown interest in some of his material.

A track starts playing in my head:

> *I've been blogging for a couple of years; earlier this year I wrote a piece*
> *about a best-selling business book. The author contacted me and asked if he*
> *could publish my material on his site. A best-selling author, no less.*

Woah! I check myself again, aware that I am about to 'try hard'. My attention has gone from 'out there' to 'in here' – my emotions and reactions to Michael's story – just as I did in the Cycle One recording.

Aware that I'm not aware of him, I direct my attention back to his voice.

He says: 'When people asked me what I did and I told them that I ran a company and they'd want to know more, I'd be thinking 'Oh, no – I really don't want to talk about it'. I thought that I wanted the spotlight, but once I had it, I found I wasn't a good enough actor to be there.'

The acting metaphor resonates with me; I am thinking about being centre stage for parts of my career. When I was a Communications Director, hosting those press conferences, acting as spokesman on TV news stories etc. High profile, creative, lots of attention…

I have a feeling of empathy – 'emotional knowing' (Van de Loo, 2007) – into which I want to tap; to give him the opportunity of exploring it further by tapping into the metaphor he's using. I offer: 'In this theatre you've described, if you're not the actor in the spotlight, what role do you have?'

(I avoid 'not the actor in the spotlight *anymore*' and 'what role *will* you have?' because in being present, I hope that Michael can experience his own Presence too, not focus on past or future.)

There is a long pause. I sit with the silence, giving him the chance to either think of an answer or to decide if he wants to share his answer. For the first time in the session there is a connection, as we fix eye contact. He's considering me and the moment.

'Do you know the TED conferences?' he asks. I nod. He says 'I see myself as Chris Anderson' (the originator of the event). 'I'm sitting at the side of the stage, providing the platform on which others can perform.' I wonder to myself whether he's speaking metaphorically or literally.

Michael pauses; I notice he takes a deep breath. 'In fact, I have this idea for a TED-like conference, focused on energy...' and he's in full flight about the format, the key themes, the people he would like to invite.

It is the most animated I have ever seen him.

At the end of the session, I tell Michael about my Inquiry and ask him for his feedback:

He: The first thing that comes to mind – sometimes in previous sessions you jumped onto points I'd made that weren't, in my opinion, as significant as you think. This usually happened when I was 'loose' with my selection of words.

Me: How was that today?

He: Very good. Perfect... Your presence in the other sense – listening – has always been fantastically good, and is still very, very good. Today you did more reflecting back what I've said before, – like today, you picked up on the undercurrents rather than the content, which is fantastic. That's absolutely how it should be, I feel.

This brings me back to Van de Loo's chapter on 'Listening' (ibid):

'Although one should try to be as free and open as possible while listening... there is always of backdrop of concepts, understandings and mental operations inhabiting the listening mind.'

I'm beginning to think that my notion of presence is somewhat idealised, striving towards a secular version of Buddhist enlightenment – pure consciousness being directed at all times.

Indeed, if the 'starting situation' (Perls et al., 1951) is that the human brain is wired to form gestalts, then I should not be surprised when mine tries to do that each time a client offers a stimulus.

Being aware of that and bracketing it each time is perhaps the best state of presence that I will achieve?

In Cycle Two, I realised that a single spotlight isn't enough. Focusing on just the words is too narrow. The field of the coaching relationship also needs illuminating; what happens with the client, with me, between us.

If my spotlight is Attention, my floodlights are Awareness.

I think awareness is the second pillar of presence in a coaching relationship, and helps me understand why I 'tuned in' to Gestalt therapy as a foundation of my practice: 'its only goal is awareness and its methodology is the methodology of awareness' (Clarkson, 2004).

It informs both the session and the outcome for the client: increasingly clients say that they notice themselves noticing more about themselves. 'Awareness by itself brings about a new experience and a new challenge and a new challenge to awareness' (Naranjo, 1970).

However, I also notice a meta-level of cognition: awareness that I am aware. This is a kind of mental Mobius strip that twists on itself, resulting in awareness of awareness but not awareness of the client. The resolution is a deep breath, then the re-opening of all channels to receive.

The current vogue labels this type of practice 'Mindfulness', originally championed by Jon Kabat-Zinn (1994, 2001) as an 'effective intervention for treatment of both psychological and physical symptoms' (Shapiro et al., 2006). If there is a shortage of definitions for presence, there is a glut for mindfulness (e.g. Bazzano, 2010; Bishop et al., 2004; Childs, 2007; Germer et al., 2005; Harvey, 2009; Siegel, 2011).

I find that having a mindfulness/meditative technique or routine *does* impact self-awareness and provide grounding for relational practice:

Mindfulness is the inner state in which we can observe ourselves in action. *The mindful coach knows from his awareness his own feelings and thoughts, when he is serving the client and when not.* (italics added; Silsbee, 2010).

But most important for me is the realisation that mindfulness isn't just about the *mind* – it's equally about the body.

When the experiential body is fully awake as an extended form of consciousness, the person is thereby attuned to the whole of the immediate spatial and social environment... Presence at the centre of where you stand. (Heron, ibid)

Which is as good a definition of awareness as I have found so far.

From Cycle Two into Cycle Three...

Maintain **awareness** of what's happening in the field

Share more of my in-the-moment experiences – especially **somatic** ones - with the client

CYCLE THREE – GETTING PHYSICAL

I begin work with two new clients, high-potential managers in a global organisation. Our coaching contract is to help prepare them for promotion.

Client – Gurdev: Before our first session, I read Gurdev's 360-degree profile document. A couple of his leaders, two of his clients and a handful of colleagues have rated him on a range of behaviours and outputs. Gurdev consistently rates himself higher than the collective perception of those around him, in many cases scoring himself 100%.

And yet, when I ask him what he'd like to talk about, his response is a mix of super-confidence and confusion:

> *I know I have what it takes to be the CEO of a company, and that's what I'd like to be. But there are some times when I just freeze in a meeting or in a conversation, and I don't know what to say. So I defer.*

He tells me about recent preparation meetings for a review meeting with a senior customer. Four of his colleagues all participated. Gurdev was mute throughout.

As he speaks about the meeting, I take a closer look at him. Tall, wide-shouldered, athletic, sculpted hair, a broad smile on a broad open face. I suppose the US term could be a 'jock'. Publicly, an easy confidence and slight swagger, he prompted some level of countertransference in me, intimidated by his physicality.

So here I am, sitting in a one-on-one with a client who is presenting a problem, and I have already judged him. Not phenomenological, without unconditional regard, no bare attention.

'...so it really worries me. Put on the spot, I kinda turn into a tree.'

The vivid metaphor brings me back to the present. I ask him to tell me more. He says that in the spotlight he puts down roots and doesn't budge. It is all about being solid. He references another meeting from earlier in the week: 'I know I was talking – I don't know what about! – but I know that I became completely immobile.'

I think of the Change Principle, and the essence of focusing on the present; 'raising awareness of what is happening now, rather than what happened 'then'' (Critchley, 2010).

'And how are you now?' I ask.

'Pretty much the same', I could see that from the neck down he was not moving at all. No hand gestures or leg crossing or fluidity in his shoulders and torso. It was as if he had been carved from wood.

In that moment, I remembered D.J. Siegel's (2010) idea of interoception, perceiving the interior of the body, and asked Gurdev what he noticed about

157

his body in that moment. He frowned and tilted his head slightly to one side. 'Whad'ya mean?'

It's a critical moment. I can ask him again, seeking a cognitive answer, or I can encourage him truly to work with his *Sensation* through *Recognition* to reach *Mobilisation* (the first three stages of a healthy cycle of experience: Clarkson, 2004). I posit that there's a disturbance somewhere, perhaps *Desensitisation*?

I ask him to close his eyes and to bring his attention to his chest. What did he notice?

'Tightening, I guess. Yes – tight. And my heart is going a little quick.'

For the next few minutes I guide his attention around his body, asking him to observe what is happening. Occasionally I remind him to breathe – a deep diaphragm breath – which he smiles about as he lets it out. During this time, I am completely focused on Gurdev as a person in the room, someone who is willing to put their trust in me, and is letting me sit in a room with him going through a guided body scan (R.D. Siegel, 2010).

I am mindful of the learning from Cycle Two, and my reading of Rodenburg's (2009) breathing and projection exercises. Perhaps this moment is as much about Michael's presence as mine.

When we finish, I ask him how it felt. He says that doing it had felt silly at first, but he had found it relaxing the more he thought about it – not is a drowsy way, but just more relaxed being in the chair, being with me. 'I gotta tell you, I was quite worried about coming to see you. I didn't want you to think I was a jerk.'

I had assumed there was only one with this feeling – but by Suspending my Self and its fear of looking foolish – I was able to try an experiment, asking Gurdev to 'actively explore himself... and act upon his own judgement in carrying it out' (Zinker, 1977).

As with Michael in Cycle Two, I used my awareness to help Gurdev raise his awareness of his somatic experience, to 'be where and what he is... stand(ing) in one place in order to have a firm footing to move' (Beisser, 1970).

CLIENT – ISABEL

She starts the session very calmly, telling me that in sessions with a previous coach she had become teary, so I should expect it. I find this vaguely reassuring; she is being upfront about how she might respond; it was as if she is preparing me for the worst.

She also says that she knows exactly what her problem is, and that she'd like to talk about connecting with people at an emotional level.

While I like the clarity of the contract, I feel nervous at this point but let the feeling pass as I concentrate on what she is saying and how she sits – straight-backed, away from the chair, her hands cradled on her lap. There was something prim, proper about her, like a schoolgirl reciting her tables.

'I am very good with data,' she says. 'I can do analysis very easily. And I am quick, you know. But I have seen recently that it's not always the best thing to do. Sometimes the other person has other things on their mind, they don't want the answer, and they want to talk. But I always go straight for the problem solving. I miss things. I do not connect.'

She is very anxious now, balancing like a small bird on an electric wire. I ask her about her background.

She: 'Ever since I was a girl I always wanted to be the best in class, the best. When you have parents with very high expectations, you have to. I had to be perfect.'

Me: 'To please your parents?'

She: *'I suppose so. But it also meant that the teacher's would leave me alone. They only picked on the girls who didn't know the answer. So if I was perfect I could be invisible.'*

Me: 'Are you trying to be perfect now?'

She: 'I guess so. If I get it all right here (at work), then they'll leave me alone.'

I notice the language: 'they'll leave me alone' and sense a Deflection from the actual question. I clarify: 'I meant *now* now. In this room, with me. Are you trying to be perfect?'
Isabel thinks for several moments, then shrugs: 'I don't know.'
We sit in silence for a few moments and I wonder about us getting stuck. I ask her what she does outside of work.

She: 'I like to get away. To nature. To walk – with my husband. Not talk, just see things in nature. Leaves. Trees. Rocks. I notice things.'

Me: "Things? How about people?"

She: 'I don't know how to.'

I sense incredible loneliness, and offer that as an observation – unsure whether that's a legitimate response or significant projection, my values onto her.

159

'Maybe,' she pauses. 'Not all the time. But there are occasions when I would like to connect with people, and I don't know what to do. How do I start? They are so complicated. I don't know where to begin.'

For the first time in the session, she holds eye contact. It feels like such a plea, and a signal of permission. Instinctively I offer her a chance to connect further with me, and ask her to pull her chair from behind the table and we sit, knees-to-knees, hands on laps.

'You said you notice things when you're out on your walks. Well, I want you to notice things now. We're going to take turns. We each start with 'I am aware...' and then tell me what you're aware of in that moment. I'll start:

Me: 'I am aware of the small flower on your hair band' (intention: immediately personal to set the tone).

She (**hesitantly**): 'I am aware...of...the sound of the air conditioner.' (I note the deflection of the personal to the least animate thing in the room).

Me: 'I am aware of the hinges on your glasses' (intention: to offer her common ground – be are both wearing spectacles).

She: '....I am aware...of...the sound of the car outside.'

Me: 'I am aware of the twitch in your right cheek as you smiled' (intention: positive feedback, acknowledging her smile).

She: 'I am aware of the flip chart papers on the wall.'

Me: 'I am aware that so far you have not been aware of me' (intention: bring her awareness to her awareness).

A pause. She flushes and tears. (That didn't land too well; did she think I was admonishing her? I can see that this is tough for her).

She: 'I don't know what to say.'

Me: 'Name whatever the first thing is you see.'

A pause.

She: 'I am aware of your frown.'

Me (**encouraging**): 'That's good. I am aware of your hands on your lap.'

She: 'I am aware of your shirt.'

Me: 'I am aware of the brown of your eyes.'

She: '...I am aware of the single hair growing between your eyebrows.'

We explode with laughter.

I sense complete connection in this moment; an intimacy of contact. She has entrusted me into her personal space, I have been open to whatever comments she could bring into the room.

She stands, exhales a long breath and holds out her hands. I stand to shake one of them, and instead she hugs me.

I feel completely present. Not just my listening and empathy, but my somatic experience, my emotional resonance with another human being in need who placed trust in me. It's Buber's genuine dialogue:

> *each participant really has in mind the other or others in their present and particular being and turns to them with the intention of establishing a living mutual relation between himself and them* (Buber, 2002)

SUSPENSION OF SELF

At the beginning of this inquiry, I tried to explain why I chose presence as my topic in the context of why I coach:

> *Because when it goes well, when I really connect with the client, something very powerful happens for me. It's a stillness, a calm, when the 'chattering monkeys' of the mind switch off, and all I experience is a presence to what's happening immediately in front of me.*

That happened with Gurdev and Isabel.

I was very aware for much of the time, and in the crucible of a single coaching hour, attended with laser-like focus. And yet, I think there is a third quality that heightened my presence and the impact that had on the clients: Suspension of Self.

It sounds rather spiritual to include the Buddhist tenet of 'No Self' as the third pillar of presence. And yet, when Professor Ralph Stacey spoke at an Ashridge seminar, he evoked much of that teaching when referencing the work of social-constructionist George Herbert Mead:

> Communication interaction constitutes consciousness... Mind is then understood as the action of a body directed to itself as a kind of private

161

role play, while that body is gesturing and responding to other bodies...
Mind is then understood as a silent conversation with oneself... (Italics
added, Stacey, 2006).

Compare that with Zen master Dogen: 'To study Buddhism is to study the
Self/To study the Self is to forget the Self/To forget the Self is to be at one
with others' (Epstein, 1995). Is that not a Self that is 'social through and
through'? (Stacey, ibid).

It seems to concur with the more recent interpretations of the Buddhist
canon (Gombrich, 2009) that the Sanskrit term 'atman' means 'No
Unchanging Self' – the implication that is it forever changing. Why? Because
the Self is in continual contact with other Selfs, and responding to them in a
constant dance of stimulus-response-stimulus-response.

So the Self I take into a coaching session is a constructed Self –
constructed by my interactions with society in general, and the client in
particular. Similarly constructed is the Self that my client brings in. This
gives greater meaning to the Hawkins and Shohet (2006) 7-Eyed Model as an
instrument through which to view the context in which the client is not only
working, but is actually being constructed.

More specifically, we are co-constructing one another's Self in the session
– which makes the Suspension of Self much easier to entertain because I am
not suspending 'me'; I am suspending a social construction. Letting go of
that construct – and just 'being' with my somatic responses to what is
happening in the room – has a noticeable impact on my attention and
awareness.

> **From Cycle Three into Future Coaching...**
>
> **Suspension of Self** leads to deeper connection with client

LEARNING FROM THE INQUIRY

I am sitting in a Kingsway (in London) meeting room, having my final supervision session of the year. My dissertation is mostly written, and I am very
much clearer on what I have learned and my framework for presence and the
importance of the somatic experience:

- I am more sensitive of the impact my mental habits have when I am
  less-than-mindful, and bracket them more readily before and during
  a coaching session

- I am more aware of the role my body plays when being with a client,
  and attend more acutely to the somatic responses that happen in
  dialogue.

Yet, I am once again doubtful of my contribution:

> *I don't know what value I provided. I know the theory – I know that I wasn't*
> *there to problem solve – but if I'm not creating answers, then I still ask*
> *myself 'what's my contribution?'*

I wonder how far (or how little) I have travelled in the past two years of study?

My supervisor offers me a story – about a long-standing senior coach who charges for an hour what I charge per day. What is it about him that reassures his clients into paying top dollar? In essence, is that he is comfortable in his own skin, and doesn't feel the need to *prove* anything when he is with his clients.

As shown in Cycle One, my default setting is problem solving: bring me an issue, and while we might talk around it, explore it, inquire within it, I know that at the end of the session I will be able to pull some good ideas – and possibly the solution – out of the bag, like a magician pulling coins from the air.

Put that to one side, and I have no parachute. And the further I fall, the greater the anxiety. ('Don't panic', says the voice in my head; 'there's always the box of tricks for emergencies').

For all my reading and reflection on this, I still find true presence uncomfortable. What if we don't come up with an answer? What if, when I lay myself completely open to this client, s/he doesn't want to play? What if their previous coach was a constant source of good ideas? What if, what it, what if?

Early in my Ashridge studies, I declared that I was worried about being able to retain the models and frameworks that were being presented, and using them in my practice.

One of the faculty offered me Bion's advice:

> *In every consulting room there ought to be two rather frightened people: the*
> *patient and the psycho-analyst. If they are not, one wonders why they are*
> *bothering to find out what everyone knows.*

At the end of this inquiry, the cause of my doubts is no longer trying to retain the models and frameworks while coaching: rather, it's trying to release them.

Presence in a coaching relationship means being prepared to free fall.

AFTERWORD

Another room, another ticking clock.

The PC tower under my desk hums, and for the first time I notice that it's not a uniform sound. There's a tiny judder every few seconds. Is there a problem?

I am sitting in my chair, crossed-legged, hunched forward as I write this sentence, my left arm draped over my right thigh, my right elbow on the desk. I am aware that my back aches, and that I should reposition myself, but the text is flowing so I'll stay with it.

Except I don't. My body demands attention; my spine straightens and my head rotates left and right atop my neck.

I notice I just wrote 'my spine straightens' rather than 'I straighten'. When it happened, 'I' didn't play a part. My body self-corrected without me.

Since writing my dissertation, there have been many moments of presence in coaching sessions. Awareness and attention have heightened my sensitivity to key words that unlock suppressed thoughts or micro-movements that signal emotions beneath the social surface. I don't try to interpret; I just name them.

My experience being with clients has become enriched and many report they feel listened to by a 'calm presence'. Of course, the moment I try to grasp at it, it disperses like a dandelion in the wind. I have learned that presence is an outcome, not a goal.

Attend to the other; be aware of the field; suspend the self.

Now I am sitting upright at my desk. The PC hum is constant, although it's no longer a hum. It's a slightly different tone; more a reverberation.

Has the noise actually changed or is it just my posture that affected me hearing it?

Tick-tock. Tick-tock.

CHAPTER 9

DEVELOPING SELF-CONGRUENT GOALS. 'DOING LESS, BEING MORE.'

MY INQUIRY QUESTION

THROUGHOUT my coaching work I have witnessed extraordinary moments of transformation in my clients and seen the consequent changes in their lives. I wanted to better understand those moments which were transformational in the leaders' development.

> I strongly believe in the importance of goal setting as a key element of purposeful personal and organisational change. What intrigues me is the agreement about goals and tasks as a core dimension of a strong and productive working alliance.

This was my claim at the outset of this inquiry. The research question I started with was:

'How does the way I help my clients work towards desired goals impact on them?'

And as a sub-question:

'In what ways does helping my clients develop self-congruent goals that are aligned with organisational goals influence their development?'

My interest was mainly in exploring to what extent the connection between the leader's personal goals and their organisation's goals impacts on them and their transformation.

The inquiry into helping my clients develop self-congruent goals is based on my work with a client whom I call here 'David'. I kept a diary on my work with the client, looking through the lenses of my research question. In constant iterations I reflected on my personal experience of research, underlying assumptions, themes and data and I had various reflective and supervision sessions.

MY OWN HISTORY WITH THE INQUIRY QUESTION

WHAT DO GOALS REALLY MEAN TO ME?

Right from the very first interaction I had with peers, a rather disturbing question began troubling me: 'What do goals really mean to you?' Working on this inquiry raised my awareness about the mental constructions that derive from my academic studies and from my professional experience (as a consultant in corporate communication and organisational development). My studies in Business Management and Economics were based on the theory of systems dynamics and cybernetics where organisations were considered as organic living systems. In contrast, the methodologies applied were of a linear nature: analyse where you are, define a tangible, measurable goal, then act and keep things under control. Thus, the focus was always on result orientation, on outcome and achievement. In my professional life a core element was to 'design the future from the future'. In my practice as a PR-Consultant and later on as a consultant and facilitator for organisational development, I was used to working towards a predefined goal, which was agreed upon with the client at the outset.

I am mindful that these influences underlie my assumption that the process of setting and working towards goals is a core element of purposeful personal and organisational change. Yet my feeling was that this was not the true reason for my approach to working with coaching clients. Still struggling to answer my colleagues' questions I kept pondering. Then there was a turning point which is best illustrated by an extract from my reflective diary:

> When working on this inquiry, particularly when reading literature, I notice that my attention is on specific terms. Not often on 'goal', never on 'performance', but on 'choice', 'self', 'well-being', 'meaningful'. Noticing this I find myself wondering: What is the question I am really asking myself? I suppose it is something like 'How can I help leaders achieve their business goals in an organisational context while still striving for their self-identified, personal goals?" While writing these words I feel baffled ...... this is exactly the kind of question that has been raised by several of my coaching clients. The issue of 'How to be and remain oneself as a leader while attaining organisational goals?' is actually one of their key concerns.

Looking back on my professional journey I now realise that this longing to 'feel truly alive' has guided my personal and professional life and ultimately my practice as an independent coach.

My work with clients is not about a distinct goal or a position. More specifically, it is something that can never be achieved in the sense of 'now I've got it and I can keep it'. It is fluid, here and there. In this inquiry I would like to find out more about these transforming and fulfilling moments.

CONGRUENCY – AWARENESS OF WHAT ONE IS IN CONTACT WITH

My desire to explore the aspect of 'congruence' in more depth changed the focus of my inquiry and I modified my research question accordingly:

'In what ways does helping my clients develop goals that are congruent with themselves and their organisations impact on them?'

For the purpose of this inquiry I chose the following definition of 'congruence':

Congruence is the term we have used to indicate an accurate matching of experiencing and awareness. It may be still further extended to cover a matching of experience, awareness and communication (Rogers, 2004)

I realised how much I felt drawn to the notion of 'being in contact with' as a pervasive element of congruence. I therefore continued to explore this concept in more depth in the context of coaching. I recognised four dimensions of contact that may play a crucial role in my coaching:

- Client's contact with himself (mentally, physically, emotionally)

- My contact as coach with myself (mentally, physically, emotionally)

- Contact between the client and me as his coach (coaching relationship)

- Contact between the client and the organisation (context).

Looking through these four lenses I explore the notion of developing self-congruent goals by sharing with you my experiences and reflections on my work with my client David, focusing on the first three sessions and the reflective conversation I had with him. I will describe in detail what my intentions and observations were, what happened during the shift from a state of incongruence to congruence and later on what my findings were.

CORE INQUIRY – MAKING USE OF INNER AND OUTER ARCS OF REFLECTION

DEVELOPING CONGRUENCE AS A LEADER: MY WORK WITH DAVID

David and I had worked together twice before when he was promoted to a new position and was therefore facing new challenges. As a director and Head of Private Client Business, David and his department (250 staff) were responsible for a crucial business area of a large Insurance company. His boss, who was a likely candidate for a top management position, had recently appointed David as his representative. Consequently, he had delegated some complex tasks to David who then found himself in a 'multitasking' position, being responsible for a variety of tasks and acting in different roles.

Our initial professional contract was about how to improve his efficiency and effectiveness in dealing with his present job and managing his department in order to gain more capacity for the extra tasks his boss had assigned to him. Although he had already improved the effectiveness of his department substantially during the previous year, his concern was to further increase it in order also to handle the extra work to be done. I sensed a pattern there: do more of the same.

PURSUING 'EXTERNAL' GOALS – NOTICING A FEELING OF INCONGRUENCE

David's readiness to change and develop was closely related to his new boss Marcus who was new to the organisation and was considered to have high potential. He told me that he genuinely looked up to Marcus and felt motivated by him. David was used to getting along well with line managers, feeling at ease when dealing with hierarchical issues, yet I noted a new way of perceiving his boss.

Excerpt from my diary:

I note that he describes what his boss Marcus wants from him; his concern is meeting the additional expectations of his boss. This is so unlike David. He doesn't mention what truly matters to him, what he wants to accomplish, only what matters to his boss. He probably suspects new career opportunities. When listening to him I have the feeling that he is not in touch with his own interests, his main focus is on Marcus. Obviously Marcus has a distinct perspective; he knows what he needs from David, as his representative, to achieve what he wants for himself. But does David really know what he wants himself?

What became apparent when reflecting on the nature of David's intentions was that they were aligned with his line manager's aims. Moreover, they were congruent with the organisational aims. His division was responsible for the management and control of claims. Increasing competition in the market put pressure on the organisation. Consequently, a modification of the strategy had been initiated. The main focus was now on cost efficiency and lean management and on revised external positioning of the organisation. The implication for David's department was to sustainably increase the competitive capacity of the claims management department. Therefore his own ambitions with regard to the increased efficiency of his department were aligned with the strategic changes.

CLIENT NOT IN CONTACT WITH SELF

When David talked about his situation I noticed that what he said was not in line with the way he said it. Being receptive and attending holistically I realised that although addressing strategic topics his focus was on short-term aspects and details. Although he said he was motivated to approach the new tasks, he used terms like 'I need to...', 'I have to...' When describing how well he was doing and how confident he was in his current position his tone was almost nagging. While speaking about the future he was leaning back in his seat. Instead of radiating the determination he was talking about, there was a lack of energy in his body language. What he said did not match his nonverbal expression. What he described was not consistent with his behaviour.

When listening to David I felt like I was listening to a variety of voices – body, mind, heart, spirit – that were not talking the same language, telling me different stories. I felt as though the fragments did not converge into a whole, similar to what Clarkson (2004) describes as 'sensory awareness'. I started feeling fragmented myself, in my body, mind and spirit, like a collage of bits and pieces, all kinds of colours and facets, not comfortably connected to each other.

CHALLENGE TO RAISE SELF-AWARENESS BY ASKING A GOAL-ORIENTED QUESTION

Based on this sensory experience my feeling in this first session was that the goals David had described in our contracting were not connected to his personal self. I could have confronted David by pointing out the discrepancies I noticed between what he said verbally and nonverbally or by addressing my sense of fragmentation. Instead I chose to ask a goal-question. My intention was to raise his awareness by shifting the level of questioning and reflection. I asked David:

'David, let's imagine you as a 'one-man-business' in the context of the organisation you find yourself working for. Picture yourself as an entrepreneur – what would be your vision?

Reflecting on this experience in more depth helped me to realise my genuine desire to help my clients notice when they stop choosing or when they let others choose for them. I became aware that at the heart of my coaching is my own intrinsic desire to help my clients 'to be that self which one truly is', to use Soren Kierkegaard's words (in Rogers, 2004).

CHAPTER 9

GOING TO A PLACE OF NOT KNOWING – CONTACT BETWEEN CLIENT AND COACH

The moment I asked the goal-oriented question I noticed a change in David's facial expression. There was pain. I instantly knew that the question was vital because of the long silence afterwards. I noticed his eyes moisten. He averted his gaze, avoided looking at me. I felt his pressure to answer. I heard my inner voice saying: 'Stay with the moment...'. His answer, still in a firm voice, was:

'I don't know exactly... I don't think I can respond to that question right now. Let me think about it between now and the next session.'

For a moment I felt tense, as if an enormous pressure was tightening my chest. It hurt. What was difficult for me was to notice the pain and vulnerability on his face yet maintain an adult ego state instead of switching to a 'nurturing parent' ('I'm sorry, I didn't want to hurt you, how can I help you now?...'). I recalled my tendency to let the client off the hook, which had been an issue in supervision. I heard my inner voice saying to myself and simultaneously to David: 'It's ok, ok...' This is my mantra, my conscious effort to offer acceptance and stay with the client in difficult moments. I was aware that what was required from me as a coach was a 'contactful presence' in the sense I later read about:

> Contactful presence tends to be less focused and to promise less by way of specific outcomes. Rather, it relies on development of great trust in the apparent depth of commitment by the consultant to stay with the client through what may be a difficult struggle (Nevis, 2005)

CONNECTING MOMENT – CLIENT IN CONTACT WITH SELF

David's response to the goal-question revealed that he was in an uncomfortable place. My concern in that moment was that my asking a question around goals and his inability to answer could have impacted our relationship in such a way that I would have been considered the critical parent thus potentially turning him into an angry child. I felt that, especially in this moment of insecurity and vulnerability, it was important – for both of us – to stay highly receptive, exploring what happened on a subtle level. I chose to ask David:

Me: 'What is the relevant question you are asking yourself?'

There was a long pause. He was thoughtful, his energy level slowing down; he seemed to look inside, listening. After a while he said:

David: 'The question is: Where would I want to be in this organisation two years from now? What would I want to be, what would I want to be doing two years from now?'

His answer sounded and felt real. His face was relaxed; he looked straight in my eyes, his voice firm and agreeable. He seemed willing to be affected and to respond with acceptance, allowing himself to be who he was in this moment. My inner response was not so much about what he said. It was the way he said it. It just felt like, 'this is David'.

EXPLORING FROM A PLACE OF SELF-CONGRUENCE: LETTING GO

I had challenged David to step out of his comfort zone. From there we did not move straight into exploring self-congruent goals. At the beginning of our second session he was in a different place, a place which raised questions from within. 'Will I be able to face the new reality? How about having enough time for my family? Moving to another level might be a risky place to be. So one asks oneself: Is this what I really want?' Walking in unfamiliar territory made him not only get in touch with himself, becoming aware of his being ambiguous about his future profile; it also made him realise that he had to let go. He was comfortable and successful in his present position and familiar with the appropriate leadership practices. Before thinking about new prospects it was important for him to think about the other side of the coin carefully. What would he lose, have to let go of?

Staying with his doubts and concerns was congruent in the sense that he was aware of his present experience and he articulated it. I consciously refrained from any pushing. Being in contact with himself in a new, still unfamiliar place required clarification of those questions first. It was an important in-between time, during the second session and before the third session. It enabled him to free himself from doubts and get ready for generative thinking.

EXPLORING FROM A PLACE OF SELF-CONGRUENCE: SHAPING WHAT MATTERS

When we met for the third session, I immediately recognised that he had moved on to new ground. It was as though he was not looking backwards any more, just forwards. He had this fresh, sparkling look in his eyes and emanated a lively, powerful energy. He was keen to explore the new territory and we contracted to think about his future professional profile in more depth.

The challenges were still the same, and he still did not have the exact answer. The shift was about his altered perspective and source of energy. Now being congruent, in contact with his self, his inner voice was the source of his exploring and defining his future professional profile. From there he went on thinking from a new angle. It seemed as if he was now pulled in a

171

self-chosen direction, instead of being pushed to accomplish things in order to meet others' expectations. David's concerns regarding the effectiveness of his department ('How can I resolve...?') became background; what mattered, his future self ('What would I want to be...?') had become foreground, fresh, clear, engaging.

MOBILISATION OF SELF AND RESOURCES – CONTACT WITH THE ORGANISATION

In the third session, when David wanted to explore future scenarios in more depth and think about his future professional profile, we had moved consciously from the field of 'outcome focus' to 'exploring' (Sills, 2006). The place where he was now was still challenging, but in a generative way. Instead of zooming in and focusing on the 'how' and 'more of the same' he now explored the multiplicity of the different perspectives and meanings that were in play. What would it be like to work on more strategic levels? What would the role of a COO be like? What opportunities does his relationship with his boss offer?

The further he developed blueprints, the more I could see his energy rising. Developing and setting his own congruent goals clearly prompted the mobilisation of resources. David seemed determined, his voice was firm, his language precise and to the point; what he said was congruent with the way he said it. When discussing an upcoming annual appraisal session with his boss in the same session I noticed that his uncertainty and reluctance had disappeared. Still open and thinking in options, he seemed clear, assertive, his senses aligned with his intentions in the self chosen direction. From developing new awareness came excitement, energy and increased self-confidence.

CONGRUENCE WITH ORGANISATIONAL GOALS: A QUALITATIVE SHIFT

As mentioned earlier in this paper, David's aspirations were already aligned with the organisation's and with his line manager's. As leader of a crucial business area he was committed to making a significant contribution. His heightened awareness prompted an even stronger, direct bonding with the organisation; he wanted to make a difference, not only to his department, but to the entire organisation. My view is that before the shift from incongruence to congruence there was more of a split in the sense that David was working for the organisation towards goals that were imposed on him, whereas developing self-congruent goals increased his commitment to making a significant contribution and created an even more direct link between his intentions and the organisation's strategic goals.

I am conscious that in this case a basic alignment between the client and the organisation was established at the outset. The intentional shift from incongruence to congruence intensified this relationship in the desired direction. I suspect that in the case of an initial misalignment of the client's perspective and the organisation's, the effect would have differed.

LEARNING TAKES PLACE AT THE BOUNDARY

I am conscious that my approach challenged David to step out of his comfort zone, to a place of 'not knowing'. On the established basis of mutual respect and empathy and by maintaining the adult-adult relationship, the question I had raised ('David, let's imagine you as a 'one-man-business' in the context of the organisation you find yourself working for. Picture yourself as an entrepreneur – what would be your vision?') was embraced by the client. For both of us this moment was hard to endure, as described above. In our reflective session later on he addressed this stretch explicitly from his perspective:

Me: 'In what ways did you benefit from our coaching sessions?'

David: 'Your viewing my self and my situation from a completely outside perspective, especially your asking questions nobody else asks me, above all critical questions. This is challenging, this is what I appreciate about our conversations.'

Me: 'In what sense?'

David: 'Well, when you cornered me, em, I was sitting here then, not knowing what to say. This was actually very tough, but it proved worthwhile because I was feeling uncertain, and then I gained clarity about why I felt this uncertainty. I didn't find the solution here, right away, but I then knew where to go from here, feeling able to work it out and find a way on my own.'

THINKING, FEELING AND ACTING FROM AN INNER PLACE

Looking back I realise that the shift from incongruence to congruence was like accessing a state of attention that allowed David to shift the inner place from which he thinks, feels and functions. When that happened in the third session, he was connected with his present self and at the same time with a future space of possibility that started to emerge. After 'letting go' (in the second session) this state was about 'letting come'. What became apparent when reflecting on our conversation was that we went from his initial focus on 'how can I achieve', to exploring 'what I really want' which then allowed the emergence of new insights originating from an inner place: the 'who I am'. This inner place was also a source for the new resources and energy required. David described this process in the following way:

> At the outset my goal was about how I could manage to get all this done, then we looked at the situation from a more long-term perspective, more like 'What do I want in the future?' ... This made sense. It was a challenge though, because in the beginning I was only thinking about the 'How?' How can I solve the problems? Then the focus was on the 'What?' What do I actually want? ... This is the danger, I am mainly in the 'How?' instead of thinking about what I actually want, I get caught there.... These were the most difficult questions, because the clarity was missing, therefore, when it is about the 'What?', I tend to think about the 'How?' again, and thinking about the 'How?' would be much easier. But then we switched to another level, to a much more important level, which is about what I really want, about my own development. Once this is clarified, it makes sense to go back to the 'How?' ...

Meaning making for and with professional coaches

My contact as coach with myself – staying in touch with my experience when I struggle

I recall the moment when my tutor said to me: 'The best learning might happen when going through pain.' And: 'It might be a paradox – in order to learn, to get to know more, you might need to go to a place first where you do not know'. Throughout the inquiry process I had to endure a state of *not knowing*, of moving from question to question and feedback to feedback yet still not clearly having the answer. This was a painful place for me to be. I started to see parallels between my own learning journey as a coach and the development I observed in my clients. Going to a 'place of not knowing' has been central to my clients' way of becoming congruent leaders, similar to my own path towards becoming a more congruent coach.

At first I struggled to share my inner story. Did I dare to communicate the full degree of congruence which I felt? I sensed a risk of vulnerability, a fear of rejection. Part of the feedback I received on my first drafts was along the lines of '... just describe in detail how you felt at the time, don't try to understand....' I then became more and more aware that my struggle was not only a matter of 'do I dare to communicate ...' but also of 'am I capable of...?'

Well, it was exactly the 'just this' that for me as a non-native speaker seemed practically unattainable. Moreover, when choosing Carl Rogers' definition of 'congruence' I realised that this endeavour was actually a crucial part of the research question I had chosen: 'Congruence is the term we have used to cover a matching of experience, awareness, and *communication*' (Rogers, 2004). In October I wrote in my diary:

> *Writing about something in a foreign language might be an additional linguistic challenge. But this is about putting my inner self into words. Sometimes my feelings or thoughts literally get stuck in my throat. I realise that my ability to put my experience into words often surfaces after a detour of reading and translating, looking for the words that matched my thoughts and feelings. Apparently this was an indirect approach which involved, at some point, understanding.*

Looking back on this struggle, the language issue might have been the crucial catalyst which evoked my real inner learning process of becoming more genuine, with no façade, accepting myself just the way I am. Allowing myself to acknowledge that struggle and note it in my journal was a turning point. It felt like a relief. I had reached a critical point at my very centre where I felt congruent and authentic, both in the moment and on reflection. From there I could move on, trusting the process and letting my thoughts and feelings emerge.

'I'M OK, YOU'RE OK' – CHALLENGING IN A CLIMATE OF ACCEPTANCE

When taking this piece of coaching to supervision I realised that only in a climate of realness and empathy can the client's self-congruence be challenged. The premise was my genuine caring as a coach, a caring that is unconditional, not evaluative, signalling 'I'll accept you as you are' (Peltier, 2001). On deeper reflection with peers later on I also realised that I may offer my client genuine caring, being non-evaluative, whereas the crucial, more challenging factor for me is to stay 'ok' towards myself with the same non-judgemental stance – 'I'm ok, you're ok' in its most genuine sense.

Therefore I resonated strongly with a tutor's statements about 'Ego States': 'You cannot not have Ego States (subpersonalities, the DNA). That's who you are as a unique self. To become more of, the best of, your unique self you first need to acknowledge it, what you are made of, attend to them with loving care, manage them, bring them to peace and integrate them with your adult.' The key here for me is to stay alert, acknowledging my inner response, embracing it with acceptance and integrating it with my adult. Whenever I start to feel sorry or guilty or even angry, pointing at myself in a evaluative way, the congruence of the adult-adult relationship might be negatively affected – e.g. in the above situation my changing to a critical parent state could have affected David, resulting in him changing to a child state, seeing in me another boss who has expectations.

PERSONAL CHANGE AND LEARNING: LESSONS FOR MY PRACTICE

STAYING WITH THE CLIENT WHEN HE IS IN A DIFFICULT PLACE

This learning journey encouraged and enabled me to stay in touch with my experience when I struggle. Before, I tended to leave that uncertain, vulnerable part of me outside the room. I tried to isolate my feelings and stay 'neutral' in order to focus entirely on the client. Why? Because I was very judgemental towards myself. It had been the pressure I felt as a coach to 'do it right'; it was my fear of dealing with vulnerability and uncertainty whilst my inner drive to 'be perfect' pushed me towards 'avoiding' instead of 'allowing'. Following the natural curve of learning and development with its highs and lows has helped me to overcome this fear and to bring myself as a whole to coaching, embracing the risk of openness and vulnerability. Consequently, I now feel more comfortable staying at the client's side – staying in contact – when he is in a difficult place where the real learning takes place.

OUT OF GENUINENESS AND ACCEPTANCE EXCITING THINGS HAPPEN

As this research has progressed my deepest learning was about 'accepting myself'. I believe that acceptance is at the heart of 'staying in contact'. Being fully congruent implies accepting me as a whole, in every moment.

I have learnt that a sensory process requires acceptance, not judging the process of experience, yet considering my subtle emotional and physiological responses as an important source of data. I relate to Rogers' words: 'I want to accept all of these feelings, ideas, and impulses as an enriching part of me. I don't expect to act on all of them, but when I accept them all, I can be more real; my behaviour, therefore, will be much more appropriate to the immediate situation' (Rogers, 1995). On the basis of my experience I have realised that I can only offer my client a climate of acceptance when I accept myself, prizing each emerging facet of my experience, of myself. I have found that if I can help bring about a climate marked by genuineness and understanding, then exciting things happen. In that sense my effectiveness as a coach, I believe, is related to the quality of relationship that I am able *mutually* to experience with my clients. And this in turn, is largely a consequence of my relationship with myself.

A NEW PERCEPTION OF GOALS: CREATING YOUR FUTURE SELF

One of the characteristics of Executive Coaching is working with leaders who are embedded in a relational context called 'organisation'. From a

Gestalt perspective you could see an organisation as a relational field which – in a holistic sense – serves the individual as the context for personal development, allowing him to develop as a congruent whole, while being part of a larger whole. I should therefore view an organisation as a useful territory, as a life space, to help an individual grow and develop in a self-directed way. The organisational goals may thus be considered as a dynamic frame, challenging the leader to develop his own congruent goals by testing boundaries, stimulating him to stretch and to explore new ground.

In my role as a coach I find myself striving to provide a space of empathy and realness to support and encourage the leader to step out of the comfort zone and grow from within through developing goals that link the present inner self with a future professional self in a way that raises energy from inside. Looking back on my work with David my emerging assumption is that by accessing our centre, by connecting with our self, we simultaneously generate a new awareness of our present being as well as of our 'future self', about 'becoming'. Scharmer (2007) describes this capacity to connect to a future possibility as 'generative listening', a form of listening in which you go through a subtle but profound change that connects you to a deeper source of knowing, including the knowledge of your best future possibility and self. In our very centre, I believe, we also find all the resources and the energy necessary to go on.

MY PERSONAL CONCLUSION

'DOING LESS, BEING MORE' – OFFERING PRESENCE IN COACHING

I set out believing that experiencing aliveness requires action. My assumption was that in order to experience peak moments of being, peak performance was required. This approach might be appropriate and useful in certain circumstances; however, I have realised that I got into a pattern of 'this is the only way', having transferred some of this pattern into my coaching practice. My bias was that what was expected from me as a coach was to *deliver* in order to add value. This inquiry has helped me to come to terms with my ceaseless need for efficiency and to recognise the value of just being present and mindful.

Writing this caused me to remember a profound, revealing experience – that I had almost forgotten – when visiting the giant Reclining Buddha in Bangkok, a 46 metre-long statue at the rear of which dozens of small bowls were placed. There is a ritual of purchasing a bag of coins and then walking past the bowls putting one coin in each. Standing at the back of the seemingly long line I found myself thinking: 'What would be the fastest way of doing this?' Thus walking quickly along the line, I caught up to a young Thai man in front of me who was walking slowly in a meditative fashion from bowl to bowl. I will never forget his look – and my feeling of shame and shock – when he turned to me, puzzled, then gently signalled to me that it would be OK to pass him... How could I possibly have thought about efficiency in such a context? This man's calm and gentle gesture made me slow down – looking back not just in that moment, but in the long run.

Going to a place of 'being' might not imply action. Moreover it implies becoming aware of my pace, tuning in with the client and myself in a sensory way, attempting to be mindful, using all the clues available: our emotions, thoughts, physical sensations, in the moment reactions, and sense of self.

Focusing on offering genuine presence has become a key ingredient in my coaching practice. It is recognised by my clients and becomes more and more appreciated as a specific quality of time, and a space where purposeful transformation can take place.

BECOMING WHO WE ARE – AN ON-GOING JOURNEY

As the findings in this chapter derive from one specific client situation you might find yourself wondering: In what ways has this coaching development affected my work with other clients in different organisational contexts?

I would like to highlight two core aspects, which in my coaching practise have proved to be effective in multiple situations.

Presence as a core principle

By being fully present in the 'here and now', I offer my clients a space which allows raised awareness and genuine reflection. I consider this island of calmness a stop-over that allows a shift to another level of quality-thinking as a key ingredient of the journey into self-awareness and developing effectiveness.

In my coaching practice this would mean, for example, that I do not coach by the hour, with a predefined beginning and end, watching the time closely. Instead I provide what I call 'quality time'. To make the 'here and now' accessible for my client I offer him the opportunity to arrive within a certain time frame, within which the coaching starts whenever he feels ready, and it is over when it's over. In this flexible setting the coachee has a chance to slow down and relax, free his mind and get ready for quality thinking, for challenging exploration and sometimes for a deep dive into profound reflection. According to feedback from clients, they highly appreciate this sort of 'timeout' which is a unique experience given the fact that their habit is constant rush and time management that counts the minutes or even the seconds. Although we might tackle challenging issues during the session, this setting allows the coachee to experience flow. The willingness to allow such a process, to tune in and slow down, to explore and 'surf' on the wave of pure experience without having a fixed goal in mind, sometimes results in an outcome beyond expectation. As these congruent steps forward are connected to the client's self, to his inner resources, I also consider this approach as an important contribution to his resilience.

'True north'

In the midst of the vast dynamics and ever increasing demands we experience in modern life, many leaders face enormous complexity along with unanswered questions that often cause disorientation. In my experience, staying centred and calm in the midst of this intensity, still radiating commitment, being able to make decisive decisions and giving others a clear sense of direction, 'becoming more of who you are' becomes a vital focus. Working consciously with all the facets of congruence enables them to move forward in a process of potentialities, rather than working towards some fixed goal.

Applying this attitude and approach in my coaching sessions serves the leader as a 'true north', helping him to find his own sustainable way through the jungle while encouraging others and allowing them to follow. This seems to be useful not only in terms of being professionally successful, but also in terms of being resilient and staying healthy. By cultivating a genuine and authentic presence, founded on realness and empathy on my side, I find a response in every client that has chosen me as his coach, enabling him to shape his personal future, to enhance his professional performance and thus adding value to the company.

CHAPTER 10

DEVELOPING MOTIVATION: A JOURNEY OF AWARENESS, INSIGHT AND NEW THINKING.

PROLOGUE

'Here you must run as fast as you can, just to stay in place. And if you wish to go anywhere you must run twice as fast as that.' (Lewis Carroll, *Alice in Wonderland*)

I N life and on the Ashridge programme it sometimes felt as though I couldn't run fast enough or be good enough. Sometimes I felt stressed, sometimes I jumped off one running track onto another that looked more enticing. Yet at other times the world felt great no matter what was going on.

The Ashridge programme started a journey that helped me see how I experience the world around me. As I stopped running, the reality of my motivation and stressors started to show themselves and in that 'seeing' insights arose and change has occurred.

I started my inquiry looking at what I saw as challenges in clients or prospective clients who might not be fully engaged in coaching. As I look back, the challenge was never with them, it was always with me.

This chapter outlines a personal journey that has helped me see what was really happening in working with clients whom I found 'challenging'. My insights have significantly improved how I support my clients whatever their level of motivation.

MY HISTORY WITH THE INQUIRY QUESTION

As I considered possible inquiry topics, I noticed I was frequently taken to thoughts of client's and coach's issues and challenges in coaching. I talked of a client's stuckness or resistance, of times when clients talked about moving forward but failed to make progress to a greater or lesser extent.

As I looked at how the topic showed up for me I noticed times as a coach where I felt challenged or frustrated. Times when sessions felt 'flat' and where I wondered what had come into or what had been taken out of the coaching process. Sometimes I had the sense of the client not being fully engaged with the coaching process and wondered was it the quality of the relationship, the contracting or something else? At its core I wondered what could I be doing better?

My tutor challenged me regarding what lay behind my musings, he observed my use of 'stuckness', 'flat', 'not engaged', 'resistance'. My meaning-making was that this was related to the motivation of the client.

After much reflection I settled on the question: 'What is the impact of Motivation on the Coaching Process?' The subquestions were: 'How can I work with my clients motivation to achieve a more effective coaching relationship?' and 'What is the impact of my motivation on the coaching process?'

I also realised that the topic of motivation had a strong resonance at a personal level. There were times in the past when I had goals that I seemed to feel strongly about but on which I would not move forward. I couldn't understand why, and was frequently frustrated by this behaviour.

Over the previous two years I noticed I had discussed the topic of clients' motivation with peers, especially when clients are referred for what might be considered remedial purposes . I shared the concern expressed in Battley (2006) that for coaching to be successful, the client needs to possess intrinsic motivation and that simply completing coaching to satisfy the request of the organisation is probably insufficient to support lasting change.

At this stage I believed that I tried to help the prospective client find potential personal wins from coaching i.e. to raise their motivation. I realised that I believed for coaching to be really effective the decision to establish a coaching relationship needed to be theirs and not their managers. After further discussion I would ask them for their decision. I termed this as the client 'crossing the line'. This was a symbolic step to show their commitment, at least in my mind.

Yet something did not feel right. I felt as though something was missing. I was focused on the start of the coaching relationship. But what was happening through the cycle of coaching?

Prior to coaching I had a successful general management career and was viewed by many as very capable and successful. However, I was also aware of a lot of self doubt and fear as to whether I was good enough.

As I think about my past, two strands have come forward into my inquiry.

Firstly I started to look at my motivation when I changed companies. I noticed that frequently I had two sides to my motivation. I would be both excited by the new opportunity and also would have the concern, named by Clance (1985) as the Imposter Syndrome, about whether 'my luck' would run out and I would be found out in my existing role. I am now aware that in some of the moves I made I was happy to escape. I now wonder whether the mix of these two motivations helped me to move earlier than I might have done and whether I missed opportunities to grow further in these organisations. Maybe this was part of my desire to support others through coaching.

The second strand related to writing my dissertation. I really enjoyed the reading, the action research and the journal writing. However I found myself with a personal battle with the piece of writing that would be read and assessed. Where did this come from? What was motivating me or what was lacking in my motivation? As I reflected, I became aware that major written pieces of work e.g. large scale proposals, complex business plans, etc., have always felt challenging to me. There would always be a delay in completing them, ultimately I would complete them when the pain of not completing them was greater than the pain of completing them. My sense was that the pain came from the concern of 'will it be good enough, how will I be judged?'

In my reflections, I am surprised that I recall that, around the age of seven, being made to stand at the front of the class for completing a piece of written work incorrectly. I had tried to be creative as I was finding the task easy, however I was very strongly chastised. I was normally a top performer and had never been told off in this way before. I am also aware that in those years nothing was ever good enough in my father's eyes, or that at least is my recollection.

Maybe my inquiry might point to some of the story of my past.

As I looked at different definitions of motivation this one from the Collins dictionary resonated with me:

> Motivation, *Psychol.* the process that arouses, sustains and regulates
> human and animal behaviour.

Maybe this enquiry would shine a light on behaviour that would help my clients and myself.

CYCLES OF INQUIRY

SELECTION OF CLIENTS

My inquiry process involved working with two existing clients over three sessions each. I also included a new client where I used the initial discussions with the sponsor and client and a coaching session in the inquiry.

The two existing clients were included because I felt that they were not getting the full benefit of the coaching sessions. I had a feeling that there was a stuckness and possibly something limiting their engagement with coaching.

The third client was a sales manager referred for what might be termed remedial reasons and where I thought there might be intrinsic motivation issues.

PAYING ATTENTION

As I started my initial inquiry sessions, I decided to bring my attention to motivation in the session and see where it took me. With James, someone I had worked with for some time, I had a client who was positive about coaching, was happy to be a reference for prospective clients and spoke enthusiastically about the benefits he was gaining.

However, I had a concern that he was not getting as much from coaching as he might be able to. He sometimes appeared to be unprepared for the sessions, he was frequently late and at times did not follow through on all his actions. I had a sense of a ceiling that he was putting on himself. I decided I would take a direct approach and be curious about whatever turned up.

James was a little late for the session, and I noticed I was feeling frustrated by this. I decided to ask him how motivated he felt about this session. I was surprised by his response, he snapped, which was unlike him, saying he was here and was motivated. I was taken aback and felt quite uncomfortable. I paraphrased the question and we had a conversation that appeared to help him. He acknowledged he 'wasn't fully in the zone' and knew he was rushing. He expressed feeling guilty that he was late and it was an issue he had in many situations.

I didn't feel good about my first 'inquiry' session but reflected on what had occurred. I noticed that I was frustrated with him being late for another session. I wondered if I had used the question in an accusatory way. I noticed the judgment I had on how I thought he should be behaving.

Whilst I felt my question had landed badly, it had landed on something that appeared was a challenge for the client and myself. I recognised that at times I have avoided raising things that cause me concern and try to coach my way around them. I had a sense of sometimes leaving valuable items untouched when they need to be acknowledged and if appropriate explored. What was my motivation to do this?

I started to question where my interest was focused. In my journal I noted

I'm seeing motivation challenges occurring at different levels. What am I interested in? Is it the client's motivation for coaching and how the client engages with coaching or am I interested in exploring their 'motivation' in

relation to the topic that they bring?...... I'm noticing that I seem to have
a need for them to be in a good place as they start the coaching session, I
want them to be highly motivated to spend this next two hours well and I'm
wondering what's necessary for this to occur.

I noticed that I seemed to have a view of a right place from which to start
a coaching relationship, yet this seems at odds with the goal of coaching to
help someone move forward over a coaching engagement. It's about the
ending not the beginning. I had a sense of 'should' about the start.

The second client in my inquiry was Ellie, a very bright and capable
manager in a large pharmaceutical organization, in her mid 30's. She had a
technical background and had moved into a management position on the
commercial side of the business. While she was doing a key job well, her
manager felt she was capable of more.

I included Ellie in this inquiry as I was feeling frustrated that she wasn't
getting as much out of the coaching as she could. She was always on time,
always completed her actions and compared to many clients was very organised. However she always resisted any push to stretch herself in her
commercial or organisational dealings.

I had noticed that I always felt as though I was only seeing half the person
who was in front of me. I also wondered if she was concerned about the relationship I had with her manager and whether this had got in the way of her
being fully present for coaching.

Shortly into the coaching session I sensed there was more going on than
we were discussing. At what felt an appropriate moment I mentioned our
discussion and raised the topic of goals and motivation. Ellie commented on
my intuition and shared that her attention was on something else; she was
pregnant and had not shared this with anyone at work at this point. She
wanted to get to an appropriate time in the pregnancy before informing her
manager and team.

I congratulated Ellie and then felt guilty about my earlier thoughts mixed
in with concern about where to go now. What should I do, do we stop, surely
it would be wrong to talk about business and career at a time like this? In the
end I asked how she would like to use the session. After consideration she
thought that it would be useful to talk about what it would mean both in the
short and medium term.

On reflection I noticed that I was still feeling uncomfortable and my
internal focus was on being appropriate, whatever that meant in my world.
We spoke about Ellie's goals and priorities and what she would want or need
to do when she told the company.

She shared fears that she had and that she had been wanting to wait until she had reached a key stage for herself. I had a sense of her being in limbo, I did not ask a question on this and on reflection I know I could have asked a question in an open and supportive way. However in the moment, it seemed as though I too went into a state of limbo, I was afraid of saying the wrong thing. This was a sensitive and delicate time and I wasn't sure I had the necessary skills.

My reflections after this session initially showed concern about my performance. We had finished early and I had decided this meant it was a poor coaching session. I felt I had not supported Ellie as much as I could have done. I had got lost in my fears and was concerned about the risk of doing the wrong thing, in this mode I noticed I lost curiosity and being fully present with Ellie.

In supervision I saw that I had helped Ellie with being able to talk and think about her pregnancy and how she might approach her work environment. I was also pleased that she trusted me and felt able to share the information about her pregnancy.

The topic of counter transference was raised. While I have no children, my brother and sister-in-law have been trying for children for many years. Despite IVF they had not been successful. I have seen the challenge and pain that this has caused. Over the years I saw these as very precious and dangerous times with a lot of care and attention required. I wondered if my response was a counter-transference and I had got caught in the headlights of my family's angst.

This also led me to look at other counter-transference that may appear in my role as coach. In particular I looked at the concerns I had with motivation and stuckness. I thought about the way I felt when I believed I was motivated but took no or little action. Did my concern about my clients' stuckness reflect my own personal concerns? Allcorn states that

> elements of the coach's life are also displaced onto the client, which then influences the coach's analytic understanding. (Allcorn, 2006)

Allcorn also comments on the subconscious nature of this automated response and the fact that some of it may become conscious. Whilst I noted it had become conscious I was sure aspects still remained unconscious. This was an area where my awareness could increase further but I saw it needed to be brought lightly so that it didn't affect my state of mind or my coaching.

GETTING LIGHTER

Whilst I felt there had been learning, my initial sessions had felt a little forced around the area of motivation. For the next sessions I decided to just bring my attention to motivation, at whatever level it occurred. I would aim to hold it lightly and respond if my sense was that it would be beneficial to the client. Roberts and Jarrett (2006) comment on the Leuzinger-Bohleber study and the importance of: 'interventions offered cautiously, creatively, and within a continuous process of reflections and exchange.'

Downey (2003) talks about the importance of *'managing oneself'* as a coach, that is the thoughts, opinions and judgements that you might have of the client. He also talks about the importance of intent and says that understanding your intent 'enables questions to flow with little or no effort and with greater accuracy.' I see this as tuning into a supportive and productive space and helping me to connect with my positive motivation layers. I also see it as acknowledging and letting go of other layers that have a negative outcome such as fear and avoidance. From this position I hoped to move closer to the core tenets of a relational coaching approach.

Ellie arrived early for our session, she was upbeat and lively. She wanted to use the session to look at how she could deliver her existing challenging deliverables, pull forward a transition that would have taken place during her maternity leave and bring in a replacement who could cover her leave effectively.

My sense was that her motivation was high, I noticed she was very clear in describing what she wanted to work on, she was leaning forward and her voice tone and body posture were very purposeful.

As we concluded she commented that it was a great session and was probably the most productive we'd had. I commented on her energy and focus and asked her how it compared to our previous sessions. She commented that this was personal to her and felt very important, previous items were more 'nice to haves' and were things others had suggested as focus areas.

As I reflected on this, what stood our for me was the area of intrinsic versus extrinsic motivation as discussed by Battley (2006), and the importance of self-concordant goals explored by Sheldon and Elliot and referenced in Bono et al. (2005). Ellie's language and energy was pointed at things that felt very important to her. What I also noticed was that in discussing what was important about these items during the coaching session she connected further with these areas and her motivation around them increased more.

In James' next session he started by commenting about the last session and how he had thought about his motivation and preparedness for his coaching. He said he felt he wasn't always living up to his intentions and that the reflection exercises had been very useful in thinking about what he wanted and what was getting in the way.

In my journal I noted that an intervention that I felt had gone wrong and caused discomfort had helped a client in a significant way. I again thought about my level of challenging and whether I sometimes constrain it because of a fear in me. If I wanted to raise the quality of my coaching did I need to challenge this aspect of my behaviour?

We quickly went into the topic. He was concerned that his way of running the business had lost its entrepreneurial flair and risk-taking, he had let it move to more of a job and he felt this threatened the medium term position of the business and was at odds with the longer term plans.

His circumstances had changed over recent years. He had been divorced, did not own a home and felt a new set of parental, partner and financial duties. As he explored what his 'steadier' behaviour was providing, he discovered a different set of values and needs that were being satisfied.

James observed that the two positions were in conflict for him. Over the remainder of the session he came up with an approach and actions that could support the safety he wanted and allow the entrepreneurship to be brought back into the business in a way that felt right to him.

At the end of session James commented that he hadn't recognised the conflict that had existed in his goals and behaviour. The insight gained from exploring his motivations and seeing there was a 'positive' reason for his behavior appeared cathartic and opened up a route for him to accommodate his two positions.

As I reflected on the session afterwards my thoughts were taken to Lichtenberg's (1989) psychoanalytic theory of five motivational systems and the proposal that 'the five systems all function to develop, maintain and restore the cohesiveness of a self or self-organisation'. I related to the complexity of each system having its own layers and hierarchy and his further question of 'does a higher level integration exist, one that constantly works to organise and stabilise dialectic tensions and hierarchical shifts between the five motivational systems'. This complexity and the suggestion of a constant tension and movement made sense in explaining the constant ebb and flow I saw in myself and clients when there appeared to be conflicted elements or ambivalence.

My sense making was that we are always motivated; however we are not always aware of the motivational layer that has the upper hand. My earlier view of a lack of motivation seemed misplaced. There is always motivation, but at times it may not be pointing in a direction of our or others conscious aspirations.

Overall I felt great after this session. There was direct feedback indicating a great benefit to the client and I also felt I had learned a lot from it.

In parallel, I saw that my positions of avoiding discomfort and wanting to be a better coach might be in conflict for me. I was becoming aware of the tensions and movement occurring in me.

BARRIERS REVEALED

For the next session with James I decided to recontract about what I might raise in the session. As mentioned earlier, I had observed that I avoided raising 'issues' or being direct about some things that I observed or felt in a session. I believed it related to wanting to please people and be seen to be good. However I also saw that at times I wasn't responding to the reality of what was in front of me. If I was avoiding honesty in regards to what was happening in the coaching relationship I felt I was missing potential critical moments as described in De Haan (2008).

This realisation disappointed me. I wondered about the quality of my earlier coaching, what had I missed? What might have happened if I had been more honest? But I also knew I had done good work, if I could bring this in it would make it better.

The recontracting went well and I described a greater openness and directness with which I wanted to make sure he was okay. He replied he would appreciate it, and thought it would help; he also commented that at times he felt I hadn't always said what I was thinking. This hit me hard; authenticity, congruence and the quality of relationship ran through my mind. I had to work hard to get back on track and I told myself I could think about it later.

As I think about the underlying goals driving this behaviour I am reminded of the negative psychological contract in Sills (2006). The comment that, if the contract is not clarified with care, the hidden agenda can come into room resonated strongly with me. I felt that as well as recontracting with the client for the benefits as outlined in Sills (2006), it was also an important piece of symbolic recontracting with myself. My intention was again to bring my attention to motivation and be clear and clean in my questions or observations.

As I reflected afterwards, I noticed how positive I felt as I started this session. James' energy and positivity was also very tangible. Whilst I had been hit by his comment about my possible unspoken thoughts, I was also now seeing them as possibilities. I recognised that self-management was a key coaching skill, but I wondered if I had been over-managing and holding back.

If I could let more of myself into the session, could I help the synergy even more? While I felt his comment had caused a rupture, it felt like it had provided me with a critical moment (De Haan, 2008) that deepened the relationship.

The importance of the coaching relationship is a constant theme in coaching literature. As I started exploring my behaviour, I started to notice how my reaction (conscious and subconscious) to my clients and my perception of their motivation was impacting my relationship with them.

I became aware that, at times, I wasn't always fully accepting the client and where they were. In supervision and in discussion with my tutor I become aware sometimes of thinking about myself as 'you should be'... 'doing better', 'trying harder', 'doing something else'. Despite having developed as a coach with very satisfied clients I noticed I was sometimes bringing 'you should be' into my thoughts about clients.

At the end of the third session with Ellie I noticed I was both pleased and frustrated. While Ellie was positive and she made progress on the items she identified, my mind went back to the frustration I had felt previously regarding what I saw as a lack of stretching goals. I noted this frustration but did not have any answers.

The learning came some time later. At an Ashridge workshop, we spoke further on psychological contracts, the unspoken expectations we carry into most if not all of our relationships. As I thought of Ellie's sessions, I realised I had a set of goals for Ellie based upon my thinking, yet these had not been explicitly agreed with Ellie.

McGonagill voices this tension

> *I wish to take the stance with my clients that openly advocates an ambitious vision for their development, yet respects their right to decide for themselves the level of aspiration they think makes sense.* (McGonagill, 2002)

I recognised I did not always have this balance and sometimes had a sense of frustration if my aspiration was not embraced. I recognised that I carried unstated Psychological contracts into some of my coaching relationships. This pointed to the criticality of clear contracting, which I sensed would reduce the tensions that I sometimes felt. It was critical that I, as well as the client, were clear on the contract.

A NEW CLIENT

When I started this inquiry I decided I wanted to include a client who was new and also who was referred for what might be termed remedial reasons.

I mentioned my inquiry when separately I spoke with the sponsor and the client in my initial discussions. As these early discussions directly impact my coaching I decided to include them in my inquiry.

SPONSOR CONVERSATION

I was contacted by Peter, a US based manager I knew well. He asked me to meet Martin, who was responsible for their small European team based in the UK. Peter felt Martin was struggling in developing their business and with establishing good working relationships with the US team.

I had a detailed discussion with Peter about what he saw as challenges and also to outline how coaching would work. As I reflected back, I noticed how my questions focused on his thoughts and motivation for this activity. I asked what he thought of Martin, what did he want to achieve, what where the challenges, what had he tried, what options had he considered, why was he looking at my services?

Afterwards, my sense-making was that I had brought a sharp focus onto a critical topic for him and the associated goals, risks and rewards. By explaining the coaching process in relation to his motivational drivers I believed he agreed to the proposed structure more readily. We agreed I would speak with Martin the same week and if Martin and I agreed to work together we would have a conference call with Peter as part of our initial session.

I realised I had not considered the sponsor in my original thoughts on motivation in the coaching relationship. Yet, it is frequently the key to the initial stages. Firstly the decision to invest in coaching, secondly (sometimes) the decision on which coaches to consider and thirdly their involvement to support effective contracting, clear feedback to the coachee and if appropriate to be available for dialogue with the coachee.

In this instance, because of the established relationship, I felt the conversation had gone extremely well and provided an excellent starting point if a coaching program was subsequently agreed. I wondered how it would have gone if it was someone I did not know. I felt sure that sometimes, with behaviour leaning towards a desire to impress and a fear of saying the wrong thing, I might be in a mindset that does not support being truly effective.

This felt as though it could be the subject of a separate inquiry. The Sponsor is often on the periphery of the main coaching relationship and yet is frequently pivotal to it. The Coaching Triangle is highlighted in coaching literature and at Ashridge as a critical consideration. Whilst I thought I understood it, by including this session in my inquiry it brought unconscious aspects of my behaviour into the conscious. So now we have the motivation of the Sponsor, Client and Coach. I am drawn to the significant benefits if they are aligned and to significant issues if they are mismatched.

MARTIN – INITIAL MEETING

As I thought about this meeting, my thoughts went to remedial coaching and my previously-stated need for the client to show their commitment and figuratively 'cross the line'. In a research discussion I had on this topic, an executive coach who came from a psychotherapy background believed that some people need to 'wallow' in the present before they can move forward. He would be comfortable with them appearing lost and unmotivated. I

191

wouldn't sign them up and he would. This had earlier led me to reflect and question my approach in this area, this was a model I had tacitly built and was operating. Now as I started to reflect on it I was starting to question my rigid structure around this. I decided to be curious, inquire about his motivation but to drop my 'crossing the line' requirement from the discussion.

I found Martin open and felt I quite liked the person in front of me, who seemed to be welcoming any help he could get. We agreed that we would work together.

As I reflected on my thoughts about this meeting, I noticed some of my automatic thoughts were on an expectation that Martin would have issues about coaching and I would need to be 'clever'. I spent many cycles on this. I wondered about my meaning-making, why did I expect people to behave in a negative way, and even if they did why did I see it as significant. My reflection on this went on over a number of days. Firstly I decided that I do tend toward a negative expectation, I justified this on the basis of being better prepared. Then I saw my expectation was negatively impacting my preparation.

I believed that I took a humanistic approach. However I felt that in carrying in these concerns at the level I did, I was not embracing the core conditions of empathy, warmth and acceptance espoused by Rogers (1961). I recognised that in times of self created concerns I would be moving away from attributes I believed were key to developing an effective coaching relationship.

While this initial session was before the coaching sessions of this relationship, I felt it hit something that I know has surfaced in full client sessions. At the motivation level, is my behaviour trying to protect me or make me better prepared? Does it take away some of the ease and flow I feel in other sessions?

I found it a very beneficial cycle and at the end was left with the question of how I can notice when I move away from a mindset that has acceptance, empathy and warmth at its core.

My realisation of the negative perspectives and expectations that I sometimes carry into my early meetings caused me concern initially, but on reflection provided an insight to an area I could develop.

My conversations with the sponsor made me realise the potential for a positive impact on the coaching programme if you can start to understand the true motivation of the sponsor.

MARTIN – FIRST COACHING SESSION
The first formal coaching session with Martin included a conference call with Peter to discuss perspectives, goals and feedback.

My plan for this session was to try to increase my acceptance for whatever might come up and not to focus on my perception of potential problems. In the past I would be thinking about managing the first part of the session so that we got into a valid and well prepared place before the phone call. I had a sense this could get in the way.

Following a highly productive start we moved to the conference call. Martin and Peter's discussions focused my attention on the interplay between motivation, connection and contracting. Helping them both look at what was really important about the topics they raised seemed to shift gears in the quality of thinking and communication that both Peter and Martin enjoyed. Additionally, while it wasn't a conscious part of my plan, we touched on areas that brought the unstated psychological contracts into the discussion.

The discussion moved to feedback and previously I would have felt a need to lead them to what I saw as a 'quality' approach going forward. I took a back seat simply asking questions and they naturally moved to a more constructive dialogue. This quality of dialogue was commented on by both Peter and Martin, and continued to improve through the coaching programme.

I felt the session had gone really well. As I reflected afterwards I noticed I had taken some of my more controlling preparation and behaviour out of the session. (It was a reduction, it certainly hadn't all gone). Now I wanted to see how I might bring that into the rest of my coaching.

PERSONAL CHANGE AND LEARNING

Looking at the summary in my original dissertation I have the sense of someone trying to provide an overview whilst still stuck in the middle of the journey. I pointed to layers of motivation, noticing tensions and movement, gaining understanding and seeing preferences. I think I was still battling through the trail.

Over the next two years I continued my research and practise. This summary includes that subsequent learning. I now feel as though I have climbed a hill and can look back on my journey with greater clarity.

The journey was much more about my motivation and behaviour than I originally expected. It also strongly informed me about my clients.

As I look back, I notice my thinking, feeling and state of mind more clearly. These are strongly informing and directing my behaviour. But these are not fixed, they change, sometimes in an instant.

I see my clients and prospective clients operating in the same way. Their thinking, feeling and state of mind in the moment will be informing and motivating the person in front of me.

As a coach I see I provide my best support when my state of mind is healthy and not cluttered by unhelpful and invalid thinking. It is from a healthy state of mind with clarity of thought that I can be fully present, listen well to the client and use my intuition and offer interventions creatively, lightly and with connection.

As I think about my clients, I see the same challenge. Whatever their goals, whether they have requested coaching or been proposed for coaching I believe helping them get into a healthy, quieter state of my mind with greater clarity of thinking will help them raise awareness, have insights and develop new thinking and fresh motivation on whatever topic we are working.

When talking with a client, I now see it is the end point that is important and not the starting point. There are some prospective clients where we agree that we are not a good fit and that is to be expected. But now I have curiosity not judgement or insecurity at the start.

I also notice that providing a challenging intervention from a place of curiosity has a very different feel to challenging from a place of insecurity or judgement. I notice I challenge more authentically and do not have the feelings of discomfort about which I was concerned before.

A significant piece of learning was in seeing the model I was applying in my coaching. Argyris and Schön (1974) describe the 'theory of action' comparing what we say versus what we do – our espoused theory versus our theory-in-use. The inquiry provided a framework to make me aware of my model and my gap. The gap surprised me and a significant benefit I gained from Ashridge was greater awareness.

The work I introduced to manage myself and raise my awareness proved of significant value. West and Milan (2001) split it into two parts. Firstly, 'minimising the impact of the coach's needs, preconceptions, judgements, and so on, on the coachee'. My intention was to notice where my attention was on items that were not relevant to the coachee and then acknowledge them with the intention of letting them go.

Secondly, West talks about 'maximising one's own performance as a coach'. Here my focus was on thinking consciously about my intent for the session with the client. It is a short simple process and has proved effective. I now prepare less than I did and find I get less in my own way. I am always aiming to respond to wherever the client in front of me is. I am not thinking of my methods or following a process. If I am pointing in the right direction, have connection and little on my mind the right steps normally come.

Of course, like everyone, at times my mind gets noisy, or my intuition misses the mark. I still find myself in the unknown and sometimes get a feeling of uncertainty. But I don't take these occasions as seriously now, I see them for what they are, simply the creations of my thinking. This will sometimes release them or sometimes reduce their impact and I can bring my attention back to the client and their journey.

Final thoughts

I now see a small number of things that are critical realisations for me as a coach. I would like to restate them as I close.

Firstly, there were times in coaching situations, where I felt uncomfortable. I associated those with my client. I believed I was responding to where the client was. In fact I was responding to the thinking and the feeling I was having in that moment.

A noisy mind and associated uncomfortable feelings are not the ideal place to generate feelings of empathy, warmth and acceptance.

As my mind quietens it is much easier to become fully present, truly listen and form a deep connection. This I believe is the key to a powerful coaching relationship.

From this place the coach can help the client to enter a quieter and clearer state of mind where they can start to see things with greater clarity. The client is the only one who can truly see what is going on and what is important. They will listen at a much deeper level to their own seeing than to that which the coach sees. Unhelpful motivational drivers lose their power and energy moves to that which is truly important.

This is the place where insight and change occur...and motivation springs anew.

CHAPTER 11

MANAGING TRANSITIONS: GAINING PERSPECTIVE ON PERSONAL CHANGE

PROLOGUE

THE focus of my action research is on those individuals who are experiencing changes in their job responsibilities and environment, and how coaching might help these clients. The main issues seem to revolve around the disruption of familiar patterns and relationships and the potential for psychological disturbances. Perceptions shape our realities and there can be many hidden assumptions when changing roles. Some clients embrace the opportunities and some resist change, dependent to an extent on their mindsets and the context in which the job change occurs.

Changes initiated by the client may hasten their progress through the transition. Before making the leap they have usually come to their decision after thinking through the likely consequences, although there can always be unforeseen challenges along the way. It seems that those who have job changes imposed on them can take a longer and more complex journey in thinking through and making the necessary adjustments.

This inquiry was conducted shortly after some major changes to my role. Inevitably, these personal experiences influenced my thoughts and feelings and contributed greatly to the inquiry and to the value I hope you will derive from reading this chapter.

THE INQUIRY QUESTION

'What is the impact of coaching on clients who experience changes in their job role?' Change is said to be the only constant in business and the pace seems to accelerate each year, triggered by mergers, acquisitions, competitive growth or just the eternal search for a structural nirvana. And so, to what extent can coaching help clients make sense of their responses to these changes and support them through the transition?

I'm old and wizened enough to remember when business structures and the roles within were reasonably stable. Only mergers or big shifts in strategy might shake the tree. I fondly recall when, back in the 1990s, my CEO declared an eighteen-month moratorium on further alterations to a new organisation structure and job families. Employees in new or substantially different roles were able to draw breath and concentrate on rebuilding their momentum after the anxieties and changes created by a merger and the attendant job reductions. Few business leaders would now have the courage to make such a bold move.

Most of the big changes of organisation and role that I have experienced over the years have been positive and beneficial, albeit that the benefits can some time to emerge. But in recent years I have closely observed business leaders who constantly 'tinker' with reporting structures and roles and thereby create a permanent climate of instability and confusion. Many of my clients have described the impact of this 'nonstop change', with the constant disruption of familiar patterns and relationships. Individuals, somewhat punch drunk by the continual shifts in their accountabilities and perspective, struggle to work through a process which provides comfort, reassurance and 'closure'.

William Bridges (2003) proposes the creation and communication of overall business designs within which the various changes can be seen as integrated components, so that all involved can make some sense of them. But I think this is somewhat elusive in today's reactive world and in complex and somewhat opaque multinational companies. And my personal experience over the last ten years is that you are just coming out of the last changes and beginning to make sense of the new order when the next big wave hits. Peter Senge et al. (2005) have demonstrated that a focused awareness on the whole situation of a person experiencing change helps them to make better sense of their thoughts and feelings and can provide better insights and solutions. So, while an holistic approach to organisation change may not always be possible, coaching which enables deep reflecting and the sensing of potential solutions should undoubtedly help the client.

MY OWN HISTORY AND THE INQUIRY

As I draw this dissertation together I have been coaching within a corporate HR role for ten years. My clients have been managers and leaders who have sought me out with a particular issue or have been referred to me because 'we think she might benefit from your support'. I have noticed how many of these clients have presented personal issues associated with changes in their role. It seems to me that situational factors can have a significant bearing on the way in which the individual makes sense of and responds to the changes. From my coaching and my own personal experiences, I know that how thoughts, feelings and behaviours are triggered by the loss of roles, status and familiar environments and are fed by concerns and curiosities about new responsibilities, changes in relationships and the impending journey through a process of transition. As Gyllensten and Palmer (2006) have observed in an IPA study, change in the workplace creates stress and turbulence and there is evidence that coaching can support the individual in their sense-making and so help to alleviate this. My personal experience is that there can be real excitement about new responsibilities, relationships and possibilities, but events may also heighten self-doubt and can cause behavioural patterns of stuckness when one is challenged to operate or think differently.

In this year, as this action research was conducted, I have faced some unexpected changes. I have left my employer, a recently-merged business whose values I felt I could no longer support. And, despite being a long-time observer of the impact of change, I have completely underestimated the effect on my personal balance and sense-making. A global merger forced major changes to my role and many of my close colleagues were made redundant. An unattractive climate gradually developed in Europe from what felt like an aggressive takeover rather than the fabled 'merger of equals'. I became very uncomfortable as a leader in this new culture and unhappy to be associated with what I believed were expedient decisions delivered unprofessionally. The new political power-base shifted away from me and offices were closed. I became a home-worker, acutely missing the camaraderie and close daily contact with esteemed colleagues. My strongest feelings have been around the new organisation not being interested in or respecting my previous attainments. As a coach, and as observed by Ulrich (2000), I recognise the importance of helping a client honour their past whilst creating a new future. But there was no appetite or mechanism within the new company to help me do this. My slate had been wiped clean. And, with the benefit of this self-reflection, I was experiencing the effects of 'boundarylessness', as described by Cohen and Mallon (1999). Ultimately, I took advantage of yet another reorganisation to leave. So I am now undertaking this inquiry into job change with some wounds still not totally healed but with the great opportunity for some serious self-analysis and sense-making. I am curious to understand how these disturbances have informed my judgement as a coach and how conducting the inquiry is influencing my personal thoughts and feelings.

ACTION RESEARCH

Work role transitions are clearly important periods in an individual's life, particularly as one's career and life goals develop. People are increasingly

199

defined by and make sense of their personal world through work-based relationships, their job status within the workplace and the wider social standing of the role. Any significant changes in a job are therefore likely to have psychological consequences for the individual.

How job change is taking place requires an understanding of the effects of social change on organisational life. For example, as studied by Sally Bibb (2008), the views of 'Generation Y' (born between 1980 and 2000) about their careers and capacity for change are different from previous generations. They tend to challenge prevailing organisational cultures and ways of managing. Other researchers have considered the impact of social isolation and the absence of community when employees move their jobs to home-working or into virtual teams. Adrian Carr (2001) has analysed those behaviours which reflect a 'dislodgement of identity' and are often associated with grieving and loss. My observations are that apparent irrational behaviour, caused in particular by imposed job change, is an expression of a deeper unconscious response. Individuals respond to what is happening to them. Their ideas and their ways of thinking affect the way in which they respond, and the forces that establish and reorganise their mindsets come from within as well as from outside.

Therefore it seems to me that coaching should provide that self-analysis and reflection which enables individuals to develop their perspectives in a new light. It should also help them consider the consequences of their plans and actions, question whether their ideas and attitudes are valid, and consider the possible outcomes. I now describe my observations, thoughts and feelings during parts of coaching sessions with two job-changers. Their names and occupations have been changed to ensure personal confidentiality.

NICOLE IS THE NEWLY APPOINTED CEO IN A HOSPICE

She initiated this career move, having led a similar but smaller business. Nicole is driven to achieve high standards in all she tackles. Previously, she has prided herself in developing and maintaining harmonious relationships with a wide range of staff and trustees, despite their sometimes conflicting interests. She was a very popular leader in her previous role and misses the camaraderie they all enjoyed. She is determined to succeed in her new role but is very concerned about her relationship with a key colleague. This person is the original founder of the charity and is still very active in supporting the day-to-day operation of the hospice, coming in for two or three hours every day. Although the founder has formally relinquished her previous role as Chair of the Trustees, her constant presence in the hospice effectively means that she is still viewed as the figurehead of the charity by the staff and many of the patients. Many of the other trustees are friends and appointees of the founder.

Nicole wants to make her mark and demonstrate leadership but is also keen to maintain the best of relationships with the omnipresent founder. Her challenge, simply, is how to manage the relationship to create the space and opportunity with which to develop the business in a more commercial way – for example, making improvements in the fundraising processes to finance a planned expansion.

Nicole says "It just seems that she (the founder) is everywhere, following me around. I really want to show friendship and I obviously respect the huge personal contribution she has made over the years. If I can't find a way round this I'll have to leave – but I don't want to give up on it. There must be a way of meeting her apparent need for continuing power and recognition and giving me the space and support I need to change things. The previous CE was a friend of hers who just did as he was told."

'My intervention probably wasn't the best, I can see that now. Advice I received a number of years ago comes to mind: 'be careful when you are the only female in a team, you might become the emotion carrier in the group'. Could it be that I was overplaying or over-compensating the emotion part? I frequently had coachees crying in my session with them, but am I qualified to deal with that? I have a sense that I can handle it respectfully and feedback from coachees is they appreciate that I'm not taken aback when strong emotions are expressed.'

'My intervention probably wasn't the best, I can see that now. Advice I received a number of years ago comes to mind: 'be careful when you are the only female in a team, you might become the emotion carrier in the group'. Could it be that I was overplaying or over-compensating the emotion part? I frequently had coachees crying in my session with them, but am I qualified to deal with that? I have a sense that I can handle it respectfully and feedback from coachees is they appreciate that I'm not taken aback when strong emotions are expressed.'

We discuss the founder's actions and what Nicole thinks her motives might be. Initially she thinks that the founder resents her presence, even though she was, as a trustee, party to her appointment. She stresses to me her need for 'only one cook in the kitchen' and this seems to be a major part of her previous leadership experience. She admits that she can be quite combative and likes to take the final decisions. Although she maintains that she takes advice and input from others, it seems to me that Nicole likes to be in total command and struggles with the notion of sharing power. I put this to her but she is not happy to accept it. Nevertheless, as our conversations continue, she empathises more with the founder's position and begins to identify the changes in the dynamics of the business that her appointment has triggered.

> Nicole says "I realise the charity is the biggest thing in her (the founder's) life. She's a widow now – I think she comes in every day for companionship. Perhaps we can keep talking about this – if I could help her find a useful role – I need her public support and her position in the local community to make the expansion successful."

Nicole gradually identifies more with the founder's position and recognises that they have to find a way of working together. At one stage in our third coaching session, and while appreciating Nicole's challenges and dilemma, my feelings and focus are drawn really strongly to the founder. Based on Nicole's input, I have built up a vivid picture of this lady who has contributed so much to the local area in creating and developing the hospice and whose whole life clearly continues to revolve around the charity and the daily 'goings on'. Nicole and I spend some time imagining the sort of issues that the change in chief executive must be giving her – the change from a relationship with a treasured friend to one with a relative stranger who is not too approachable. The process of exchanging these thoughts and feelings enables Nicole to see things from another's perspective.

From this coaching experience, I note that an obvious outcome of job change is that changes subsequently follow in relationships, knowledge and power. A new leader can cause changes in the group dynamics and these, in turn, impact directly on relationships. Clearly, the role and power of the founder was unknown to Nicole before she arrived and has had a dramatic impact on the way she expected to do the job, based to a large extent on how she had operated previously. As our coaching conversations continued, Nicole increasingly realises that she might be viewed as a threat by the founder through bringing new ideas into the charity, presenting these to various colleagues and thereby undermining the founder's social position. Our joint coaching challenge becomes how to design and build the bridges which could get the founder on her side, particularly with the big changes to fundraising processes that Nicole is proposing. It seems that a positive approach for Nicole might be initially to involve the founder directly in her thinking, to build her initial understanding and support and then present her proposals more widely in such a way that it is clear that the founder has been 'consulted' and is giving her tacit support. We start to work on how Nicole can understand and control her emotions so that this form of collusion can work effectively.

Our coaching journey has enabled Nicole to view her situation from different perspectives and, importantly, from the viewpoint of the founder. An important part of the process was my personal reflections on what I felt the founder might be feeling. I feel this was a key intervention in that it enabled the client to share deeper thoughts with me and start to develop a path and strategy by which she and the founder could be 'reconciled' and work together effectively. Nicole is now more self-aware and has experimented with different approaches to communicating and delegating. I also observed her use of metaphors in describing her loss of the relationships in her old company and her frustrations with the founder. It seems that, prior to my interventions and a shift in her sense-making, she was stuck in what had been a previous successful leadership behaviour pattern and was really struggling to understand why this was not working.

BEN IS A NEWLY-APPOINTED LEADER OF AN IT CUSTOMER SERVICE FUNCTION

Ben has been moved unilaterally into a new role. He is particularly frustrated by the failure of his new team to 'connect with their customers'. The business has recently gone through a merger and Ben's previous part of the business was particularly 'customer-orientated'. He had worked hard to build this ethos into the culture and operational structure. He is now really frustrated by being forced to preach the message again, particularly as he is meeting resistance to this. Our conversations identify that he has always set high standards for himself, as inculcated originally by his parents. He acknowledges that he can be very intolerant of those whose standards do not meet his and can be quite blunt and direct in setting targets for his team members.

> Ben says "I do tend to be "telling" rather than listening. But, while I accept they've been successful, the new customer feedback is shocking. They just need to get out more and not hide behind their desks. I'm going to tell them how it is."

It seems he has been involved in virtually continuous change in the business structures and in his role for five years. I intervene to suggest that he may have become immune to the strains of transition and to the effects these might have on others. We agree that he will pay more attention to the detail of the resistance messages and, by exploring with me his own feelings and responses to change, use this to understand and empathise with his team's behaviour.

Over four sessions Ben works to understand more about the concerns and anxieties of each member of his direct team. We role play to help him understand better one particular individual who is adamant that he doesn't need to visit his customers regularly. This process helps Ben to identify and respect the different individual viewpoints around him and his directive style seems to soften, although another crisis throws him back to a dictatorial stance. The process of his self-reflecting on his own experiences through continual job change also helps his personal sense-making. It seems that his recent progression through a series of leadership roles has been relatively unplanned and unsupported. He has often struggled to make sense of the changing perspectives and challenges and has felt like 'a ship at sea'. My personal and HR observations are that this is not an isolated case, as studied by Hall (1995). Many organisations pay scant regard to supporting leaders in maintaining their clarity and a sense of equilibrium.

I conclude that the coaching support has helped to reduce his initial frustration and he does now subscribe, at least in my presence, to a less controlling style in which he takes some time to understand others' points of view and where their emotions might be coming from. We agree that he has a 'must try harder' view of his self, which I recognise strongly in myself, and this creates his stuck behaviour when he could profit from taking a different perspective and moving to think and behave differently. We also discuss the generally debilitating effect of continuous change on him and his team. I introduce the concept of a staged transition and he recognises that he has been effectively stuck in a series of 'neutral zones' (see below) in subsequent transition processes. Through this long and stressful period, he has never found real closure in any one of a long series of organisational changes. And, until now, he has not had the stimulus or opportunity to examine his sense-making and consider changes he might need to make in his own thinking and behaviour.

A TRANSITION MODEL

The work of Amado et al. (2001) analyses the transitional nature of change. William Bridges (2003) describes three critical stages of a successful transition and I find this transition model developed by Bridges to be a very useful construct for both coaches and clients to use when talking and thinking through a job change. It enables the job-changer to broaden their perspective in terms of a wider transition process, and offers a continuum, rather than just a focus on specific issues and ad hoc challenges. Although a simplistic model, it enables the client to plot where they are in the transition process and to label their various thoughts, feelings and behaviours in terms of the three distinct zones. My prime concern is that it is presented as a linear process and with the suggestion that psychological adjustment and sense-making is taking place only in the neutral zone. My observations from this inquiry are that an individual is reacting constantly and adjusting throughout the transition. For example, Nicole's concerns about the loss of her previous colleagues was being aired at the time we were discussing her 'new beginnings' and her tactics for progressing in her new position.

Zone One – "endings, losing and letting go"
The start of the transition: letting go of old ways and identifying and dealing with losses.

Zone Two – "the neutral zone"
An in-between time: the old is gone but the new is not fully operational. Critical psychological adjustments and sense-making are taking place.

Zone Three – "new beginnings"
Coming out of the transition, developing new identity and experiencing new energies and a renewed sense of purpose.

MEANING MAKING FOR COACHES

My observations are based on only a few cases. Nevertheless, it appears to me that the circumstances of the change, whether largely sought by or imposed on the individual, have a bearing on how the jobholder copes emotionally. Ben clearly struggled with the imposed nature of his new role. I observed resistance to change and stuck behaviours based on previously successful outcomes. I observed the need to manage though a grieving process and for clients to feel that they are making progress through some form of transition process. I also observed the effect of job change on a client's broader life transitions and their sense of career and social standing. Through this inquiry, I have become far more conscious of such 'external' factors.

Because of the wide range of issues that job-changers present, I have worked to help them develop deeper self-understanding and sense-making about their situation and challenges. I have worked hard to maintain an unconditional regard, using interventions to help their sense-making and using our personal and joint feelings as data. It seems that I am able to use examples of my experience of change, together with my own self-disclosures, to build rapport and create an empathetic relationship.

I notice how I have focused on the client's use of metaphors to describe their deeper thoughts and feelings. I encouraged them to use their past experiences to make sense of current challenges. I use my experience of transitions to enable clients to build a sense of where they are in an overall process. I use the work of Michael Watkins (2003), to encourage their awareness of the need for planning and strategising. Watkins has created a road map for leaders to create momentum, build credibility and secure early wins, and has analysed the requirements for success in making different types of transition. I know that, when in transition myself, my main internal voice is often about 'trying harder' while checking on whether changing values are still congruent for me. In considering how this comes into play with my clients, I believe that I concentrate on repressing the former, but might well introduce counter-transference whenever the subject of values comes up. It's my hobbyhorse.

I also think that the client's assumptions about and preparedness for the job change are important areas of study for the coach. As I know personally, it is easy to remain in the same, previously successful, behavioural and thinking pattern, seemingly ignoring the fact that changes actually may be required by the new circumstances and job challenges. Self-reflection through coaching can help the client to analyse and make better sense of the reality of the new role and their expectations versus the reality. The coaching process can help the client to experiment with planned actions ahead of implementation and then reflect on the outcomes and re-plan.

THROUGH MY OWN PRISM

Inevitably, I connect with my clients and make sense of my observations through my own prism – my personal meaning of what I see, feel and interpret and how these have developed from my own experiences of job change together with my current approach to coaching. It seems that, through the period of this inquiry, I am placing a high emphasis on the role of power and being more explicit about imposed rather that sought changes. Inevitably, I feel heavily influenced by my personal experiences of the last two years – the impositions created by the merger and my struggles to deal with alienation. But inherently I do recognise the uplifting nature of change, creating new opportunities and allowing one to dream a dream and then make it happen. I did notice this with Nicole, who was excited to move to a new employer and used these emotions to drive her determination to be a success. But, preoccupied with the impact of impositions, I wonder what I have missed and experienced in my observations and, as a coach, as my clients disclosed their feelings.

Where the job change has a backdrop of seemingly never-ending organisational turbulence, this can also affect the client's psychological attachment. As explored by Travaglione and Cross (2006), the effect of being a 'survivor' through this turbulence can affect psychological equilibrium and our sense-making. In these circumstances, I am feeling strongly that the pursuit of longer-term corporate purpose will not always engender loyalty, stability, commitment and a sense of security in the employee. This has obviously been a big personal issue for me.

Personal learnings

I was acutely aware of Ben's cynicism about his life of continuous change and his sense of not making progress and spinning his wheels. I noticed this transference of his thoughts into our coaching relationship and recognised that, at these moments, I became a particularly receptive listener, sharing similar cynical internal thoughts about corporate life but working hard to keep them to myself.

I notice that my interventions increasingly tend to be facilitative rather than directly confrontational. I have identified a range of catalytic interventions, as identified by Heron (2001). For example, my asking Nicole about what other ways she could communicate with and influence the founder enabled her self-discovery and put her on the road to adopting different behaviours and new tactics. I notice that my informative interventions in this inquiry have often been about introducing the concept of a longer and more complex transition process than the client can see. I sense that the client cannot always see the wood for the trees and that my information is about the size and nature of the forest. I have noticed that I do view it as quite a dense forest to be traversed, and I guess that reflects my recent personal experiences.

I had moments of stuckness and despair with Ben. I noticed how both his hopes for job success and the personal value he placed on dedication were under attack. I used a supervision session to role-play how I might get myself unstuck and, through some informative interventions, we got his style onto the agenda. This created a critical moment, in that it shifted our focus to thinking through practical steps, and gave us both some hopes that he could really galvanise his troops. It was a good example of enabling the client to face up to his life not being as simple and controllable as he wished. The shift that followed enabled him to think about practical steps, re-establish his sense of purpose and begin to trust his own judgement again. He looked and said he felt more comfortable. Ben had also revealed that he had lost confidence in the business. This was another critical moment which propelled us into examining how he could manage with these feelings until things started to settle down in the company. This refuelled my personal commitment to help him as I was flagging somewhat before this shift occurred. I sense that we both experienced, in parallel, a feeling of new vigour and resolve.

Theories at the heart

The Rogerian core values of focusing on the client with an unconditional regard are very much at the heart of my coaching style (Rogers, 1961). The development of an empathic relationship is also at the heart of how I operate. It works well and it makes me feel worthwhile. It creates the platform for the client's self-analysis and reflection, and a climate in which to develop ideas in a new light. I now recognise that I worked hard to contain both my client's and my own emotions. On one occasion Ben vented his anger but then wanted quickly to move off to safer territory. But I persevered with directing his focus on his feelings of anger, maintaining a boundary and helping him move eventually to a higher level of thinking about why he felt so emotional.

Making sense of what I hear from clients and what I am experiencing myself is a critical component of successful coaching. I have identified my own inner voices and drivers when I am in transition during live coaching and during my writing of the inquiry notes. I also use appreciative enquiry very frequently and I like it used on me. Invariably it brings positivity into the conversations, delivered via facilitative interventions. I use it when I identify or sense a client's recurring patterns. I asked Nicole if her need for control was a regular pattern of thought. I asked if she had ever achieved anything by taking a different stance with colleagues. It was successful in reminding her of a more collaborative project she had succeeded in, back at university, and it moved us on to consider different tactics in her relationship with the founder.

I have paid attention to the psycho-social processes in my clients, in which they make sense of themselves in relation to others. It is clear that job change creates new relationships and new expectations from others and how we are regarded. I have paid attention to and invited clients to consider the impact on social factors in their external world as well as on psychological factors such as their personal beliefs and values. At one stage, Ben sensed that his status in the business was under scrutiny and attack. At the same time he had a deep belief in his ability to overcome obstacles through hard work, but that was not working. The coincidental effect of these pressures was, I believe, undermining his self-confidence and that was feeding his anger.

COACHING AS A TRANSITION PROCESS ITSELF

I am interested to note that the coaching relationship can be compared to the stages of a change transition process, and that the content of coaching a job-changer may also follow a similar path. One begins by attending to the starting point of the change and to what were the triggers and immediate reactions. Then, as the coach builds the relationship, the attention moves to deeper and broader considerations and to taking stock from a wider perspective. Eventually, the client and coach start to focus on stepping up to the new responsibilities and analysing the new environment. But this somehow demands too linear a rate of progress and closures. Many clients will present a more complex map where, for example, issues of loss are surfacing alongside considerations about their challenging new relationships.

WHAT MY CLIENTS MIGHT SEE

I think my clients might see my espoused values. I strongly believe that companies should be open and honest in their communication of change. Coaching and support is really valuable, irrespective of the extent of the turbulence for the individual. I know, from my clients' feedback, that they recognise and value my experience of companies in transition. I believe they are attracted to me as a coach because of this 'wisdom' in company-initiated change. Historically, I have been less likely to reference my own personal experience of change but that is now changing as I see the value of self-disclosures and as I understand much more about what I have gone through.

CONCLUSIONS

To a large extent, I commenced this inquiry with the strong belief that coaching can support job-changers. After all, that has been my personal coaching experience in recent years and my experiences in the live coaching used in this inquiry have confirmed this. So, yet again, the findings confirm the views of the researcher! The impact of coaching provides the job-changer with the opportunity to develop their personal sense of the situation. Forms of stress can often accompany the various stages of the job change, as the client gains a deeper understanding and begins to experience the consequences. Coaching can help build the job-changer's capacity to manage their anxieties. Difficult questions can be posed and 'what if' questions can be explored. Based on an effective coaching relationship, the client's reflecting and imaging can help create greater clarity, enable them to see things in a different light and better gauge their challenges and plans.

This project has undoubtedly helped my own personal transition through the second half of what has been a notable year. Initially I had some doubts about my abilities to undertake the inquiry properly. I was looking backwards and noting that I had never undertaken anything like this before. Then I started to prepare through reading and conversations with peers. And finally I became really energised when planning and conducting the live coaching, using supervision to build perspective and then committing my thoughts into this dissertation.

As a critical input to this inquiry I have reflected on my own history role of job change. I've had a long and exciting career, with many twists and turns, but have never really looked back with any degree of focus. I have been amazed by the power of self-reflection in this regard and have really enjoyed the opportunity to mull over long-past details and identify historical (and hysterical) patterns of behaviour and thinking. Apart from a few notable occasions when I have chosen to move company in order to progress my career, I now recognise that most of my job changes have been imposed rather than sought. I now recognise that, at these times, I had a strong emotional need to buy into the business changes that were directly affecting me. But I also accept that many business decisions are never crystal clear and can often defy close scrutiny and analysis. And so over the years I believe I have become more accepting of imposed changes. I also recognise that I have developed a strong focus on the connection between the company's values and vision and my HR role within these, rather than just an allegiance to specific leaders. I believe this results from my experiences of continual job change and my observations on and experience of the 'survivor syndrome', as researched by Baruch and Hind (2000). Also, my internalised view of my 'psychological contract', as defined and researched by Bennett and Durkin (2000), has gradually evolved to become more to do with my personal vision of my role, my impact on the business and my congruence with the values in action.

From a psychodynamic perspective, it seems that my unconscious driver is to be congruent with the values of the business. From a cognitive behavioural stance, it seems that I am well programmed when I am clear about my role and responsibilities and know my boundaries pretty well. But I am poorly programmed when unclear on these and where the hierarchy of accountability is ambiguous. Through this year, from a humanistic perspective, I have been affected by and responding to an unhealthy environment and particularly with the loss of colleagues. And, with surviving colleagues, it seemed that everyone else was focused on their own personal agendas and no one was interested in me. This has been my own personal 'dislodgement of identity'. I have been feeling definitely an acute sense of grieving.

The peer coaching I have received throughout the year has been immensely valuable and cathartic. The on-going cycle of inquiry has definitely provided me with a process of re-engagement and that rare opportunity to look back and analyse certain phases in my life. As I have said, I have pondered on historical decisions on which hitherto I had spent absolutely no time. I still cannot believe how little time I have spent reflecting on the good things in the past! I still have a few unresolved issues about my personal changes this year, but feel better able to make sense of these and articulate my feelings more constructively. The process and the content of the inquiry have taken me on a really good journey, albeit accompanied by a few doubts and a little bit of procrastination, and it has been timed perfectly.

EPILOGUE

DEVELOPING OUR CAPACITY TO BE AFFECTED IN RELATIONSHIP

AFTER 11 page-turning chapters brimming with coaching experiences it is hard not to admire these coaches for the courage and rigour they have mustered in entering into their experiences and really allowing themselves to be touched by them. I have been reading chapter after chapter concluding quietly to myself: 'Here is a coach with whom I'd really value spending some time'.

The capacity just to experience and be touched by experience provides the groundwork for coaching, and yet is still rather rare in our field. Countless practitioners shy away from just exploring with their client what this experience right now may be telling them. They would much rather respond actively to their experience, weigh in with their own views or structure the remainder of the session with the help of their 'coaching skills'.

It does not help those coaches who are trying to engage in an honest inquiry with their clients, that there is such a contrast between rigorous inquiry and authentic conversations on the one hand and the cultures of most businesses and organisations on the other, which unwillingly seem to encourage their leaders to be strong, have answers, provide certainty not doubt, lead with confidence, flatter and project their brand not themselves, keep their feedback to themselves, etcetera.

I would surmise that all such coaches' responses and clients' cultures are mainly in place to avoid being in this experience right now for much longer: to avoid being exposed to ambiguity, to uncertainty and to the many unresolved issues of their organisations. It is our own anxiety that moves us away from our experiences and, in particular, away from the unresolved aspects of our experiences. This is why so much courage is needed to carry on just sitting with our own experience as it meets us, fresh, without judgement, and sceptically curious.

On reading this book I have admired the refreshing fondness for inquiry and the ability to 'just experience'. I have been thinking about how these coaches will preserve their freshness when 'inquiry' is a practice of the past for them, or when their coaching assignments and organisational contexts may become more stressful and challenging. How are they then going to maintain their inquiry stance of 'just experiencing', how are they going to stay fresh and lively without prejudging what might emerge?

HOW CAN WE PRESERVE OR RENEW OUR STANCE OF INQUIRY?

Some studies of psychotherapy outcomes have shown novice therapists attaining a higher effectiveness than experienced practitioners (see, e.g. Dumont, 1991). This may serve as a reminder that freshness and an inquiry stance are constantly in danger of compromise, during the course of a coaching career. The easier 'coach approach' will always be the more formulaic and interventionist one, particularly in the face of anxiety or stress.

It is important therefore to ask ourselves regularly, how *can* we maintain our inquiry stance? What helps us to maintain our freshness?

The usual answer to this question about remaining fresh, unprejudiced and open minded, is twofold: (1) engage in regular supervision and (2) undertake further development activities such as skills practice or conferences with the latest ideas. This answer is often summarised by three letters, the acronym of Continuing Professional Development, CPD. Apart from the fact that it is sometimes hard to see how Continuing Professional Development keeps us fresh and open minded, there is also a hidden paradox inherent in the ideal of CPD for executive coaches.

This paradox stems from the fact that the coach wishes to retain or preserve the freshness and openness of a 'beginner', whilst also acquiring greater robustness and 'seniority' in the face of difficult assignments. The paradox reminds us of the 'castle and battlefield' metaphor of Roger Harrison (1963): on the one hand a strong *container* is needed and on the other *vulnerability* to allow the coach to be affected and really touched by her coaching experiences.

Coaches therefore come to CPD both to increase their sensitivity (as when they muster the courage to bring a really shameful or exposing issue to supervision) and to strengthen their resilience (as when they seek reassurance regarding a difficult decision they have had to make).

In an earlier article (De Haan, 2008) I have looked at ways of resolving this paradox, through analysing 60 coaches' own words about their critical moments in coaching, i.e. their descriptions of moments when they felt particular strain in maintaining their capacity to 'just experience'. 69 critical moments as reported by sixty coaches were content-analysed with the help of grounded research. In that analysis a picture emerged of *doubts*, which the coaching process opened up for these coaches, and of which CPD may help them become more aware, explore and even lay to rest. In fact, content analysis of the descriptions of the 69 critical moments showed that in every single description doubts of the coach came to the fore. The attendant uncertainties and feelings of not knowing appeared only at first glance to be by-products of coaching. In actual fact they were more like the groundwork or starting point for coaching, as stated also in the Prologue of this book.

Some critical moments in the collection that opened up some sort of rupture in the coach-coachee relationship (De Haan, 2008), hinted that the strains are sometimes resolved in a way that leads to a deterioration in the coaching, i.e. by a coach becoming less perceptive and less sensitive; and often at the same time also less robust and less self-confident. Through doubting during critical moments coaches might gain a thicker and thinner skin, but they also stood to lose much of their sensitivity and robustness.

Ideally, one would want to see coaches do the opposite: become both thicker and thinner skinned at the same time. The question remains, how can this be achieved? How can the paradox of 'castle' and 'battlefield' (Harrison, 1963) be resolved? How is building one not going to be to the detriment of the other?

A THICK AND A THIN SKIN REGARDING ONE'S DOUBTS AND CHALLENGES

Studying the critical moment descriptions more deeply provided a fresh way to look into the doubts themselves. It was possible to perceive a certain *hierarchy* within the many doubts expressed in the 69 critical moments (De Haan, 2008):

1. *Existential doubts*, in which the professionalism of the coach and the nature of the coaching intervention are called into question by the coach. Among the 69 critical moments, 17 clearly raised existential doubts, and they are essentially existential questions about self, or 'Who' questions ('Who am I to do the coaching?', 'Who am I to propose something different?', 'Who is it this coachee needs?' etc.).

2. *Relational doubts*, in which the nature of the relationship with the client and the boundaries of the coaching are called into question by the coach. Among the 69 critical moments, 24 clearly raised relational doubts, and they are essentially 'What' questions ('What is going on between us right now?', 'What is still part of this coaching relationship, and what belongs elsewhere?', 'What if I say what I think about this: will he hold it against me?').

213

3. *Instrumental doubts*, in which the guidance and process of the coaching conversations are called into question by the coach. Among the 69 critical moments, 28 raised mainly instrumental doubts, and they are essentially 'How' questions ('How do I deal with such themes and issues?', 'How do I structure this conversation?', 'How to respond right now: a summary or a probing question?').

In this hierarchy it appears that, if the earlier, more profound doubts have not been resolved, the more instrumental doubts cannot yet be addressed. Conversely, if the coach is experiencing less profound doubts, we can assume that the deeper ones have been laid to rest – even if only temporarily and unsatisfactorily. Many doubts have their origins with the coachee and the material. It is the coachee herself who comes to the coaching with an array of doubts and queries, or 'issues'. These can be of a relatively superficial, instrumental nature; of a deeper, relational nature and, finally, of a more personal and existential nature. Coaches work with their clients' doubts on several levels *whilst* being exposed to their own doubts as well.

The conflicts within the coach around developing a thicker or thinner skin exist on all these levels but, over time, one would hope for a way of resolving them in a hierarchical way. A 'well-functioning' coach has acquired a reasonable self-confidence with respect to existential doubts, and some self-confidence with respect to the relational and instrumental doubts, whilst being at the same time open and even vulnerable in these latter areas. Maintaining one's freshness as a coach may therefore mean that most of the existential doubts have been laid to rest and many of the instrumental doubts have been resolved, so that for this coach most doubting takes place in the *relational* arena, where she consistently struggles to relate to this particular client at this particular moment in time.

Continuing professional development (CPD) should in principle help executive coaches with all of their doubts, moving them generally towards more and more conscious exploration. The images of a 'thicker' and 'thinner' skin, or of the development of more 'backbone' and 'heart' (O'Neill, 2000), are relevant here. It seems coaches would do well to develop a thicker skin (or, more backbone, more self-confidence) when it comes to their instrumental doubts, and perhaps also their existential doubts, whilst developing a thinner skin (or, more heart, more vulnerability) when it comes to their relational doubts. CPD should help them in creating a well-defended 'castle' (Harrison, 1963) for their instrumental and existential doubts, whilst at the same time creating a much more exposed 'battlefield' (again: Harrison, 1963) for their relational doubts, so that they dare experience and perhaps mention the doubts they have about this particular coaching relationship as it enfolds.

Remaining fresh: staying on as a good enough coach

In conclusion I believe that to be a 'well-functioning' or 'good-enough' coach longer term means acquiring the ability to explore one's own doubts and questions in the moment, and to greet what comes next with sensitivity. Like Descartes in his famous *Meditations*, coaches will realise a significant turning point when they shift their attention away from the many doubts, uncertainties and anxieties that beset them during the coaching, and towards the activity of doubting itself, which can be regarded as both a starting point and a *raison d'être* of their professional activity. Descartes' famous saying *Cogito Ergo Sum* can then be rephrased for coaches as 'I doubt therefore I coach'. This sense of doubt leads to coaches developing both their thick skin ('existential and instrumental grounding') and thin skin ('relational openness'), simultaneously.

Maintaining freshness means maintaining the inquiry stance that has underpinned the experiences in this book. It means being able to defer judgement on our experience as we engage with it. This includes deferring judgment on the 'material' of coaching, i.e., being able to see the issues as the client sees them whilst also maintaining a separate, curious stance regarding how else the issues could also be viewed. For this freshness we need to maintain our 'backbone', our ability to 'contain' emotions, or our 'thick skin' within the sessions, whilst also maintaining our 'heart', our ability to be 'touched' by emotions, or our 'thin skin' within the sessions.

Within the inquiry process the thick skin stands for the rigour or discipline of inquiry, the application and commitment with which we engage. Within coaching this is represented by the regularity of the sessions, the clear boundaries and agreements in the coaching contract, and the reliability of the neutral space and the timing of sessions. It is also the capacity to find and trust a place of ease and rest within one, and of remaining serene in the face of the unknown, ambiguity, or serious doubts.

Within the inquiry process the thin skin stands for the capacity to be touched, without filtering or judgement, whilst taking in the experience as fully and openly as possible. Within coaching this is represented by the openness and receptiveness of whatever the client may bring to a session. It is also the capacity to enjoy moments of connection, surprise and quiet compassion together with one's clients.

If we think about it in these terms, the simple act of 'just experiencing' may entail a whole lot more than it seems to entail if we only read the Sceptical admonitions that were quoted in the Prologue. 'Just experiencing' now means that we feel comfortable in our own skin; we feel that our skin will protect us and will signal to us any challenge or threat. 'Just experiencing' means trusting that our skins – our perceptual apparatus included – are supple, fresh, yet resilient and protective, so that we can begin to offer this protection and this freshness to others and, in particular, to our clients. 'Just experiencing' means being comfortable within one, comfortable with new experiences and comfortable with not knowing what to do, not having the answers, and even not understanding or grasping what is being presented to us.

So much comfort and so much freshness seems a very bold requirement when one thinks about it. Perhaps this is why so few philosophers took the Sceptical route even in Antiquity, and most preferred to remain enveloped within the comforting axioms, hypotheses, half-truths and idiosyncrasies of ideology.

Well done to the coaches in this book, for leaving, at least temporarily, the comforting slumbers of existing doctrine and formulaic practice, and endeavouring to experience coaching just as it presented itself to them in conversation.

AUTHOR PROFILES

Ann Baldwin: Ann has run her own executive coaching business since the mid-90s. Her clients are directors, partners and those hoping to reach that level in medium to large businesses and organisations. She works primarily as a one-to-one coach. She considers coaching to be the most challenging and rewarding work she has done and is grateful to her clients for all they have taught her. Ann gained her MSc in Executive Coaching in 2010. She is a former partner in a large accountancy practice, panel member for the selection of partners, office managing partner and executive board member.

Nicola Carew: Nicola founded CWL Coaching (www.cwl-coaching.co.uk) in 1996 and has developed a practice working with diverse industries from blue chip to emerging organisations. Her work is informed by a person-centred approach and she is passionate about helping individuals flourish in organisations through executive coaching, co-coaching and bespoke group programmes. She gained her MSc in Executive Coaching from Ashridge in 2011. Nicola is also a volunteer business mentor and progression mentor with the Prince's Trust, supporting disaffected young people to get established in society; and a member of the Royal Society of Arts Social Enterprise and Coaching Networks.

Stephanie Conway: Stephanie is a senior manager and leadership coach at Google. Working in sales operations and management, she has managed cross cultural teams and global projects, and has lived and worked in four different countries. The international nature of her work means that she has 'virtually' coached middle and senior managers in EMEA, the U.S.A. and Asia. Stephanie holds a diploma in Business, Executive and Personal Coaching and is an accredited coach with Ashridge and the Association for Coaching. For the latter she also works as head of operations in Ireland on a voluntary basis. She gained her MSc in Executive Coaching from Ashridge in December 2011.

Erik de Haan: Erik is organisation development consultant, executive coach and supervisor. He is the Director of the Ashridge Centre for Coaching and programme leader of the Ashridge Master's (MSc) in Executive Coaching, and the Ashridge Postgraduate Certificate in Advanced Coaching and O.D. Supervision. Erik is also Professor of Organisation Development and Coaching at the VU University of Amsterdam. He has written more than a hundred articles and seven books in different languages, among which are *Fearless Consulting* (2006), *Coaching with Colleagues* (2004; with Yvonne Burger), *Relational Coaching* (2008), *Supervision in Action* (2011) and *Coaching Relationships* (2012; edited with Charlotte Sills).

Jude Elliman: Jude has been delivering coaching and team development for over 20 years, partnering with in-house HR and HC professionals to create tailored, leadership programmes. She has worked with FTSE 100 Companies and International Professional Service Firms, plus a range of not-for-profit organisations, sector skills councils and small manufacturing companies. She now specialises in coaching experienced leaders and their boards, supervising coaches in their practices and working with individuals at key transition points in their lives – www.listeningpartnership.com. Jude gained her MSc in Executive Coaching from Ashridge in December 2011.

Jacqui Hazell: Jacqui has over 25 years' experience of optimising company-wide, board, team and individual performance. She has worked within FTSE 100 companies and other large and complex organisations as a director of a range of business functions and lead OD /change programmes. At www.Hazellconsulting. com her focus is on senior management coaching, mentoring, team facilitation and organisation development and consultancy both in SME's and large corporate organisations. She also works as an associate with leading consultancies, coaching and developing individuals and teams and also supervises the work of other coaches and consultants. Jacqui gained her MSc from Ashridge in 2010.

Andrew Martin: During a career spent largely in global US technology companies, Andrew has led international HR teams in designing tactical and strategic solutions and delivering these into complex organisations. Within Unisys, and as a UK Board member with Lucent Technologies, he supported leaders and their teams through mergers, acquisitions, divestments and other significant upheavals. He first came into coaching through his role as a trusted advisor to those facing major personal transitions resulting from ever-changing technology and market conditions. Andrew studied at Ashridge in 2007-8 and now provides independent coaching support and HR consultancy advice to international clients.

Saskia Mureau: Saskia is a business leader in sales and marketing with a passion for people development. She has worked in multinationals in the Oil and Gas industry for over a decade in various leadership roles, managing multibillion dollar business units. Saskia likes to be a thinking partner to business professionals both within and outside her company on individual and in group learning settings. Her customer portfolio is truly international and diverse. Saskia has been an Ashridge accredited coach since April 2011 and gained her MSc in Executing Coaching from Ashridge in December 2011.

Paul O'Connell: Paul has been working as an executive coach and facilitator for seven years. Previously he spent 25 years working in Sales, Sales Management and General Management in the Technology sector from blue chip organisations including Hewlett-Packard to small and medium-sized private US companies where he ran the UK or European sales operations. He now works with executives, helping them raise performance by helping themselves and their teams to understand and operate more frequently in their best State of Mind and highest Quality of Thinking. He gained his MSc from Ashridge in January 2010.

Nick Pounder: Nick is HR Business Partner and a member of the UK and Ireland management team of an international biopharmaceutical company. His role provides opportunities for formal and informal internal coaching and he also commissions work from external executive coaches. Nick has extensive experience developing teams and individuals within businesses achieving rapid growth and change. Before being attracted to HR Nick held senior sales and marketing roles building iconic consumer brands such as OXO and Robinsons Soft Drinks for Campbell Soup Company and Reckitt & Colman. Nick will achieve his MSc in Executive Coaching in 2013.

Paul Rutherford: Paul came to coaching after 25 years working in start-up ventures and blue chip corporations. He held line management roles in Xerox and IBM, and was responsible for the personal development and team performance of up to 150 people across 16 countries. Latterly, he was a Board Director of a pan-European search firm, providing career coaching to hundreds of candidates and clients. He now designs and delivers development programs for global organisations, coaches executives 'who have reached a plateau or lost their mojo' and writes coaching haikus at www.paulrutherford.com. Paul gained his MSc from Ashridge in December 2011.

Christina Wanke: Christina has been a facilitator, coach and organisational consultant and has run her own consultancy for over ten years. Previously she held marketing roles at IBM and later on gained extensive experience in communications and project leadership as a PR advisor and board member for a PR agency. Christina holds a degree in Business Administration (MA) from the University of St. Gallen, Switzerland and has coached a range of management teams and leaders from CEO's to directors and junior managers. Her current work focuses on effectively linking personal transition and people processes to business outcomes. Christina completed her MSc in Executive Coaching at Ashridge in 2008.

GLOSSARY OF TERMS

* signifies a term that can be found in this same Glossary

ACTION RESEARCH

Action research is a progressive reflective process initiated to address an immediate issue or an inquiry question. Action research is led by individuals to improve the way they address issues and solve problems. Action research involves the process of actively participating in an organization change situation whilst conducting research. As designers and stakeholders, researchers work with others to propose a new course of action to help improve their work practices. Kurt Lewin, then a professor at MIT, first coined the term 'action research' in 1944. In his 1946 paper *Action research and minority problems* he described action research as 'a comparative research on the conditions and effects of various forms of social action and research leading to social action' that uses 'a spiral of steps, each of which is composed of a circle of planning, action and fact-finding about the result of the action'. This is where the idea of 'cycles of inquiry'* comes from.

ATTACHMENT

Attachment is conceptualised as a core, biologically based instinct which informs behavioural and motivational drives. John Bowlby introduced the concept in a series of papers starting in 1958 with 'The nature of the child's tie to his mother'. Bowlby also hypothesised that individual differences in the functioning of this 'attachment system' are linked to individual working models of self and others. Infants become attached to adults who are sensitive and responsive to them in social interactions, and who remain as consistent caregivers during the period from about six months to two years of age. When infants start to crawl and walk, they begin to use these attachment figures as a secure base to explore from and to return. Responses from caregivers (usually parents) lead to the development of patterns of attachment. These, in turn, form internal working models which will guide the individual's perceptions, emotions, thoughts and expectations in later relationships. Behaviour associated with attachment is primarily the seeking of proximity to an attachment figure.

CONGRUENCE

Congruence was defined by Carl Rogers to refer to the compliance between ideal self and actual self. Congruence is one of Rogers' three 'core conditions' (unconditional positive regard, empathy* and congruence) that he conjectured for helping conversations to be effective. It is the state of being where we experience significant alignment between how we want to be, how we are experiencing ourselves and how we are being experienced by others. Congruence is therefore a state of internal and external consistency, perceived by others as genuineness or sincerity. Congruence can also be used for the compliance between a feeling or emotion, and the manner in which that emotion is being expressed.

CYCLE OF INQUIRY

From the earliest days of action research* (Kurt Lewin, 1946) the inquiry process has been seen as essentially and necessarily circular in nature, and as consisting of spirals of planning, action and fact-finding about the results of the action. Cycles of inquiry are entirely natural: the nature of our attention, which is by and large sequential and ever drifting, means we cannot hold attention to an object of inquiry for a very large time. Attention automatically drifts away and is then purposefully brought back to the object of study, often with a difference in perspective. This course of events, which may only take seconds to complete, demonstrates time and time again, that inquiry proceeds by cycles.

EMPATHY

Empathy is a skill building on reflective-self function*, and can be defined as being aware of and sharing in states of mind as they occur to another person, in the present moment. In other words empathy is the capacity to recognise states of mind or feelings within another person. One needs a certain amount of empathy to be able to feel compassion.

FIRST, SECOND AND THIRD PERSON INQUIRY

Action research* can be thought of at the level of individuals, the small group, and wider organisational and social entities. According to Reason and Bradbury (2001), first person action research skills and methods address the ability of the researcher to foster an inquiring approach to his or her own life, to act awarely and choicefully, and to assess effects in the outside world while acting. Second person action research addresses our ability to inquire face-to-face with others into issues of mutual concern, for example in the service of improving our personal and professional practice both individually and separately. Second person inquiry starts with interpersonal dialogue and includes the development of communities of inquiry and learning organizations. In third person inquiry the process moves beyond the relatively contained and small scale practices of first and second person action research to stimulate inquiry in whole organizations and in the wider society.

INNER AND OUTER ARC OF REFLECTION

Marshall (2001) describes action research* using the inner arc as perceiving, making meaning, framing issues, choosing how to speak out, and so on. She looks for 'repetitions, patterns, themes, dilemmas, key phrases that are charged with energy' and works with a 'multi-dimensional frame of knowing; acknowledging and connecting between intellectual, emotional, practical, intuitive, sensory, imaginal and more...'

Outer arcs of attention on the other hand move outwards (while the inner arc is still engaged) through 'actively questioning, raising issues with others or seeking ways to test my developing ideas.' There is a considerable amount of overlap with first-person and second-person inquiry*.

MINDFULNESS

Mindfulness ('sati') has its origins in Buddhist psychology as a spiritual or psychological faculty that is considered to be of great importance in the path to enlightenment according to the teaching of the Buddha. It refers to a psychological quality that involves bringing one's complete attention to the present experience on a moment-to-moment basis, in a kind of non-elaborative, non-judgmental, present-centred awareness in which each thought, feeling, or sensation that arises in the field of attention is acknowledged and accepted as it is. Mindfulness can therefore be seen as attentive awareness of what is going on in the present moment.

PHENOMENOLOGICAL INQUIRY

Phenomenological inquiry is an approach to psychological subject matter that has its roots in German idealist philosophy. Those engaged in phenomenological inquiry focus in-depth on the meaning of a particular aspect of their experience, assuming that through dialogue and reflection the meaning of the experience will be revealed and reviewed. Language is viewed as the primary symbol system through which meaning is both constructed and conveyed. The purposes of phenomenological inquiry are description of, interpretation of, and critical self-reflection into own experience. Central are the notions of intentionality and caring: the researcher inquires about the essence of lived experience. In phenomenological

223

philosophy (and in particular in the work of Husserl, Heidegger, and Merleau-Ponty), 'experience' is a considerably more complex concept than it is usually taken to be in everyday use. Instead, experience (or being, or existence itself) is a relational phenomenon, and it is defined by qualities of directedness, embodiment, and worldliness, which are evoked by Heidegger's term 'being-in-the-world'.

REFLECTIVE SELF-FUNCTION

Reflective-self function or mentalization was introduced by Peter Fonagy and others in 1991 and can be described as an awareness of what is going on in the minds of self and others, in the present moment. Reflective-self function can be understood as a form of mindfulness*, and has been shown to be correlated with secure attachment* (see De Haan, 2012).

REFLEXIVITY

Reflexivity generally refers to circular relationships between cause and effect. A reflexive relationship is bidirectional with both the cause and the effect affecting one another in a situation that does not render both functions causes and effects. Reflexivity therefore refers to an act of self-reference where examination or action 'bends back on', refers to, and affects the entity instigating the action or examination. Reflexivity is therefore a way of reflecting that takes account of the activity of reflecting itself and our own presuppositions during reflection, whilst changing them as well.

RELATIONAL COACHING

Relational coaching firmly understands the relationship between coach and client to be at the heart of effective coaching and to be a central vehicle for learning and change. Coaching relationally means recognising that the client's agenda will be defined by their organisational context, so, at a more indirect and subtle level, will the coaching relationship between client and coach. Relational inquiry is to pay attention to what goes on between coach and client, i.e. to make the relationship with the client explicit, because it is likely that such an exploration will cast new light on the client's relationship with his or her organisation. The coaching relationship becomes a forum for understanding stale patterns and transference*; and for experimenting with new ways of being in relationship. Relational approaches began in the 1980s in New York as an attempt to integrate interpersonal psychoanalysis' emphasis on the detailed exploration of interpersonal interactions with British object-relations theory's ideas about the psychological importance of internalised relationships with other people. Relationalists argue that personality emerges out of the matrix of attachment* relationships or formative relationships with parents and other figures.

TRANSFERENCE/COUNTERTRANSFERENCE

Transference was defined by Freud in *Zur Dynamik der Übertragung* (1912) as that part or those parts of the person's highly individual, highly personal and largely unconscious loving impulses which is not being satisfied in her relationships. Freud suggests that everyone will repeat one or several of such 'clichés' regularly in the course of a lifetime. Transference is a phenomenon characterised by unconscious redirection of feelings from one person to another or the redirection of feelings and desires to a new person, and especially of feelings and desires unconsciously retained from childhood. The idea of transference is clearly a precursor to the idea of attachment* as transference also conceptualises earlier relationships to become working models of later relationships. Countertransference is the same phenomenon of emotional entanglement as experienced by a consultant, coach or therapist in working with a client in a helping relationship.

TRANSFERENCE/COUNTERTRANSFERENCE

REFERENCES

Allcorn, S. (2006). Psychoanalytically Informed Executive Coaching. In Stober, D. R. and Grant, A. (2006). *Evidence based coaching handbook: Putting best practices to work for your clients*. Hoboken, NJ: John Wiley.

Amado, G., Ambrose, A. and Amato, R. (2001). *The transitional approach to change*. London; New York: Karnac Books.

AMEC 2 handout: Reflective Inquiry: an introduction and overview March 2009.

Appelbaum, S.H. and Roy-Girard, D. (2007). Toxins in the workplace: Affect on organizations and employees. *Corporate Governance: The International Journal of Effective Board Performance, 7*(1), 17-28.

Argyris, C. (1991). Teaching smart people how to learn. *Harvard Business Review, 69*(3), 99-109.

Argyris, C. and Schön, D. A. (1974). *Theory in practice: Increasing professional effectiveness*. San Francisco, CA: Jossey-Bass.

Bachkirova, T. and Cox, E. (2007). Coaching with emotion in organisations: Investigation of personal theories. *Leadership and Organization Development Journal, 28*(7), 600-612.

Bakan, D. (1966). *The duality of human existence: Isolation and communion in western man*. Boston, MA: Beacon Press.

Barber, P. (2006). *Becoming a practitioner researcher: A gestalt approach to holistic inquiry*. London: Middlesex University Press.

Baruch, Y. and Hind, P. (2000). Survivor syndrome – a management myth? *Journal of Managerial Psychology, 15*(1), 29.

Battley, S. (2006). *Coached to lead: How to achieve extraordinary results with an executive coach*. San Francisco, CA: Jossey-Bass.

Bazzano, M. (2010). Mindfulness in context. *Therapy Today, 21*(3), 32-36.

Beisser, A.R. (1970). The Paradoxical Theory of Change. In Fagan, J. and Shepherd, I. L., *Gestalt therapy now: Theory, techniques, applications*. Palo Alto, CA: Science and Behavior Books.

Bennett, H. and Durkin, M. (2000). The effects of organisational change on employee psychological attachment: An exploratory study. *Journal of Managerial Psychology, 15*(1-2), 126-147.

Bentz, V. M. and Shapiro, J. J. (1998). *Mindful inquiry in social research*. Thousand Oaks, CA: Sage.

Berger, P. L. (1997). *Redeeming laughter: The comic dimension of human experience.* New York: Walter de Gruyter.

Berger, P. L. and Luckmann, T. (1967). *The social construction of reality: A treatise in the sociology of knowledge.* New York [etc.]: Anchor Books: Doubleday.

Berne, E. (1961). *Transactional analysis in psychotherapy: A systematic individual and social psychiatry.* New York: Grove Press.

Berne, E. (1964). *Games people play: The psychology of human relationships.* London: Penguin.

Berne, E. (1972). *What do you say after you say hello?: The psychology of human destiny.* New York: Grove Press.

Beyer, C. (2011) Edmund Husserl. In Edward N. Zalta (ed.), *The Stanford Encyclopedia of Philosophy (Summer 2011 Edition).* Stanford, CA: Stanford University. http://plato.stanford.edu/archives/sum2011/entries/husserl/.

Bibb, S. (2008). Selecting and developing generation Y. *Selection and Development Review,* 24(5), 9-11.

Bion, W. R. (1961). *Experiences in groups and other papers.* London: Tavistock.

Bishop, S. R., Lau, M., Shapiro, S., Carlson, L., Anderson, N. D., Carmody, J., Devins, G. (2004). Mindfulness: A proposed operational definition. *Clinical Psychology: Science and Practice,* 11(3), 230-241.

Blickle, G., Schneider, P. B., Perrewé, P. L., Blass, F. R. and Ferris, G. R. (2008). The roles of self-disclosure, modesty, and self-monitoring in the mentoring relationship: A longitudinal multi-source investigation. *The Career Development International,* 13(3), 224-240.

Block, P. (2000). *Flawless consulting: A guide to getting your expertise used.* San Francisco, CA: Jossey-Bass/Pfeiffer.

Bluckert, P. (2006). *Psychological dimensions of executive coaching.* Maidenhead: Open University Press.

Bowlby, J. (1977). The making and breaking of affectional bonds: I. aetiology and psychopathology in the light of attachment theory. *British Journal of Psychiatry,* 130, 201-210.

Bowlby, J. (1988). *A secure base: Clinical applications of attachment theory.* London: Routledge.

Boyatzis, R. E. and McKee, A. (2005). *Resonant leadership: Renewing yourself and connecting with others through mindfulness, hope, and compassion.* Boston, MA: Harvard Business School Press.

Bridges, W. (1986). Managing organizational transitions. *Organizational Dynamics Organizational Dynamics,* 15(1), 24-33.

Bridges, W. (2003). *Managing transitions: Making the most of change.* London: Nicholas Brealey.

Brockbank, A. and McGill, I. (2006). *Facilitating reflective learning through mentoring and coaching.* London; Philadelphia: Kogan Page.

Brown, P. T. (2011) 'What happens in GAUSsian Space?' Time to Think Collegiate 13th October 2011.

Brown, P. (2012). *Neuropsychology for coaches: Understanding the basics.* [S.l.]: Open University Press.

Bruch, H. and Ghoshal, S. (2003). Unleashing organizational energy. *MIT Sloan Management Review,* 45, 45-52.

Brunning, H. (2006). *Executive coaching: Systems-psychodynamic perspective.* London: Karnac.

Buber, M. (1958). *I and thou.* New York: C. Scribner's.

Buber, M. (2002). *Between man and man.* London: Routledge.

Carr, A. (2001). Understanding emotion and emotionality in a process of change. *Journal of Organizational Change Management,* 14(5), 421-436.

Carroll, M. (2009). Supervision: Critical reflection for transformational learning, part 1. *Clinical Supervisor,* 28(2), 210-219.

Carroll, M. and Gilbert, M. C. (2005). *On being a supervisee: Creating learning partnerships.* London: Vukani Pub.

Cavicchia, S. (2009). Towards a relational approach to coaching – integrating the disavowed aspects. *International Gestalt Journal,* 32(1), 49-80.

Cavicchia, S. (2010). Shame in the coaching relationship: Reflections on organisational vulnerability. *Journal of Management Development,* 29(10), 877-890.

Chambers Harrap. (2003). *The Chambers Dictionary.* Edinburgh; [Paris]: Chambers Harrap.

Childs, D. (2007). Mindfulness and the psychology of presence. *Psychology and Psychotherapy: Theory, Research and Practice,* 80(3), 367-376.

Clance, P.R. (1985). The imposter phenomenon. *New Woman,* 15 (7): 40-43.

Clarkson, P. (2002). *On psychotherapy 2: Including the 7-level model.* London; PA: Whurr.

Clarkson, P. (2004). *Gestalt counselling in action.* London: Sage.

Cohen, L. and Mallon, M. (1999). The transition from organisational employment to portfolio working: Perceptions of 'boundarylessness'. *Work, Employment and Society: Journal of the British Sociological Association,* 13(2).

Cohen, L. and Manion, L. (1994). *Research methods in education.* London: Routledge.

Connor, S. (2010) Professor of Modern Literature and Theory, Birkbeck, University of London. *In Our Time.* BBC Radio 4 programme, 25 November 2010

Cope, M. (2004). *The seven Cs of coaching: A definitive guide to the collaborative coaching.* Harlow: Pearson/Prentice Hall Business.

Critchley, B. (2010). Relational coaching: Taking the coaching high road. *Journal of Management Development,* 29(10), 851-863.

Critchley, B., Higgins, J. and King, K. (2007). *Organisational Consulting: A relational perspective: Theories and stories from the field.* London: Middlesex University Press.

Cunliffe, A. L. (2004). On becoming a critically reflexive practitioner. *Journal of Management Education,* 28, 407-426.

Damasio, A. R. (1994). *Descartes' error: Emotion, reason, and the human brain.* New York: Putnam.

Darwin, C. (1872). *The expression of the emotions in man and animals.*

Day, A., De Haan, E., Sills, C., Bertie, C. and Blass, E. (2008). Coaches' experience of critical moments in the coaching. *International Coaching Psychology Review*, 3(3), 207-218.

De Haan, E. (2007). Ten Commandments for the Executive Coach. *Training Journal -Ely-*, (Oct.), 51-55.

De Haan, E. (2008). I doubt therefore I coach: Critical moments in coaching practice. *Consulting Psychology Journal*, 60(1), 91-105.

De Haan, E. (2008). Becoming simultaneously thicker and thinner skinned: The inherent conflicts arising in the professional development of coaches. *Personnel Review*, 37(5), 526-542.

De Haan, E. (2008). I struggle and emerge: Critical moments of experienced coaches. *Consulting Psychology Journal: Practice and Research*, 60(1), 106-131.

De Haan, E. (2008). *Relational coaching: Journeys towards mastering one-to-one learning*. Chichester: John Wiley.

De Haan, E. (2012). Back to basics II: How the research on attachment and reflective-self function is relevant for coaches and consultants today. *International Coaching Psychology Review*, 7(2), 194-209.

De Haan, E. and Burger, Y. (2005). *Coaching with colleagues: An action guide to one-to-one learning.*New York: Palgrave Macmillan.

DeYoung, P. A. (2003). *Relational psychotherapy: A primer*. New York: Brunner-Routledge.

Downey, M. (2003). *Effective coaching: Lessons from the coaches' coach*. New York; London: Texere.

Drake, D. B. (2009). Using attachment theory in coaching leaders: The search for a coherent narrative. *International Coaching Psychology Review*, 4(1), 49-58.

Duhigg, C. (2012). *The power of habit: Why we do what we do in life and business*. New York: Random House.

Dumont, F. (1991). Expertise in psychotherapy: Inherent liabilities of becoming experienced. *Psychotherapy: Theory, Research, Practice, Training*, 28(3), 422-428.

Duncan, B. L., Miller, S. D. and Sparks, J. (2004). *The heroic client: A revolutionary way to improve effectiveness through client-directed, outcome-informed therapy*. San Francisco, CA: Jossey-Bass.

Egan, G. (1994). *Working the shadow side: A guide to positive behind-the-scenes management*. San Francisco, CA: Jossey-Bass.

Eibl-Eibesfeldt, I. and Sutterlin, C. (1990). Fear, defence and aggression in animals and man: Some ethological perspectives. In Brain, P. F., Parmigiani, S., Blanchard, R. J. and Mainardi, D. (Eds.). *Fear and defence*. Amsterdam Netherlands: Harwood Academic Publishers.

Epstein, M. (1995). *Thoughts without a thinker: Psychotherapy from a buddhist perspective*. New York: Basic Books.

Etherington, K. (2004). *Becoming a reflexive researcher: Using our selves in research*. London; Philadelphia: Jessica Kingsley Publishers.

Farber, B. A. (2006). *Self-disclosure in psychotherapy*. New York: Guilford Press.

Fineman, S. (2000). *Emotion in organizations*. London: Sage.

Finkelstein, S., Whitehead, J. and Campbell, A. (2008). *Think again: Why good leaders make bad decisions and how to keep it from happening to you.* Boston, MA: Harvard Business Press.

Finlay, L. (2011). *Phenomenology for therapists: Researching the lived world.* Chichester: Wiley-Blackwell.

Flaherty, J. (2005). *Coaching: Evoking excellence in others.* Burlington MA: Butterworth Heinemann.

Fletcher, J. K. (2001). *Disappearing acts: Gender, power, and relational practice at work.* Cambridge, MA: MIT Press.

Fonagy, P., Steele, M., Steele, H. and Moran, G. S. (1991). The capacity for understanding mental states: The reflective self in parent and child and its significance for security of attachment. *Infant Mental Health Journal*, 12(3), 201-218.

Foucault, M., Faubion, J. D. and Hurley, R. (1994). *Power.* London: Penguin Books.

Freud, S. (1900) *The Interpretation of Dreams*, Standard Edition. London: Hogarth Press.

Freud, S., Strachey, J., Freud, A., Strachey, A. and Tyson, A. (2001). *The standard edition of the complete psychological works of sigmund freud vol. XIII (1913-1914), totem and taboo and other works.* London: Vintage.

Frisch, M. H. (2001). The emerging role of the internal coach. *Consulting Psychology Journal*, 53, 240-250.

Geertz, C. (1973). *The interpretation of cultures: Selected essays.* New York: Basic Books.

Gergen, K. J. (2009). *An invitation to social construction.* London: Sage.

Gerhardt, S. (2004). *Why love matters: How affection shapes a baby's brain.* Hove, East Sussex; New York: Brunner-Routledge.

Germer, C. K., Siegel, R. D. and Fulton, P. R. (2005). *Mindfulness and psychotherapy.* New York: Guilford Press.

Gilbert, M. (2008). *Becoming an executive coachee: Creating learning partnerships.* [S.l.]: Vukani Pub.

Ginger, S. (2007). *Gestalt therapy: The art of contact.* London: Karnac.

Goleman, D. (1998). *Working with emotional intelligence.* London: Bloomsbury.

Goleman, D. (2006). *Social intelligence: The new science of human relationships.* London: Hutchinson.

Gombrich, R. F. (2009). *What the buddha thought.* London [u.a.]: Equinox Publ.

Greene, J. and Grant, A. (2003). *Solution-focused coaching: Managing people in a complex world.* London: Momentum.

Gyllensten, K. and Palmer, S., (2006). Experiences of coaching and stress in the workplace: an IPA, *International Coaching Psychology Review*, 1(1), 86 – 97.

Hall, D. T. (1995). Unplanned executive transitions and the dance of the subidentities. *Human Resource Management*, 34(1), 71-92.

Hardingham, A. and Chartered Institute of Personnel and Development. (2004). *The coach's coach.* London: Chartered Institute of Personnel and Development.

Harrison, R. (1963). Defenses and the need to know. In: *Human relations training news*, 6(4), 1-3.

REFERENCES

Harvey, W. (2009). Mindfulness in practice. *Healthcare Counselling and Psychotherapy Journal*, 9(1), 3-7.

Hawkins, P. and Shohet, R. (2006). *Supervision in the helping professions.* Maidenhead: Open University Press.

Hawkins, P. and Smith, N. (2006). *Coaching, mentoring and organizational consultancy: Supervision and development.* Maidenhead: Open University Press.

Hayes, J. A., McCracken, J. E., McClanahan, M. K., Hill, C. E., Harp, J. S. and Carozzoni, P. (1998). Therapist perspectives on countertransference: Qualitative data in search of a theory. *Journal of Counseling Psychology*, 45(4), 468-82.

Heidegger, M. (1962). *Being and time.* New York: Harper.

Hellinger, B., Weber, G. and Dirksen, A. (2001). *De verborgen dynamiek van familiebanden.* Haarlem: Altamira-Becht.

Heron, J. (1996). *Co-operative inquiry: Research into the human condition.* Thousand Oaks, CA: Sage.

Heron, J. (1990). *Helping the client: A creative practical guide.* London: Sage.

Heron, J. (2001). *Helping the client: A creative practical guide.* London: Sage.

Higgins, J. (2009). *Images of authority: Working within the shadow of the crown.* London: Middlesex University Press.

Hill, C. E. and Knox, S. *(*2001) *Self-disclosure,* http://epublications.marquette.edu/edu_fac/31 pub Marquette University.

Hochschild, A. R. (1983). *The managed heart: Commercialization of human feeling.* Berkeley: University of California Press.

Holt, N. (2009, May 28). Email to Jacqui Hazell.

Horner, M. S. (1972). Toward an understanding of achievement-related conflicts in women. *Journal of Social Issues*, 28(2), 157-176.

Houston, G. (1982). *The new red book of Gestalt.* London: Gaie Houston.

Hycner, R. H. (1993). *Between person and person: Toward a dialogical psychotherapy.* Highland, NY: Gestalt Journal Press.

Ibarra, H. (2003). *Working identity unconventional strategies for reinventing your career.* Boston, MA: Harvard Business Press.

Jacobs, L. (1989). Dialogue in gestalt theory and therapy. *Gestalt Journal*, 12(1), 25-67.

Jordan, J. V. (1991). *Women's growth in connection: Writings from the stone center.* New York: Guilford Press.

Joseph, S. (2006). Person-Centred Coaching Psychology: A Meta-Theoretical Perspective, *International Coaching Psychology Review*, 1(1), 47-54.

Joyce, P. and Sills, C. (2001). *Skills in gestalt counselling and psychotherapy.* London: Sage.

Kabat-Zinn, J. (1994). *Wherever you go there you are: Mindfulness meditation in everyday life.* New York: Hyperion.

Kabat-Zinn, J. (2004). *Full catastrophe living: How to cope with stress, pain and illness using mindfulness meditation.* London: Piatkus.

Kagan, N. (1984). Interpersonal Process Recall: Basic Methods and Recent Research. In Larson, D. (1984). *Teaching psychological skills: Models for giving psychology away.* Monterey, CA: Brooks/Cole Pub. Co.

Kahler, T. (1975). Drivers: The key to the process of scripts. *Transactional Analysis Journal*, 5(3), 280-284.

Kahler, T. and Capers, H. (1974). The miniscript. *Transactional Analysis Journal*, 4(1), 26-42.

Karpman, S. (1968). Fairy tales and script drama analysis. *Transactional Analysis Bulletin*, 7(26), 39-43.

Kaufman, G. (1989). *The psychology of shame: Theory and treatment of shame-based syndromes*. New York: Springer.

Kelly, A. E. (2002). *The psychology of secrets*. New York: Kluwer Academic/Plenum.

Kilburg, R. R. (2000). *Executive coaching: Developing managerial wisdom in a world of chaos*. Washington, D.C.: American Psychological Association.

Kline, N. (1999). *Time to think: Listening to ignite the human mind*. London: Ward Lock.

Knight, S. (2009). *NLP at work: The essence of excellence*. London: Nicholas Brealey.

Kolb, D. A. (1984). *Experiential learning: Experience as the source of learning and development*. Englewood Cliffs, NJ: Prentice-Hall.

Kolb, D. A., McIntyre, J. M. and Rubin, I. M. (1971). *Organizational psychology: An experimental approach*. Englewood Cliffs, NJ: Prentice-Hall.

Lambert. (1992). Psychotherapy outcome research. In Norcross, J. C., *Handbook of psychotherapy integration*. New York: Basic Books.

J. Norcross. (eds), *Handbook of psychotherapy integration*. New York: Basic Books.

Lapworth, P., Fish, S. and Sills, C. (2001). *Integration in counselling and psycho-therapy developing a personal approach*. London: Sage.

Lapworth, P., Fish, S. and Sills, C. (2005) *Interpretation in Counselling and Psychotherapy: developing a personal approach*. London: Sage.

Lapworth, P. and Sills, C. (2011). *An introduction to transactional analysis: Helping people change*. London: Sage.

Ledford, G. E. (1985). Transference and Countertransference in Action Research Relationships. In W. M. Cooke and J. W. Cox, *Fundamentals of Action Research* (pp. 201-216). London: Sage.

LeDoux, J. E. (1998). *The emotional brain: The mysterious underpinnings of emotional life*. London: Phoenix.

Legge, K. (2005). *Human resource management: Rhetorics and realities*. New York, NY: Palgrave Macmillan.

Lewis, T., Amini, F. and Lannon, R. (2000). *A general theory of love*. New York: Random House.

Lichtenberg, J. D. (1989). *Psychoanalysis and motivation*. Hillsdale, NJ: Analytic Press.

Ludeman K. and Erlandson E. (2004). Coaching the alpha male. *Harvard Business Review*, 82(5), 58-67.

Ludeman, K. and Erlandson, E. (2006). *Alpha male syndrome: Curb the belligerence, channel the brilliance*. Boston, MA: Harvard Business School Press.

Luft, J. A. (1955). *The Johari window, a graphic model of interpersonal awareness, Proceedings of the western training laboratory in group development*. Los Angeles: UCLA.

REFERENCES

Machlowitz, M. (1982). The great imposters. *Working Women*, 7(2), 97-98.

Mackewn, J. (1997). *Developing gestalt counselling: A field theoretical and relational model of contemporary gestalt counselling and psychotherapy.* Thousand Oaks, CA: Sage.

Malan, D. H. (1979). *Individual psychotherapy and the science of psychodynamics.* London; Boston, MA: Butterworths.

Malan, D. H. (1995). *Individual psychotherapy and the science of psychodynamics.* London; Boston, MA: Butterworths.

Mann, D. (2010). *Gestalt therapy: 100 key points and techniques.* London: Routledge.

Marris, P. (1996). *The politics of uncertainty attachment in private and public life.* New York: Routledge

Marshall, J. (2001). Self-reflective Inquiry Practices. In Reason, P. and Bradbury, H., *Handbook of action research: Participative inquiry and practice.* London; Thousand Oaks, CA: Sage.

Maslow, A. H. (1943). A theory of human motivation. *Psychological Review Psychological Review*, 50(4), 370-396.

Maslow, A. H. (1966). *The psychology of science: A reconnaissance.* South Bend, Ind.: Gateway Editions.

McDermott, I. and Jago, W. (2001). Brief NLP therapy. London: Piatkus.

McDermott, I. and Jago, W. (2001). *The NLP coach: A comprehensive guide to personal well-being and professional success.* London: Piatkus.

McGonagill, G. (2002) The Coach as a Reflective Practitioner: Notes from a Journey without End. In Fitzgerald, C. and Berger, J. G. (2002). *Executive coaching: Practices and perspectives.* Mountain View, CA: Davies-Black Pub.

McLeod, J. (1998). *An introduction to counselling.* Buckingham: Open University Press.

McLeod, J. (2009). *An introduction to counselling.* Maidenhead: McGraw-Hill / Open University. Press.

Mead, G. H., Morris, C. W., Brewster, J. M., Dunham, A. M. and Miller, D. L. (1938). *The philosophy of the act.* Chicago, IL.: The University of Chicago Press.

Mead, G. H. and Morris, C. W. (1934). *Mind, self, and society: From the standpoint of a social behaviorist.* Chicago, IL: University of Chicago Press.

Miller, A. (2008). *The drama of the gifted child: The search for the true self.* New York: Basic Books.

Mindell, A. (1985). *River's way: The process science of the dreambody: Information and channels in dream and bodywork, psychology and physics, taoism and alchemy.* London: Arkana.

Myers D. and Hayes J.A. (2006). Effects of therapist general self-disclosure and countertransference disclosure on ratings of the therapist and session. *Psychotherapy (Chicago, Ill.)*, 43(2), 173-85.

Myers, I. B. and McCaulley, M. H. (2003). *MBTI manual: A guide to the development and use of the myers-briggs type indicator.* Mountain View, CA: CPP.

Nanamoli, B. and Bodhi, B. (2005). The middle length discourses of the buddha a translation of the majjhima nikaya. Boston, MA: Wisdom Publications

Napora, J. (2010). *Stress-free diabetes.* Alexandria: American Diabetes Association.

234

Naranjo, C. (1970). Present-Centredness in Gestalt. In Fagan, J. and Shepherd, I. L. (1970). *Gestalt therapy now: Theory, techniques, applications.* Palo Alto, CA: Science and Behavior Books.

Nevis, E. C. (2005). *Organizational consulting: A gestalt approach.* Santa Cruz, CA; New York: The Gestalt Institute of Cleveland Press; Distributed by The Analytic Press, Inc.

Newton, T. and Napper, R. (2010). Transactional Analysis and Coaching. In Cox, E., Bachkirova, T. and Clutterbuck, D. *The complete handbook of coaching.* London: Sage.

O'Brien, R. (2001). An Overview of the Methodological Approach of Action Research. In R. Richardson [ed.], *Theory and Practice of Action Research.* João Pessoa, Brazil: Universidade Federal da Paraiba.

O'Neill, M. B. (2000). *Executive coaching with backbone and heart: A systems approach to engaging leaders with their challenges.* San Francisco, CA: Jossey-Bass.

O'Neill, M. B. (2007). Executive coaching with backbone and heart a systems approach to engaging leaders with their challenges. San Francisco, CA: Jossey-Bass.

Palmer, S. and Whybrow, A. (2007). *Handbook of coaching psychology: A guide for practitioners.* London; New York: Routledge.

Parkinson B. (1996). Emotions are social. *British Journal of Psychology* (London, England: 1953), 87, 663-83.

Peltier, B. (2001). *The psychology of executive coaching: Theory and application.* New York [etc.]: Brunner-Routledge.

Perls, F. S., Hefferline, R. F. and Goodman, P. (1951). *Gestalt therapy: Excitement and growth in the human personality.* London: Souvenir.

Pooley, J. (2004). Layers of Meaning: a Coaching Journey. In Huffington, C., *Working Below the Surface* (pp. 171-190). London: Karnac Books.

Reason, P. and Torbert, W. R. (2001). The action turn: Toward a transformational social science. *Concepts and Transformation Concepts and Transformation,* 6(1), 1-37.

Reason, P. (1988). *Human inquiry in action: Developments in new paradigm research.* London: Sage.

Reis, S. (1987). We can't change what we don't recognize: Understanding the special needs of gifted females. *Gifted Child Quarterly,* 31(2), 83-89.

Revans, R. W. (1982). *The origins and growth of action learning.* Bromley: Chartwell-Bratt.

Roberts, VZ and Jarrett, M (2006). What is the difference and what makes the difference? In H Brunning (ed.), *Executive Coaching: Systems-Psychodynamic Perspective.* London: H. Karnac (Books) Ltd.

Robinson E. (2010). The use of literary techniques in coaching. *J.Manage.Dev. Journal of Management Development,* 29(10), 902-913.

Rock, D. (2006). *Quiet leadership: Help people think better – don't tell them what to do: Six steps to transforming performance at work.* New York: Collins.

235

References

Rodenburg, P. (2009). *Presence: How to use positive energy for success in every situation.* London: Penguin Books.

Rogers, C. R. (1957). The necessary and sufficient conditions of therapeutic personality change. *Journal of Consulting Psychology,* 21(2), 95-103.

Rogers, C. R. (1961). *On becoming a person. A therapist's view of psychotherapy.* Constable and Co.: London; printed in U.S.A., 1961:

Rogers, C. R. (1995). *A way of being.* Boston, MA: Houghton Mifflin Co.

Rosenbaum, R. (2009). Empty mindfulness in humanistic psychotherapy. *Humanistic Psychologist,* 37(2), 207-221.

Rosenzweig, S. (2010). Some Implicit Common Factors in Diverse Methods of Psychotherapy. *American Journal of Orthopsychiatry,* 6(3), 412-415.

Scharmer, C. O. (2007). *Theory U: Leading from the future as it emerges: The social technology of presencing.* Cambridge, MA: Society for Organizational Learning.

Schmidt, P.J. (1982). Sexist schooling. *Working Woman,* 7(10), 101-102.

Seaward, B.L. (1992). Humor's healing potential. *Health Progress* (Saint Louis, Mo.), 73(3), 66-70.

Seligman, M. E. P. (2006). *Learned optimism: How to change your mind and your life.* New York: Vintage Books.

Senge, P. M. (1994). *The fifth discipline fieldbook: Strategies and tools for building a learning organisation.* London: Nicholas Brealey.

Senge, P. M. and Society for Organizational Learning. (2005). *Presence: Exploring profound change in people, organizations, and society.* London: Nicholas Brealey.

Sextus and Bury, R. G. (1993). *Outlines of pyrrhonism.* Cambridge, MA. [u.a.]: Harvard Univ. Press.

Shapiro, S.L., Carlson, L.E., Astin, J.A. and Freedman, B. (2006). Mechanisms of mindfulness. *Journal of Clinical Psychology,* 62(3), 373-86.

Shaw, P. (2002). *Changing conversations in organizations: A complexity approach to change.* London; New York: Routledge.

Sherin, J. and Caiger, L. (2004). Rational-emotive behavior therapy: A behavioral change model for executive coaching? *Consulting Psychology Journal,* 56(4), 225-233.

Siegel, D. J. (2010). *The mindful therapist: A clinician's guide to mindsight and neural integration.* New York: W.W.Norton.

Siegel, D. (2011). *Mindsight: Transform your brain with the new science of kindness.* Oxford: Oneworld Publications.

Siegel, R. D. (2010). *The mindfulness solution: Everyday practices for everyday problems.* New York: The Guilford Press.

Sills, C. (2006). *Contracts in counselling and psychotherapy.* London: Sage.

Sills, C., Fish, S. and Lapworth, P. (1996). *Gestalt counselling.* Bicester: Winslow Press.

Silsbee, D. K. (2008). Presence-based coaching cultivating self-generative leaders through mind, body, and heart. San Francisco, CA: Jossey-Bass.

Silsbee, D. K. (2010). *The mindful coach: Seven roles for facilitating leader development.* San Francisco, CA: Jossey-Bass.

Solomon, M. F. and Siegel, D. J. (2003). *Healing trauma: Attachment, mind, body, and brain*. New York: W.W. Norton.

Stacey, R. (2006). Theories of change in therapeutic work. *Clinical Child Psychology and Psychiatry*, 11(2), 191-203.

Stacey, R. D. (2003). *Complexity and group processes: A radically social understanding of individuals*. Hove; New York: Brunner-Routledge.

Stern, D. N. (2004). *The present moment in psychotherapy and everyday life*. New York: W.W. Norton.

Stewart, I. and Joines, V. (1987). *TA today: A new introduction to transactional analysis*. Nottingham; Chapel Hill: Lifespace Publ.

Stone, D., Patton, B. and Heen, S. (1999). *Difficult conversations: How to discuss what matters most*. New York: Penguin Books.

Taylor, S.E., Klein, L.C., Lewis, B.P., Gruenewald, T.L., Gurung, R.A. and Updegraff, J.A. (2000). Biobehavioral responses to stress in females: Tend-and-befriend, not fight-or-flight. *Psychological Review*, 107(3), 411-29.

Tomlinson, C. (2009, October 13th). Email to Jacqui Hazell.

Torbert, W.R. (2000). *The practice of action inquiry*. In Reason, P. and Bradbury, H. *Handbook of action research: Participative inquiry and practice*. London: Sage.

Travaglione, A. and Cross, B. (2006). Diminishing the social network in organizations: Does there need to be such a phenomenon as 'survivor syndrome' after downsizing? *Strategic Change*, 15(1), 1-13.

Ulrich, D., (2000). Coaching CEO Transitions. In Goldsmith, M., Lyons, L. and Freas, A., *Coaching for leadership: How the world's greatest coaches help leaders learn*. San Francisco, CA: Jossey Bass/Pfeiffer.

Van de Loo, E. (2007). The Art of Listening. In Kets de Vries, M. F. R., Korotov, K. and Florent-Treacy, E., *Coach and couch: The psychology of making better leaders*. Basingstoke: Palgrave Macmillan.

Van Deurzen, E. (2010). *Everyday mysteries: A handbook of existential psychotherapy*. Hove, East Sussex; New York: Routledge.

Verrier, N. N. (1993). *The primal wound: Understanding the adopted child*. Baltimore: Gateway Press.

Verrier, N. N. and British Association for Adoption and Fostering. (2010). *Coming home to self: Healing the primal wound*. London: BAAF.

Vucetic, S. (2004) Identity is a Joking Matter: Intergroup Humor in Bosnia. *Spaces of Identity: An Interdisciplinary Journal*, 3(2), 1-28.

Walker, S. P., Walker, S. P., Walker, S. P. and Human Ecology Partners. (2011). *The undefended leader trilogy*. [Great Britain]: Human Ecology Partners.

Watkins, M. (2003). *The first 90 days: Critical success strategies for new leaders at all levels*. Boston, MA: Harvard Business School Press.

Watzlawick, P., Weakland, J. H. and Fisch, R. (1974). *Change; principles of problem formation and problem resolution*. New York: Norton.

West, L. and Milan, M. (2001). *The reflecting glass: Professional coaching for leadership development*. Basingstoke: Palgrave.

Whitmore, J. (1992). *Coaching for performance: A practical guide to growing your own skills*. London: Nicholas Brealey.

References

Whitworth, L., Kimsey-House, H. and Sandahl, P. (1998). *Co-active coaching: New skills for coaching people toward success in work and life.* Palo Alto, CA: Davies-Black.

Wosket, V. (1999). *The therapeutic use of self: Counselling practice, research, and supervision.* London: Routledge.

Yontef, G. and Jacobs, L. (2005). Gestalt Therapy. In Corsini, R. J. and Wedding, D., *Current psychotherapies.* Belmont, CA: Thomson/Brooks/Cole.

Yontef, G. (2002). The relational attitude in gestalt therapy theory and practice. *International Gestalt Journal,* 25, 15-36.

Zachrisson, A. (2009). Countertransference and changes in the conception of the psychoanalytic relationship. *International Forum of Psychoanalysis,* 18(3), 177-188.

Zinker, J. C. (1977). *Creative process in gestalt therapy.* New York: Vintage Books.

Zohar, D. (1997). *Rewiring the corporate brain: Using the new science to rethink how we structure and lead organizations.* San Francisco, CA: Berrett-Koehler Publishers.